Concepts, Kinds, and Cognitive Development

1

5

LD
&CC   The MIT Press Series in Learning, Development, and
Conceptual Change

Lila Gleitman, Susan Carey, Elissa Newport, and Elizabeth Spelke, editors

Names forThings: A Study in Human Learning, John Macnamara, 1982

Conceptual Change in Childhood, Susan Carey, 1985

"Gavagai!" or the Future History of the Animal Language Controversy, David Premack, 1986

Systems That Learn: An Introduction to Learning Theory for Cognitive and Computer Scientists, Daniel N. Osherson, Scott Weinstein, and Michael Stob, 1986

From Simple Input to Complex Grammer, James L. Morgan, 1986

Categorization and Naming in Children: Problems of Induction, Ellen M. Markman, 1989

Concepts, Kinds, and Cognitive Development, Frank C. Keil, 1989

Concepts, Kinds, and Cognitive Development

Frank C. Keil

A Bradford Book

The MIT Press
Cambridge, Massachusetts
London, England

First MIT Press paperback edition, 1992

©1989 Massachusetts Institute of Technology

This book was set in Palatino and printed and bound in the United States of America.

Library of Congress Cataloging in Publication Data

Keil, Frank C., 1952–
    Concepts, kinds, and cognitive development / Frank C. Keil.
        p.   cm.—(The MIT Press series in learning, development, and conceptual change)
    "A Bradford book."
    Includes index.
    ISBN 0-262-11131-4 (HB), 0-262-61076-0 (PB)
    1. Cognition in children.   2. Concepts.   3. Learning, Psychology of.
4. Children—Language.   5. Semantics.   6. Pycholinguistics.
BF723.C5K39 1988
155.4'13—dc19   88-8973
                                                            CIP

To Derek and Dylan
and to the natural kind they represent

Contents

Series Foreword

This series in learning, development, and conceptual change will include state-of-the-art reference works, seminal book-length monographs, and texts on the development of concepts and mental structures. It will span learning in all domains of knowledge, from syntax to geometry to the social world, and will be concerned with all phases of development, from infancy through adulthood.

The series intends to engage such fundamental questions as

The nature and limits of learning and maturation: the influence of the environment, of initial structures, and of maturational changes in the nervous system on human development; learnabililty theory; the problem of induction; domain specific constraints on development.

The nature of conceptual change: conceptual organization and conceptual change in child development, in the acquisition of expertise, and in the history of science.

Lila Gleitman
Susan Carey
Elissa Newport
Elizabeth Spelke

Preface

When I was five, I rarely got up early. One spring morning however, the sun was so bright and ground so dewy that the whole world seemed to sparkle through my window. To my parents' surprise, I rushed through dressing and eating breakfast and was outside long before the usual time. I was immediately dazzled by a profusion of forsythia growing along our driveway and decided to make a bouquet for my teacher. After a great amount of tugging and bending, I proudly held several branches in my hand and showed the "bouquet" to my mother. Every branch was a different length and was pointing in a different direction. My mother asked if she could borrow it for a while and fix it up a bit. Ten minutes later, with the help of pruning shears and a parent's aesthetic eye, she reappeared with a carefully arranged bundle and said something about it being more symmetrical. "Symmetrical"...I liked the sound of that word and very much wanted to know what it meant; but then the bus arrived and I was off to school without an answer.

Once at school, I promptly sought out my senior kindergarten teacher (I remember there being several, headed by a portly silver-haired matron who talked in a high, yet booming voice, with very long vowels). I gave her the bouquet and asked her what "symmetrical" meant. She paused as if she were about to explain, but then looked at me again and said very sweetly but firmly. "That's not the kind of word you can understand at your age. You'll just have to wait a few years before I can explain it to you." My first thought was probably that it was another of those naughty words that only adults are allowed to use; but given who had used it and that it was about such a nice plant, I quickly decided that my teacher meant what she said; and it bothered me immensely. She was telling me that there were some things that children just couldn't understand no matter how hard they tried. We were somehow different, and if we did try, we'd botch it up so badly that we'd get the meaning completely wrong anyway.

I am sure this wasn't the first time I was given such a message, and I can remember it being repeated many more times throughout my childhood. Most children seem to have many experiences of this sort, including my own, with their father sometimes being an unwitting perpetrator. Even people with massive amounts of relevant experience (such as my kindergarten teacher) often seem to think that children have very different sorts of concepts from adults as a result not just of being ignorant but of representing the world in a fundamentally different way. This view is communicated to children in many ways, most far subtler than simple pronouncements that one isn't developmentally ready for the concept. These ways can include: changing of the subject, substituting a loosely related word, and promising to get back to it later.

Children usually find these encounters frustrating. It is easy to understand something being perhaps too mathematically complex or too technical (as it can be for adults), but often the "incomprehensible" concepts are neither technical nor associated with any formal discipline or large body of knowledge; they are simply different and supposedly outside of the child's conceptual arena. If you have difficulty remembering such experiences in your childhood, consider how frustrating it would be as an adult to have someone tell you that an unfamiliar word is not understandable to you because you don't have the right sort of mental equipment. It does no good, of course, to ask why one can not understand it because the explanation will undoubtedly involve just those mental capacities one lacks.

Much of this book is an attempt to understand what it is about concepts that makes children appear to be so cognitively different. If there are distinct types of concepts and if concepts themselves have different sorts of constituents, then perhaps these contrasts can be used to make sense of what develops. In the end, I will side mostly with the children, arguing that neither their concepts nor their conceptual capacities are fundamentally different from ours; but I will also try to explain the strong adult intuition of a qualitative shift in conceptual structure that occurs with development. My veteran kindergarten teacher was wrong in telling me that I simply couldn't understand, but she was also on to something that does change dramatically with development.

Acknowledgments

I have incurred a great many debts in writing this book. An enormous debt is owed to all those people who patiently read various manuscript drafts and sent me remarkably detailed and thoughtful comments. While many of the following deserve a paragraph each praising the quality and quantity of their comments, space only allows a listing; so, endless thanks to: Terry Au, Susan Brudos, Susan Carey, Jennifer Freyd, Susan Gelman, Karen Guskin, James Hampton, Chris Johnson, Mike Kelly, John Macnamara, Doug Medin, Greg Murphy, Liz Spelke, Ken Springer, J.D. Trout, and Rob Wilson. Even among this group, I have to give a special thanks to Susan Carey, whose massive set of comments were a wonderful help in thousands of ways. Susan also managed to instill maximal guilt by sending me installments of her comments while on various vacations. Nothing can make you feel more in debt to a colleague than to receive detailed and constructive comments on some of your worst chapters, with a note scrawled across the top saying "sorry that some of the references are incomplete, I had to type this while camping in Toulemene Meadows."

I have also received many comments from colleagues who have heard me talk on various aspects of the work in this book; but here the number of people to thank is simply too large. I do owe special thanks, however to several of my colleagues at the Center for Advanced Study in the Behavioral Sciences where I wrote much of the first draft of this book. These include Ann Brown, Susan Carey, Rochel Gelman, Jackie Goodnow, and Bob Krauss. Thanks also to Jerry Fodor and Phil Johnson-Laird, who each spent several hours discussing this book with me during recent visits to Cornell. One other person, looms large in influencing the intellectual content of this book, my former Cornell colleague Dick Neisser. Prior to Dick's departure we had countless discussions that planted many of the seeds for this book; and even thought he is now a thousand miles further south, he continues to be one of my closest colleagues.

All these wonderful comments didn't come free. The book has been completely rewritten once with a dramatically different organization and several changes of content, including new studies suggested by some reviewers. And it has been heavily rewritten twice more, the last time with the enormously talented help of Ann Mark, whose skill as a manuscript editor is nothing short of breathtaking. She improved the style tremendously and caught countless problems from the level of typos to conceptual muddles. All of this rewriting has caused the book to be delayed several times; and I am grateful to Betty Stanton of Bradford books for nudging me along as hard as she dared and for patiently watching deadline after deadline pass.

In my lab, many undergraduate and graduate students and research assistants have been wonderful colleagues on the studies reported in this book. These include: Robert Altman, Nancy Batterman, Norma Bacillious, Susan Brudos, Cindy Hutton, Nadine Freed, Jeff Graff, Karen Guskin, Sheila Jeyifous, Mike Kelly, Chris Kenworthy, Jackie Raia, and Lianne Ritter. They have all made doing research a much more lively and fun activity.

Although the children in our studies have come from many places, the majority have been part of the Ithaca School District. I am deeply indebted to the principals, teachers, parents and students of that district for unfailingly being of help and for being genuinely interested in the research. Warm thanks also to several area day care centers, especially to Ithaca Child Care. Many people in my department have also been of great help: Fred Horan with computers in all their manifestations, Ed Snyder with shopwork and fixing most anything, Edie Clark and Linda LeVan with research administration, Joan Lawrence with last minute manuscript changes, and Kim Stockton with helping out in countless crises; but a special debt is owed to Sue Wurster who is simply the best secretary alive.

I am grateful for research funding from the National Science Foundation (grants BNS 81-02655 and BNS 83-18076) and from the National Institutes of Health (grant 1-R01-HD23922-01), and I thank the many people at both agencies who have fought so hard to keep some funding alive for basic research on cognition and cognitive development in the face of a hostile administration. With luck, they won't have to fight so hard for much longer. I also thank the Center for Advanced Study in the Behavioral Sciences and, through the Center, the MacArthur, Sloane and Exxon Education foundations, as well as Cornell University for support that enabled me to start a first draft of the book.

By far my biggest debt, however, is to my family. They have patiently endured countless times when I should have been around but wasn't. My wife Kristi has been especially long suffering, for she too expected that the long nights, the lost weekends and the general stress created by such a project would be over long before it finally was. I worked on this book during what may well end up being the busiest period of our lives with one, then two, young children and with both of us involved in demanding jobs. Throughout all of this she has been remarkably supportive and unselfish. I know that she is now probably even happier than I that the book is finally done.

Our two sons, Derek and Dylan, have also patiently put up with my preoccupations with this project as well as being a bit confused by how anyone would want to spend so much time staring at papers with a frown on his face when he could be outside sailing or swimming. Derek, age seven, has made me believe more than anything else in the great wisdom of children. I am continuously struck by the thoughtfulness and sensitivity of his questions, and I am invigorated by his tremendous enthusiasm and delight at learning about something new, even if of late it is largely about F-14 Tomcat weapons systems. Dylan, age three, shows in its purest form that marvelous sense of wonder that we all strive to retain from our childhood but which we all too often lose in the face of more pragmatic concerns.

Finally a note of thanks to two less intellectual, but nonetheless very loyal members of the family. Bonnie (10 years) has now suffered through two books, I hope she lives long enough to see the third. Daisy (6 months), on the other hand, may not last another month if she doesn't learn to stop chewing up my reprints.

Chapter 1
The Representation and Acquisition of Concepts

Any adult who interacts with a child, any traveler who visits other cultural groups, any historian who studies beliefs and attitudes of the past immediately becomes aware that others might not construe the world as she or he does. Even peers from the same culture are confronted with these issues, such as when communication fails or when one person misunderstands another. When we make such observations, we often say the others have different concepts from us; this sort of statement is especially common in discussions of children. These statements make two assumptions: (1) we know what concepts are and how to evaluate their properties, and (2) we know what it means to say, for example, that a child's concept of some phenomenon is qualitatively different from an adult's. In much of this book I will be concerned with trying to better specify and understand these assumptions. I will propose a particular view of conceptual structure and will present a series of developmental studies that use this perspective to explore whether concepts undergo qualitative changes.

Concepts

At a general level, the view of concepts adopted in this book is in accord with several recent proposals in the literature (see, for example, many of the chapters in Neisser 1987): concepts are construed as intrinsically relational sorts of things. They are not isolated entities connected only in the service of propositions. No individual concept can be understood without some understanding of how it relates to other concepts. Concepts are not mere probabilistic distributions of features or properties, or passive reflections of feature frequencies and correlations in the world; nor are they simple lists of necessary and sufficient features. They are mostly about things in the world, however, and bear nonarbitrary relations to feature frequencies and correlations, as well as providing explanations of those frequencies and correlations. If it is the nature of concepts to provide such explanations, they can be considered to embody systematic sets of beliefs—beliefs that may be largely causal in nature.

The notion of concepts as containing systematic sets of causal beliefs is closely linked to recent notions of concepts as being embedded in theories and mental models (see, among others, Carey 1985; Murphy and Medin 1985; Johnson-Laird 1983; Medin and Wattenmaker 1987; Gentner 1983); and I will endorse the idea that much of our understanding of concepts and how they might change over time will depend on our understanding of the intuitive theories in which they are embedded. Fully specifying the structure of theories and how they are represented and linked to concepts is beyond the scope of this book; but I will attempt to provide some details of how the beliefs that make up concepts are structured and how they relate to theories. In addition, I will argue that concepts are not just beliefs—that they in fact also contain a different form of representation that beliefs operate on and interpret.

Are the elements and/or relations that make up a given concept all of the same type, or could it have two or more qualitatively different facets associated with it that imply different representational formats? If such differences do exist in concepts, how might they be involved in patterns of development? Are different representational types observed across different types of concepts? Some concepts might be exemplar based, others dimensional, and still others composed of discrete features. Some concepts, like those for nominal kinds, might be more "classical" in nature (see Smith and Medin 1981), and others might be more probabilistic. Some concepts, such as the so-called syncategorematic ones, might be almost completely defined by their patterns of use, and others by almost pure belief. More broadly, the question of how eclectic we should be in our characterizations of conceptual structure is central to much of this book.

Concept Development

I will argue for a view of cognitive development and conceptual change that allows for qualitative change, but only of a special sort that is not stage-like. It relies on heterogeneity within concept structure, a heterogeneity that is present at all stages in a concept's acquisition and that exists in different variants for almost all concepts.

Decades of research, both anecdotal and experimental, have suggested that dramatic shifts take place in children's competency and manner of concept representation in a wide variety of areas such as conservation, causal thinking, classification, and seriation. The predominant view of this older tradition has been that the changes are relatively monolithic and represent global, across-the-board changes in basic computational and representational capacities. However, a host of more recent studies have repeatedly found that the apparently dramatic changes demonstrated in the older research were often due to task-specific artifacts or other failures on the young subjects' part to access knowledge that they actually possessed (see, for example, Flavell and Markman 1983). In light of the more recent "early competency" views, we must reconsider what phenomena the earlier researchers actually uncovered. I will attempt a partial reconciliation of these two views and will argue that neither in isolation can fully explain the phenomena of concept development.

There has been an increasing emphasis in cognitive developmental research on local knowledge systems and on how increasing expertise in such systems may account for much of the developmental change that we observe. Chi (1978), for example, performed compelling demonstrations of the memory skills of young children who were experts in such domains as chess and dinosaur lore, demonstrations suggesting that many of the dramatic changes in development may be less related to development per se and more to acquired expertise. But this too has caused unease among many developmental psychologists who are reluctant to equate development with novice/expert differences. To many, the characterization of the child as "the universal novice" seems to oversimplify what develops. I will suggest that the novice/expert contrast as originally developed in descriptions of chess-playing skills and other highly restricted "invented" domains may be a misleading way of understanding not just most cases of conceptual change in children, but conceptual change in adults as well.

Learning and Domain Specificity

Virtually all who think about cognitive development, even the most empiricist of philosophers, grant that for learning to succeed, it must be subject to certain innate constraints. The controversy rages over the nature of those constraints, ranging from the opinion that they are completely domain-general constraints at all but the most sensory levels to the opinion that there are domain-specific innate constraints at the most central, belief-laden levels of cognition. Perhaps there are sets of high-level cognitive constraints that demarcate various "mental organs," or perhaps the child is better viewed as a powerful all-purpose general computational device with few if any restrictions on learning at the central level. I will not propose new constraints on natural concepts in this book and show how they guide induction; the studies described here are not designed to uncover such constraints. They will, however, shed light on the relative contributions of general learning procedures and more domain specific mechanisms, and in doing so will suggest a promising way to model qualitative change.

Concepts vs. Knowledge

One of the dangers of proposing that concepts are intrinsically relational is the implication that they really are just the same as encyclopedic knowledge about the world. Everything is related to everything else in a vast network of roughly equal density. I will try to block this implication by arguing that beliefs tend to cluster in highly structured bundles with special properties that distinguish these clusters from the general interconnectedness of knowledge. Thus, lexical concepts are not viewed simply as the more or less arbitrary association of words to nodes in some vast network; instead, as a subset of all concepts, they tend to be associated with only particular kinds of configurations that are isolatable from other aspects of knowledge. In our folk psychology, we talk of having concepts, of "getting" new ones, and of sharing or not sharing them. This talk assumes that concepts are somehow isolatable entities distinct from our vast "web of belief." Part of this book will try to better understand what this talk is about and how the structure of concepts might be related to the structure of the world itself.

One of the best ways to start to tackle these issues is by considering some classical developmental phenomena, phenomena that seem to conflict with more recent views of concepts and concept acquisition. The phenomena, the conflicts, and some possible modes of resolution will then motivate a more extensive analysis of concepts and kinds.

Chapter 2
Some Traditional Views of Conceptual Development Reconsidered

For many years it has been claimed that children's knowledge of conceptual categories, and consequently of word meaning, undergoes dramatic qualitative changes with development. Although these changes have been described in a wide variety of ways, many of the descriptions share a theme that has commonsense appeal to the casual observer of children: young children's representations are instance bound, whereas older children are able to free themselves more from particular instances to form more "logical," abstract concepts. It is important to examine the variants of these themes more closely to see whether they converge on a common account. In this chapter I will consider whether, despite recent challenges, claims of qualitative change might still hold merit, given an appropriate model of concepts and learning.

Vygotsky

Vygotsky (1934/1986) was convinced that children's concepts, especially lexicalized concepts, were often fundamentally different from those of adults. In his view, the young child's concepts were much more tied to specific instances and immediate experience, whereas the older child referred to underlying principles and definitions. Vygotsky proposed a three-stage sequence in the natural acquisition of concepts:

1. The first stage is characterized by "unorganized congeries" wherein "word meaning denotes nothing more to the child than a vague syncretic conglomeration of individual objects that have somehow coalesced into an image in his mind....The child tends to merge the most diverse elements into one unarticulated image on the basis of some chance impression" (p. 110).

2. The second stage is characterized by "thinking in complexes" wherein "objects are united in the child's mind not only by his subjective impressions but also by bonds actually existing between these objects" (p. 112).

In a complex, the bonds between its components are concrete and factual rather than abstract and logical....The factual bonds underlying complexes are discovered through direct experience....Since a complex is not formed on the plane of abstract logical thinking the bonds that create it, as well as the bonds it helps to create, lack logical unity; they may be of different kinds. Any factually present connection may lead to the inclusion of a given element into a complex. That is the main difference between a complex and a concept. While a complex groups objects according to one attribute, the bonds relating the elements of a complex to the whole and to one another may be as diverse as the contracts and relations of the elements are in reality. (p. 113)

Concept formation at this stage therefore seems to be guided by overall similarity and seems to be insensitive to "logical unity."

3. The final stage of "true" concepts is characterized by what the prior two stages are not: abstract, logical thought wherein single principles or logically coherent sets of principles are the basis for conceptual structure. "The global character of the child's perception has been breached" and as a result "the grouping of objects on the basis of maximum similarity is superseded by grouping on the basis of a single attribute" (pp. 136–137).

Although this description omits much of the detail of Vygotsky's three stages and does not characterize the numerous substages, it captures the most fundamental aspects of the changes that occur: highly idiosyncratic instance-bound concepts giving way to more systematic organizations based on overall similarity, giving way in turn to more analytic forms. The most relevant aspect of this change is summarized nicely by Vygotsky himself: "More often than not, new phenomena or objects are named after inessential attributes, so that the name does not truly express the nature of the thing named...the result is a ceaseless struggle within the developing language between conceptual thought and the heritage of primitive thinking in complexes" (p. 132). Although Vygotsky saw true concepts as the hallmark of mature thinking, he nonetheless also believed that the adult also engages in complex-like thinking and that "we too resort to it very often in our daily lives" (p. 134). This notion of adults "resorting" to less analytic modes of representation is discussed extensively later in this and other chapters.

In sum, Vygotsky saw the major pattern of conceptual change as being one from categories formed on the basis of overall similarity among the most typical features to categories organized on the basis of just one or two principled dimensions or features. Vygotsky was particularly fond of illustrating this pattern with the child's acquisition of kinship terms, and he discussed how children initially think of "uncle" or "brother" as specified by the whole cluster of typical properties associated with uncles and brothers. Thus, young children might think that any person roughly their father's age who is warm and friendly to them and visits on holidays is an uncle. Only later do they shift to the more standard kinship definition. Vygotsky referred to concepts acquired in this way as "spontaneous" concepts in an attempt to distinguish them from "scientific" concepts, which show the opposite pattern of acquisition. Scientific concepts are taught by explicit instruction and, according to Vygotsky, are first presented in terms of definitions and only later filled out with examples and more characteristic information. Thus, in contrast to kinship terms, a concept like "exploitation" is frequently learned first by explicit definition. Vygotsky saw the two types of concepts as developing in opposite directions, eventually meeting at a point where they have both instance-bound, concrete properties and definitional ones: "the development of the child's spontaneous concepts proceeds upward, and the development of his scientific concepts downward, to a more elementary and concrete level" (p. 193). Later studies in this book will question whether Vygotsky's account of how scientific concepts are acquired is adequate for concepts in unfamiliar domains, but for the most part I will focus on the acquisition of spontaneous concepts.

The other fundamental aspect of Vygotsky's theory of conceptual change was a global, across-the-board change in conceptual structure—the view that before a certain point in development children would have great difficulty representing any concept in terms of a principled definition and after that point they should be able to do so easily for most concepts. This general cognitive metamorphosis view of conceptual change is common to many developmental theories, which claim that the very format for representing concepts changes in a fundamental manner.

Vygotsky advocated such a view for a strongly motivated reason. His ideas on conceptual change were part of a larger theory about how language changes the nature of thought. For Vygotsky, only as one comes to internalize language does one have the ability to represent concepts in any other way than via concrete instances and the simple associative principles that operate over those instances. By his account, internalized language frees children from relying on memories of specific instances and enables them to use more abstract, principled representations. This internalization process implies that the shift must occur at roughly the same time for all concepts, namely, at that point where language becomes sufficiently internalized so as to enable children to distance themselves from particular instances and thereby possess more principled representations. This view might also allow concepts to shift in a somewhat staggered order. For example, those with complex definitions might shift later since they require a more fully and stably internalized language to be able to represent them. Nonetheless, it is clear from Vygotsky's writings that, although such gradations might be allowed, he firmly believed in a general stage-like transition.

Werner

Werner's theory (Werner 1948; Werner and Kaplan 1963) is complex and employs subtle distinctions at several levels; my purpose here is not so much to explore its nuances as to identify some of the broadest themes that it might share with other developmental theories. Werner character-ized his view as an organismic-holistic approach to development in which children "move from a state of relative globality and undifferen-tiatedness towards increasing differentiation and hierarchic organiza-tion" (Werner and Kaplan 1963, 7). Werner described this shift with a variety of oppositions such as "diffuse to articulated," "syncretic to discrete," and "holistic to analytic," since he was attempting to character-ize a highly general developmental process. In fact, it was so general that its application to concepts constituted only a small part of Werner's overall developmental theory, which also referred, for example, to patterns of social interaction and music perception. Moreover, Werner wavered somewhat on the degree to which this sort of transition was a general stage that occurred at one period in development. He repeated several times that it could also be observed in adults, and yet he seemed to strongly imply a transition in middle childhood. The most likely inter-pretation is that the ability to be able to make the shift may not emerge until a certain point in middle childhood, and when it does emerge, it may apply in principle to all content domains. But it is only an ability, and a host of experiential factors determine whether and at what age the actual transition occurs in each domain.

Werner also proposed that semantic development consists of children achieving an increasing distance from the immediate concrete experi-ences with which a word is initially associated (Werner and Kaplan 1963). He suggested that words are initially bound to perceptual and perceptual-motor experiences. More generally, this becomes a claim that there is a shift from context-bound and context-dependent word mean-ings to meanings that are more independent of instances and instead refer to classes.

There is a persistent theme throughout much of Werner's writings that is closely related to Vygotsky's claims about changes in conceptual structure: namely, that children shift from instance-bound representa-tions that are global or holistic in organization to concepts that are more principled and articulated along specific dimensions. Werner and Vygotsky may have differed considerably on their theories of the mechanisms behind these developmental changes, but they were referring to similar sets of phenomena. Others have also noticed similarities between the two. Kozulin (1986), for example, in an introduction to a new edition of Vygotsky's *Thought and Language*, points out such similarities and notes that Werner's students, such as Hanfmann and Kasanin (1942), extensively adopted Vygotsky's methodological techniques and theoretical orientations in their own research.

Related Points of View

Although Werner and Vygotsky are the two developmental theorists most closely associated with a notion of concepts as shifting from undifferentiated holistic organizations to articulated, principled ones, other developmental theorists such as Piaget and Bruner have advanced related points of view. In a comprehensive review of the concept development literature, Flavell (1970) characterizes a common theme across a great many studies as follows:

> Generally speaking, there appears to be an ontogenetic shift—clearly evident in one study, less so in another—from equivalences based on the more concrete and immediately given perceptual, situational, and functional attributes of objects to equivalences of a more abstract, verbal-conceptual sort. (p. 996)

In this context he then refers to a long list of studies, including those of Piaget and Bruner.

One variant of this general view that has repeatedly surfaced in work on classification is the notion of a transition from thematic or complexive groupings to more taxonomic classificational ones. It is not necessarily the same as a holistic-to-analytic shift because the thematic stage need not be interpreted as more global—it may simply be different. Nonetheless, specific accounts show strong parallels. For example, in discussing classification skills in young children, Inhelder and Piaget (1964) note that

> they do not see how the similarities and differences which determine the "intension" of a class generate a set of inclusions which form its "extension"...making supper "belongs with" a mother although it is hardly an essential property which she shares with all mothers. True, most mothers make supper; and we could think of these "belongings" as similarities. *But such similarities are accidental rather than essential*, since not all mothers make supper (p. 36, my italics). The child...is lumping a not quite essential attribute along with the object it is supposed to define (p. 37).

Incidentally, since the supper/mother example was explicitly drawn from a study by Binet on children's definitions, we can be confident that Inhelder and Piaget intended here for the pattern to apply to spontaneously acquired concepts and not just ad hoc classification tasks.

These quotations must be qualified, however, by the broader context in which they are used. Inhelder and Piaget were primarily concerned with showing that younger children could not compare and contrast features of similarity in an objective way and were continuously being overwhelmed by thematic relations, spatial relations, and other configurational properties that grouped elements together. Thus, although Vygotsky argued that younger children form concepts on the basis of maximum similarity across all dimensions, Inhelder and Piaget wished to stress that the appropriate similarity relations were often ignored. Bruner, Olver, Greenfield, et al. (1966) make similar observations in their discussions of a movement from concrete representations to more abstract, rule-based ones.

The massive literature on learning in children (see Stevenson 1970; Gibson 1969) contains frequent discussion of how younger children fail to selectively attend to the relevant dimensions or attributes in a task because they put an equally strong emphasis on irrelevant ones. This pattern is also seen in Kendler and Kendler's (1962) work on the reversal shift in which younger children continue to operate on various dimensions or features associated with the learned concept and ignore the crucial dimension on which values have become reversed. These classical learning studies have important limitations, however; by focusing almost exclusively on artificial concepts, they minimize the extent to which other factors beyond simple weightings of features might be operative.

Perceptual and Conceptual Categories

Besides influencing investigators of language development, Vygotsky's work has independently affected researchers interested in the development of perceptually derived categories. In particular, Vygotsky's block studies suggested a model of how children learn to attend to various perceptual dimensions in categorization tasks. In the block tasks children were required to sort groups of blocks into various categories on the basis of critical dimensions such as size, shape, and color. Younger children tended to sort the objects on the basis of overall similarity between groups of blocks (that is, on the basis of how similar they were along all the possible salient dimensions of comparison). According to Vygotsky, with development, "the grouping of objects on the basis of maximum similarity is superseded by grouping on the basis of a single attribute: e.g., only round objects or only flat ones" (1934/1962, 77).

This phenomenon was replicated for many years, but only recently have advances in theories of category structure allowed us to better understand this shift in perceptual classification and how it might relate to other conceptual shifts (see several chapters in Harnad 1987 for detailed discussion of these and related issues). The most relevant advance comes from the work of Garner (1974), who proposed a dichotomy between integral and separable dimensions in the psychological representation of categories. Some dimensions of category structure appear to be easily isolated as separate units that can be dealt with psychologically. These might include shape, color, and size. Other dimensions such as hue and saturation might not be separable from the color they instantiate and thus cannot be used independently to classify color.

Garner's proposal led to the developmental speculation that performance on the Vygotsky block task might reflect an integral-to-separable shift wherein younger children treat dimensions such as color and shape as integral to the categories and cannot isolate them sufficiently for use in classification; only later do the dimensions become separable. Kemler, Smith, and Shepp (Kemler and Smith 1978; Kemler 1983; Smith 1981; Shepp 1978) have conducted a series of studies illustrating that young children often fail to isolate dimensions that are accessible to older children. In their more recent papers they have generalized this account to a broader set of categories and drawn links to other work in developmental psychology. Kemler (1983), for example, argues that the integral-to-separable shift is similar to Werner's holistic-to-analytic shift. One of the easiest ways to visualize the nature of the shift is to consider objects arrayed in a multidimensional space, as in figure 2.1.

There are two salient ways to organize the objects in this space. One technique is to sort together those that are closest overall on the different dimensions. With such a technique, objects A and B would form one cluster, and C and D another. The other technique is to group together those objects that share the same values on various dimensions, as would be the case with objects A and C, and B and D. Of course, which strategy is chosen depends not only on the age of the subject but also on the types of objects and dimensions involved. Even for adults many dimensions are of the sort that overall proximity may be an easier strategy to use. For example, if there are no obvious boundaries or reference points in the continuum of a dimension, it is more difficult to determine whether two objects share the same value along the dimension. In those cases where the dimension itself consists of discrete attributes or some sort of categorical perception is involved, however, a separable strategy might be easier to employ. Children have more difficulty using some dimensions separably and thus are forced to rely on the strategy of minimal proximity in the dimensional space, or overall similarity. This characterization

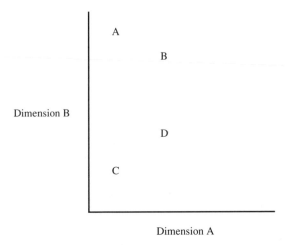

Figure 2.1
Four objects arranged in a two-dimensional space (after Kemler 1983).

of the developmental pattern illustrates in greater detail how the holistic-to-analytic view of development could be common to both perceptual and conceptual categorization.

The relations between theories of conceptual structure and the integral/separable distinction become especially clear when probabilistic models of category structure are represented in terms of multidimensional scaling solutions, as was originally done by Smith, Shoben, and Rips (1974). The basis for categorizations in such spaces as predicted by prototype theory is essentially the same as that used by an integral categorizer. Overall similarity on as many salient dimensions as possible determines membership in a category, rather than possession of one or two criterial attributes.

Spontaneous Definitions

In addition to the more theoretical research programs, there are also more purely empirical lines of work that repeatedly document similar qualitative shifts. One of the most heavily used methods for assessing developmental changes in conceptual structure is simply to ask children for definitions of terms. Much of this work has been embedded in psychometric tests such as the Binet-Simon intelligence test (Terman 1916). Terman placed considerable emphasis on the definition part of the Binet-Simon scale and noted a change with increasing age in the pattern of spontaneously given definitions from those that defined objects in terms of their uses or functions to those that referred to more abstract properties. Others also remarked on similar qualitative shifts in perform-ance on the Binet-Simon scale and on the later Stanford-Binet vocabulary test. Feifel and Lorge (1950) developed a five-category qualitative coding scheme for patterns of definitions. The most dramatic developmental result was a large increase in the use of appropriate synonyms between 6 and 14 years. The second major developmental pattern was a decrease in definitions that referred primarily to use of the object and/or to describable properties such as color (for instance, "It's yellow" for "straw"). Feifel and Lorge summarized the overall developmental pat-tern as one in which the younger children use a "concrete approach" and have "word definitions with a personal rather than a symbolic outlook" (p. 16), whereas "older children stress the abstract or 'class' features of the word meanings" (p. 17).

This concrete to abstract shift away from personal subjective meanings toward "objective" meanings is a recurrent theme in much of the older literature on children's definitions. One of the oldest accounts along these lines is by Chambers (1904), who suggested that young children have knowledge only about those things that are familiar in their immediate experience and that later they free themselves from this immediacy.

There has been a resurgence of interest in children's definitions in the last decade in an attempt to provide a more fine-grained analysis of these broader characterizations in the earlier literature. Moreover, much of this work attempts to draw connections to recent literature on semantics, concepts, and categories. Litowitz (1977) focuses specifically on the ability to define words and on what cognitive changes are likely to underlie such an ability. In her review of past work she suggests five levels of definitional competence, ranging from pointing and syntag-matic associations to "Aristotelian definitions" in which "specific defin-ing attributes or properties" are used. The most interesting level of development is a pattern of responses that Litowitz refers to as relying on "concrete examples of actual experience." Litowitz suggests that the child at this level has a specific problem in giving appropriate definitions.

> The problem is that the experience is an idiosyncratic meaning, not a social meaning. The focus is on the original instance of the word and not on the shared semantic aspects of the word. One can compare this level of definability to Vygotsky's level where the word is seen as an attribute of experience. (p. 295)

Elsewhere Litowitz refers to a general continuum from the "individually experiential to the socially shared" (p. 289). These characterizations of changes in definitions sound very much like other descriptions of chil-dren changing from an excessive reliance on typical instances to more conventionalized meanings. Litowitz also stresses that this transition is gradual and does "not [occur] all at once due to a major restructuring" (p. 302), and she cites a similar conclusion by Wolman and Barker (1965); in this respect, then, her theory differs from the more global restructuring views described earlier in this chapter. Though not specifically cited, Litowitz's views are also echoed strongly by Nelson (1985), who places great emphasis on the social milieu and the acquisition of shared meaning in the structuring of concepts.

Anglin has extensively used definition techniques and, in a recent review of work in the area (Anglin 1984), suggests that certain consistent findings emerge.

> One can postulate a continuum of word descriptions in terms of the extent to which they approximate definitions from not known, to responses based on personal experience, to characteristic features, to some defining properties, to all or most defining properties. (p. 9)

Clearly, the progression here is much the same as that proposed by Vygotsky and Werner, with the suggestion that perhaps features are more idiosyncratic in the earlier ages.

It is tempting to broaden the discussion and bring in many more studies on concept and language acquisition, classification, and novice/expert differences; but such an extensive review is not necessary to make the argument offered here. The theories and studies reviewed are sufficient to illustrate that almost a century of research has repeatedly reported similar observations about qualitative changes in conceptual structure. It is against this background that we must consider more recent criticisms.

The Traditional Themes Reconsidered

Many of the traditional theories and much of the empirical research on conceptual development have been shown to argue for development away from a holistic mode of representing concepts toward a more analytic mode. The shift is revealed by a decreasing attention over time to all the attributes that typically cooccur with a category and an increasing focus on only a certain subset of attributes that are essential to the meaning or intension of a concept. Despite the wide range of ways used to describe this shift, there seems to be a strong convergence on a common pattern.

Almost all of these theories also construe the shift as being a global reorganization of conceptual structure that occurs at a certain point in the child's development. The various theorists may have differed radically in their views of the mechanism behind this shift (as did, for example,

Vygotsky and Piaget), but for the most part they saw it to be a fundamental reorganization or evolution in the child's ways of thinking about the world. This is certainly true for Vygotsky, Bruner, and Piaget. Werner suggested such global shifts as well; but he was also careful to describe ways in which the shifts can recur in specific situations on into adulthood. Nonetheless, Werner would have held that before a certain period the analytic mode of representing concepts is virtually inaccessible to the child. The learning theorists were much more divided on the issue, some believing that there were no important changes in manner of learning and others envisioning a qualitative shift from universal "rat-like" stimulus-response concept spaces to more human, cognitively and linguistically mediated ones (for examples of these two views, see Munn 1965 and Kendler and Kendler 1962).

Such views of conceptual development are no longer popular, and the majority of current researchers in cognitive development have come to doubt their theoretical and empirical status (for examples, see several chapters in Flavell and Markman 1983). One of the most eloquent critiques of such qualitative shifts is a retrospective review of Vygotsky's *Thought and Language* by Fodor (1972), a review that, in conjunction with other of his papers (Fodor 1975; Fodor 1981), has become one of the major catalysts for the emergence of the current dominant view of cognitive development.

Fodor raises four general objections to Vygotsky's theory:

1. He argues that Vygotsky had the wrong view of adult concepts; consequently, children would be developing to a fictional end state. Vygotsky's theory of adult concepts was similar to what Smith and Medin (1981) have called the "classical view," in which the meanings of concepts can be described by lists of necessary and sufficient features. Given the now extensive literature challenging the classical view on both empirical and theoretical grounds (see, among others, Smith and Medin 1981; Rosch and Mervis 1975; Smith, Shoben, and Rips 1974), this objection is a serious one unless Vygotsky's account can be redescribed in nonclassical terms or unless some reasonable subset of concepts can be found that are closer to the classical view.

2. Fodor is especially critical of the notion of qualitative shifts, arguing that the same developmental phenomena can be fully accounted for by assuming that roughly the same computational and representational systems are shared by individuals of all ages and that what develops is an increasing ability to use these systems in a wider and wider range of tasks.

Fodor suggests that it is extremely unlikely that children and adults have different kinds of concepts for the same terms, for if so, "they must misunderstand each other essentially; and, insofar as they appear to communicate, the appearances must be misleading. Nothing less than this is entailed by the view that word meanings evolve" (p. 88). Fodor's incompatibility problem is not limited to Vygotsky's theory but would seem to apply to almost any case of purported qualitative shifts in conceptual structure. In addition to raising questions about adult-child communication, the developmental incompatibility problem asks how children could have access to even their own earlier memories. Though it has been suggested that childhood amnesia is caused by such "code changes" (for a discussion of such issues, see Neisser 1962, 1982, and Schachtel 1947), it has rarely been claimed to occur as late as the 5-to-7-year-old period, when many of these qualitative shifts in conceptual structure are said to take place. Clearly a central challenge here is to see whether it is possible to accommodate Fodor's concerns without reducing claims of qualitative shifts merely to descriptions of increasing access.

3. Closely related to objection 2 is Fodor's claim that Vygotsky's account offers no viable mechanisms of learning and conceptual development. Vygotsky seems to adhere to a hypothesis-testing model of learning, in which the child makes conjectures about possible new relations that might be central to a concept and then evaluates those conjectures against available evidence. This general model of the child as a scientist who collects data, generates hypotheses based on those data, and evaluates and modifies those hypotheses continues to be a prevalent assumption in much of developmental psychology. But if a child's concept undergoes a complete qualitative shift, any hypotheses made in the earlier representational format would be useless to the later one. In other words, how could a child in stage 1 ever learn anything that would be relevant to a qualitatively different stage 2; how could stage 2 ever emerge by any means other than maturation? Whatever is learned in one representational format is forever trapped in that format and useless to a later one because the later one would be unable to "read" it. Learning would only occur within each stage, with no carry-over to the next. Again, this criticism is hardly limited to Vygotsky's theory, and elsewhere Fodor (1975) also criticizes the theories of Bruner, Werner, and Piaget on similar grounds. He also warns that apparent qualitative changes in the manner of representation should not be confused with qualitative changes in the sorts of things the representations are about.

> One cannot, in general, infer from what is represented to the nature of the vehicle of representation....For this reason, to demonstrate an ontogenetic shift in the features of the environment that the child attends to is not more than the first step in demonstrating the very radical thesis that the medium of internal representation changes with development. (p. 177)

In this passage Fodor is challenging a particularly dramatic claim of qualitative change, namely, Bruner's notion of a stage-like change from thinking and representing in terms of images ("iconically") to thinking and representing more discursively ("symbolically") (Bruner, Olver, Greenfield, et al. 1966); and in this essay at least, he does restrict his claim by saying that there can be no qualitative differences "in the kind of way that Bruner seems to require" (p. 177). Even with this caveat, however, Fodor is making some very general claims about the implausibility of qualitative shifts in conceptual structure, and he suggests that when children talk about different sorts of things, we should not be misled into thinking that they are in general representing them differently.[1]

4. Finally, Fodor correctly points out that the centerpiece of Vygotsky's empirical enterprise, the Vygotsky block task, is not really a study on concept formation. Arbitrary conjuncts of features in short-term learning situations in which children are attempting to discover the experimenter's rule for labeling hardly constitute a naturalistic measure of conceptual development.

Fodor's objections are serious ones, extending far beyond both Vygotsky's and Bruner's specific programs of research; they require a reanalysis of the phenomena discussed in the first part of this chapter. The challenge here is to see whether a reasonable reinterpretation of those phenomena can both address Fodor's concerns and retain some version of qualitative change. Let us consider each of Fodor's points in turn.

1. *Vygotsky had the wrong view of adult concepts.* There are two answers to this objection. The first is that, for some concepts, Vygotsky may not be so far from the truth; some kinds are created largely by human convention and may have nearly if not completely definable meanings. It is no coincidence that most of the concepts that Vygotsky and others have studied are of this sort. They tend to be either totally artificial constructs for which definitions are completely clear or at least terms with highly conventionalized meanings. Thus, perhaps a qualitative shift holds for some special subset of concepts that are well defined.

The second answer is simply that one can adhere to a doctrine of qualitative shifts without holding a strictly classical view. Thus, one might argue that all concepts have probabilistically distributed features, not necessary and sufficient ones, but that the nature of such a distribution radically changes, such that young children tend to sum over all

---

1. Fodor (1981) also feels that hypothesis testing is in no way a viable model of concept learning, since one must already have the concept in order to test it. Instead, he proposes that the process is only one of concept confirmation. This argument relies on a number of controversial assumptions about the compositional nature of concepts and hypothesis generation (for further discussion, see Samett 1984).

attributes and relations that are observed to cooccur with concepts, whereas older children tend to weight just a few features and relations much more heavily. This answer may still presuppose versions of decompositionality that Fodor rejects (see for example, Fodor et al. 1980), but it does address the concern with the classical view.

2. *Vygotsky's theory entails developmental incompatibility.* This objection may be too strong for two reasons. First, it assumes that adults and children do not miscommunicate; as any parent can attest, such confusions do occur. Moreover, experts often fail to communicate with novices as do adherents of different scientific paradigms with each other. Of course, we do usually resolve such miscommunications; but we often do so in a way that relates to the second reason. Word meanings might evolve in such a way that adults retain or have easy access to what they knew as children and in such a way that they can use that knowledge in communicating with children. We often do fall back on global, primitive similarity spaces to resolve such miscommunications. Anyone who has spent time trying to talk with a four-year-old about politics, sex, or religion has surely resorted to this option.

It seems that the force of Fodor's objection here rests on a particular view of conceptual change, namely, one where the reorganization is comprehensive and broad across all concepts and where it is so fundamental that nothing remains from the earlier stages. The assumption about the breadth of the shift is a fair interpretation of Vygotsky's theory and is one of its weaknesses. However, the assumption about the completeness of the reorganization may be too strong a critique of what Vygotsky intended, as can be seen from the above quotations about adults resorting to earlier representations. (Fodor might then rephrase the problem as one of translation between the two representations; but see below.)

One way of resolving Fodor's objection is to assume that there is heterogeneity both within and across concepts. Across concepts, this solution allows us to postulate that a child may successfully communicate with an adult in some conceptual domains and not others. Moreover, if communication is possible in some domains, analogies may make it possible to gain insight into others. More important is the assumption of heterogeneity within concepts. I will argue that most concepts are intrinsically made up of both causal explanatory beliefs and sets of atheoretical relations on which the causal explanatory elements are only partially overlaid. If more associative structures are intimately related to causal explanatory beliefs and both are fundamental to conceptual structure, then access to such structures may well allow adults to communicate with children and experts with novices.

3. *Hypothesis testing cannot model qualitative change.* Assumptions of heterogeneity not only allow us to address the above concerns but also help to explain hypothesis testing. Although a child might have both representational types available to her, there may be radical shifts in the degree to which she relies on one or the other. For example, early on in a domain a child may have only the most skeletal framework of causal beliefs that guide the noticing of correlations, frequencies, and so on. By contrast, an older child or adult might have the same conceptual space heavily infiltrated with causal beliefs, such that judgments of similarity and category membership shift dramatically from being based primarily on atheoretical relations to relying on connected causal beliefs. At all points in development the child has the competence for belief-laden representations and more associative ones; but for a given concept the balance between the two may change so dramatically that the dominant representational type does indeed shift.

4. *The block tests don't assess much that is relevant here.* I don't find this to be an overly serious objection. It is certainly true that many psychologists have used artificial tasks that strain our understanding of their possible relevance to real-life cases of concept acquisition; and as I have argued elsewhere (Keil 1986a), such tasks tend to favor excessively the atheoretical components of concepts. Many of the studies described earlier in this chapter, however, are much more naturalistic in nature and report similar findings; they cannot be discarded on such grounds. Even Vygotsky also referred to a number of day to day phenomena, such as changing understanding of kinship terms.

Fodor's arguments do rule out several models of qualitative change. They rule out global across-the-board qualitative shifts in manner of representation and processing such that children in an earlier stage are fundamentally unable to have representations available to an older group. When the global change assumption is replaced by a domain-by-domain assumption, the arguments are weakened somewhat, but they still seem to work against any claim that a child at a given stage is intrinsically unable, even in a restricted domain, to have conceptual representations of the sort possessed by an older child or adult. Thus, even on a domain-specific basis, claims of fundamental competency changes in manner of processing and/or representation are exceedingly difficult to defend.

It is, of course, tempting to then try to construe all developmental change as increasing access to already present structures and representations and thereby deny any qualitative shift. Such views can easily deteriorate into a pointless, and usually unresolvable, debate about when two representations are qualitatively vs. quantitatively different.

What we call it is less important than that we capture the theme that does underlie so many past studies on concept acquisition; I believe increasing access alone is inadequate. On the assumption that dramatic changes in similarity ratings, judgment of membership in the category picked out by a concept, and processing can be construed as qualitative, I consider there to be two sorts of developmental changes that meet Fodor's concerns: (1) A shift within a domain from a predominant reliance on one kind of relation to reliance on a different kind. No claims are made here about absolute ability to have either kind of representation, so even the youngest child might have both. (2) A shift from embedding a class of entities in one theoretical system to embedding it in another. This second type of change, to which I now turn, raises new problems both with characterizing conceptual shifts as qualitative and with "tracking" concepts.

Conceptual Change and Theory Shifts

Carey and her associates (for example, Carey 1985; Smith, Carey, and Wiser 1985) have adopted a view of conceptual change closely related to that of Kuhn, in particular as best expressed in his 1977 paper "A Function for Thought Experiments." Kuhn argues against the idea that representations for concepts shift historically from diffuse, unarticulated forms to tightly organized, theoretically driven ones; he suggests, not shifts in the representational nature of concepts, but shifts in which theoretical system embraces the same, or roughly the same, class of phenomena. Smith, Carey, and Wiser see this as an excellent model for much of cognitive development and explicitly challenge qualitative changes such as Werner's holistic-to-analytic shift and Piaget and Inhelder's (1974) change from concepts of global undifferentiated quantity to more articulated ones.

> This description of undifferentiated concepts as "diffuse, syncretic wholes" commits the psychologist to the claim that undifferentiated concepts are a different *kind* of concept than differentiated ones.... Kuhn (1977)...denies that undifferentiated concepts are "diffuse, syncretic wholes" or are in any sense "intrinsically confused". Rather, they function within their theories just as do all scientific concepts. An undifferentiated concept has components which will become specific to each of its descendants. Yet as parts of the undifferentiated concept, these components make up an articulated, integrated and consistent whole. The lack of distinction between those components makes the concept inadequate in some contexts, but that is true of any concept in any theory. The descendants in turn

have united components which may subsequently have to be distinguished to make sense of further phenomena. Thus, it is the concept-as-applied to the world which leads to confusion; not the concept itself. (Smith Carey, and Wiser 1985, 180)

They argue for this position with an empirical demonstration that younger children seem to have different theoretical representations of weight and density than older children, not just less articulated ones. Similarly, Carey (1985) argues that children's concepts of animals change from being embedded in a theoretical system based on behavioral principles to being embedded in a theoretical system based on biological principles. Smith, Carey, and Wiser (1985) argue that true differentiation occurs when

> The theoretical contexts in which the undifferentiated concept ...played a role called for only one concept, one in which these components played no distinct roles. That is, these components were not appealed to differentially in the explanation of different phenomena, did not figure in separate laws, and were not explicitly related to each other in the theory....Thus it is only by analyzing concepts relative to theories in which they are embedded that we can decide how components are packaged, whether in any given case there is one concept or two. (Smith, Carey, and Wiser 1985, 181)

This is an interesting proposal; it allows for differentiation of theories and the concepts within those theories, but it denies that the concepts themselves change in representational nature. It also raises another thorny problem. How can one be sure that one is even talking about the same concept at all if concepts are relative to theories? Smith, Carey, and Wiser wrestle with this issue in the following way:

> Analysis of concepts in terms of components may seem to be incompatible with an analysis of concepts relative to theories. The two accounts are incompatible, however, only on extreme versions of each program: that is, an analysis-into-components approach which requires that all components be theory neutral and an analysis-relative-to-theories approach committed to extreme meaning holism, such that all components must change when a theory changes. On the latter account, any theory change entails conceptual change, and the task of tracing descent of individual concepts from one theory to another is impossible. Many historians and philosophers of science, however, reject such extreme views of theory change....Both Kuhn (1977) and Wiser and Carey (1983) maintain an analysis of theory change that involves true conceptual change in core concepts, although it allows for tracing descent between them.

...the core concepts in each are not intertranslatable. Descent can be traced, however, because of several properties of theories that stay fixed through change. First, successive theories can agree on some data, and some phenomena are in the domains of both. Second, some components of core concepts in successive theories remain the same and play similar roles in the explanation of common phenomena. (Smith, Carey, and Wiser 1985, 181–182)

In some sense, this last argument about "tracking" concepts across theory change must be right. We do not want every change in theoretical beliefs to make the concepts embedded in them completely different from those that were embedded before the change; yet no precise method is offered for making a decision about each instance. How much agreement on data and phenomena is needed? How much must the components of core concepts in successive theories overlap? These are obviously difficult issues, and it is hardly surprising that they are not yet resolved. Informally, at an intuitive level we often seem to be able to judge when concepts are tracked. The difficulty lies in trying to specify precise criteria that tell us how to do it.

Differentiation of the sort just described is not a qualitative change in conceptual structure. Though more theoretical relations are added, the nature of the representation remains the same. It is less clear whether radical theory change might not result in qualitative concept change. Perhaps the first theory is a rigidly unidirectional hierarchical model of causal relations, whereas the second is more of an interactive cluster. The representations for the two might have different consequences for processing and retrieval of information and for the learning of new information, and thereby seem qualitative. The dilemma is that one might want to argue that it is in precisely such cases that the concept is not tracked. A new concept has emerged in a new theoretical context that only loosely shares some extensions with the old.

Carey and her associates' view of conceptual change seems to be based on the notion that theory completely infiltrates conceptual spaces and that all entities are therefore contrasted on theoretical grounds and no others. This bias may derive from the assumption that concepts are fully specified by their relations to the theories in which they are embedded. As is clear from the above quotations, Smith, Carey, and Wiser allow for concepts to be "inadequate" in how they are applied to the world, thus attempting to account for the obvious fact that our theories do not make sense of everything in a domain, even for experts. But this view seems to rule out any atheoretical storing of information in a domain; we can only know what our theories interpret for us. It may be, however, that in all domains we also know a great deal more about relations between elements, correlations, and frequencies that have not yet been fully interpreted by the best, most relevant theory. If concepts are always a blending of both the theoretical and the more mechanical tabulation of information, a model of conceptual change quite different from that of Smith, Carey, and Wiser emerges.

Consider an example involving cars. A theory of why cars exist, what they are used for, and how subtypes are designed for specific environments tells me why there are typical feature correlations uniquely associated with car subtypes such as sports cars, sedans, and off-road vehicles. Thus, I have a coherent cluster of causal beliefs about why the features of low ground clearance, wide wheelbase, powerful high-rpm engine, and two seats frequently cooccur in sports cars and why features such as high ground clearance, short wheelbase, four-wheel drive, and roll bars cooccur with off-road vehicles. Within any of these subclasses, I have few if any theoretical or causal beliefs that I use to interpret correlations; yet I daily use those correlations to distinguish, for example, a Ford from a Chevy sedan. Theory may tell me to look at correlations between trim and hood shape and ignore the license plate, the color, and the presence of fuzzy dice; but beyond telling me to look for correlations in some domains and not others, it does not tell me which ones to look for and what their values are likely to be. This atheoretical knowledge is part of the concept because it provides a framework for further theory development; it is the structure on which future causal beliefs will be overlaid.

Thus, it seems that one way of addressing both Fodor's concerns and those of Carey and her associates about qualitative change is to postulate an ever-present heterogeneity of conceptual structure where the balance of the different parts can change drastically with development, and can do so on a domain by domain basis. Moreover, the change in balance should have clear consequences that suggest a qualitative change not just in what concepts are about or how they are used but also in how they are represented. For this account to work, a more careful analysis of concepts is needed, one that explains why both the theoretical and the atheoretical parts are needed and how they relate to each other. Equally important is an analysis of possible differences among types of concepts; for it may well be that the patterns of qualitative change reviewed in this chapter are possible only for a special subset of concepts that approximate this notion of heterogeneity. To address these issues, I turn to a discussion of concepts of natural kinds, nominal kinds, and artifacts.

Chapter 3
Natural Kinds, Nominal Kinds, and Artifacts

Are There Different Sorts of Concepts with Different Developmental Consequences?

Most of the concepts studied in more traditional concept attainment tasks, such as those described in chapter 2, either are completely artificial constructs or have meanings that are heavily influenced by social conventions and human intentions. A great many other concepts, however, refer to classes of things that occur in the world independently of human activities. Such classes of things are known as "natural kinds," because they cohere in nature as groups of entities that are governed by a common set of laws. There is no simple definition for natural kinds, but they are commonly thought to include such things as animals and plants, as well as elements and compounds. Triggered largely by the writings of Putnam (1975) and Kripke (1972a), a dramatic change has occurred over the past 15 years in how the meanings of natural kind terms are viewed, a change that raises the possibility that natural kind concepts might have representational structures different from those of other concepts such as artifacts and other more conventionally defined concepts known as "nominal kinds" (see Schwartz 1977).

The purpose of this chapter is to develop more explicitly a set of assumptions about nominal, natural, and artifact kind concepts. As argued in chapter 1, it is difficult to design and motivate empirical studies on concept acquisition without first committing oneself to a set of assumptions about what concepts are and how they are represented. A central question with such assumptions is whether concept types differ fundamentally in such a way that some types may nicely model apparent qualitative change whereas others intrinsically cannot. In chapter 2 it was noted that most prior successful research demonstrations of apparent qualitative change have focused on a highly restricted subset of concepts that might be unusually well suited for modeling such shifts, implying that other types of concepts might not do nearly as well. The possible contrasts between concept types are best understood by first considering Putnam's and Kripke's views about natural kinds; in presenting such views, they often suggest what other sorts of concepts might be like as well.

Both Putnam and Kripke criticize what Putnam (1975) calls "the traditional view" wherein

> The meaning of, say, 'lemon' is given by specifying a conjunction of properties. For each of these properties, the statement 'lemons have the property P' is an analytic truth; and if P_1, P_2, ..., P_n are all properties in the conjunction, then 'anything with all of the properties P_1...P_n is a lemon' is likewise an analytic truth. (p. 140)

Putnam illustrates in detail why a concept such as "lemon" cannot be defined by conjoining a set of necessary and sufficient properties. Atypical or abnormal members (green lemons, sweet lemons, and so on) seem to show that no one feature-category relation can be analytically true.

> There are no *analytic* truths of the form *every lemon has* P. What has happened is this: the traditional theory has taken an account which is correct for the 'one-criterion' concepts (i.e. for such concepts as "bachelor" and "vixen"), and made it a general account of the meaning of general names. A theory which correctly describes the behavior of perhaps three hundred words has been asserted to describe the behavior of tens of thousands of general names. (p. 141)

There are, Putnam points out, stereotypes that are associated with these terms, stereotypes that might consist of some probabilistic weighting of the features that commonly cooccur with members of a category, and these stereotypes may govern much of our everyday usage of these terms.

Kripke (1972a, b) also doubts that natural kind terms can be easily described by simple lists of necessary and sufficient features and illustrates the implausibility of this idea with several examples. Putnam and Kripke do not, however, wish to equate meaning with stereotypes or what Kripke calls "cluster concepts." They both go on to suggest that the natural kind terms are rigid designators, which means that they refer necessarily to a certain set of things that happen to share a set of essential properties, even though they may be unknown to most and possibly even all users of the term. Though this essentialist proposal has since been challenged in the philosophical literature for many reasons (see, among others, Donnellan 1983; Dupré 1981; Canfield 1983; Boyd 1984), the Kripke-Putnam approach has served to argue strongly against the idea that users of natural kind terms are relying on a list of necessary and sufficient features to determine their extensions. (Users may, however, believe some features to be necessary and sufficient even when they are not, a point that will be addressed later.)

Kripke and Putnam were certainly not the first to point out the problems with traditional or classical accounts of meanings as simple feature lists. Wittgenstein (1953) is perhaps best known to psychologists as arguing for the "family resemblance" view of concepts wherein no one feature of a concept is necessary to its meaning. Rosch (1975), in particular, has traced aspects of her views back to Wittgenstein. Nonetheless, Putnam and Kripke have made perhaps the most concerted attack on traditional views of meaning by arguing that there may be no simple property or properties that language users always rely on to pick out the referents of a term. Such necessary and sufficient features might in fact exist, but they are by this account rarely if ever part of an analytic meaning that is known to most users of the term in question, and they are not the criteria used to pick out the extension.

The writings of Putnam and Kripke and earlier authors such as Wittgenstein have not been lost on cognitive psychologists. Smith and Medin (1981) have chronicled the revolution that occurred in the field when Rosch and her colleagues (for example, Rosch and Mervis 1975), Smith, Shoben, and Rips (1974), Hampton (1976), and others conducted a series of studies suggesting that concepts do not have necessary and defining features. With natural kinds in particular—for example, dogs, tigers, and gold—people seem unable to give anything like a set of defining features for picking out instances. As soon as one posits a defining feature of "tiger," such as stripes, it is easy enough to describe a consensually real tiger lacking such a feature, such as a tiger that happens to be albino but is like tigers in all other respects. The conclusion normally drawn from such examples is that if any large subset of characteristic features is present, the entity is a valid member of the category, with no one feature being necessary.

These accounts argue against concepts having necessary and sufficient features for picking out their extensions. They do not, however, automatically show that the extensions in a set have no necessary and sufficient features, a contrast that is important to both Putnam and Kripke (see also Rey 1983). Unfortunately, it is often assumed in the psychological literature that the failure of subjects to list a set of essential properties for members of a kind does entail that no such properties for the kind in fact exist.

The difficulty of providing definitions is not limited to animal concepts. Similar examples can also be constructed for the other traditional natural kinds such as plants and compounds. One can easily imagine a set of flowers, each of which lacks a different characteristic feature of roses but all of which are considered roses. The same sorts of considerations can also be extended to other classes of things that are not normally discussed but are also natural kinds, such as thunderstorms, earthquakes, and diseases.

If natural kinds are "defined" merely in terms of characteristic features, then a characteristic-to-defining shift in development becomes much less of a general phenomenon, possibly restricted to a relatively small number of natural language terms (perhaps as small as 300, by Putnam's count). There would be only more characteristic features to acquire and no possibility of a shift toward defining features. Analogous shifts, such as those from holistic to analytic representations, are similarly imperiled. Thus, the century of research described in chapter 2 documenting a qualitative shift in the structure of concepts might be tightly circumscribed in terms of the relevant concepts.

Not only natural kind concepts but also many non-natural kind concepts, such as those for artifacts, may be mere collections of characteristic features. Most of the concepts empirically studied by Rosch and her colleagures have been concepts of artifacts, such as types of furniture, clothing, and vehicles, rather than natural kinds. It might seem that functional definitions can be extracted for artifacts, and yet such approaches have not fared well. A chair, for example, might be built so poorly that it does not really hold one's weight, or it might have such bad splinters that one cannot sit on it; it is nonetheless a chair. There still may be a definition for such artifacts having to do with the function *intended* by their creators, whether or not it was actually satisfied in the finished product; but these examples illustrate that there are potential problems with providing simple definitions for most artifacts.

To make matters worse, the "best-defined" or purest nominal kind terms themselves may not be safe. Schwartz (1977) suggests that "some version of the traditional theory is more or less correct about such terms" (p. 39); but perhaps even this small subset does not have the neat simple set of defining features that we had imagined. Is a continent surrounded by water on all sides, such as Australia, still an island? Is a premature infant who is my father's brother really my uncle? What about the adopted brother of my father? Philosophers and linguists are able to find fuzzy, indeterminate cases for almost any word imaginable. For example, Coleman and Kay (1981) analyzed the English word "lie" in an attempt to prove that it too must be considered a prototype concept. They chose "lie" in order to demonstrate that semantic prototypes were not restricted to "directly perceptible physical objects or [things] with physical sensations themselves, e.g. colors, plants and animals, utensils, and furniture" (p. 27). Coleman and Kay propose that in a situation where a speaker S asserts some proposition P to an addressee A, a highly prototypical or "good" lie has all three of the following features:

1. P is false.
2. S believes P to be false.
3. In uttering P, S intends to deceive A.

In line with their proposal that this list is a prototype with graded degrees of membership, Coleman and Kay argue that not only will subjects view most speech acts that have all three features as good examples of lies, but they will also often label acts that have any two of these three features as marginal but legitimate instances of lies. They constructed scenarios incorporating different numbers of these features and asked subjects to judge whether they described lies. The results suggest a graded effect of judged membership in the lie category that was predictable from the number of features present in the story.

If Coleman and Kay's analysis is correct and can be extended to other social terms, one wonders whether all terms are perhaps governed by what they call "prototype semantics." What then could an apparent, qualitative, characteristic-to-defining shift in word meaning and concept structure really be? Although the characteristic-to-defining notion may in most cases be an inadequate description of concept acquisition, it may well provide an oversimplified but easily describable way of understanding more complex and subtle qualitative shifts. There are some signs of the usefulness of such a contrast even in Coleman and Kay's paper when they suggest that a distinction should perhaps be recognized between "prototypical" and "typical" features, where "prototypical properties play a role in meanings of words, while merely typical properties do not" (p. 37). They propose that Lakoff's (1972) work on linguistic hedges may provide independent evidence for the typical/prototypical distinction. In particular, phrases such as "*x* is a regular *y*," as in "John is a regular fox," may utilize only the typical features of a concept (in this case "fox") and not the prototypical. Although Coleman and Kay do not discuss this issue in depth, it may reveal a distinction that is crucial for understanding the developmental shifts for most concepts. An unpacking of why prototypical features "play a role in meanings of words" whereas typical features do not may illustrate some fundamental limitations of the whole approach of prototype semantics that Coleman and Kay so warmly embrace in their paper. In particular, the "prototypical features" may be central to meaning just because they are not simply pure indices of prototypicality and because they *are* centrally involved in other more explanatory sets of relations (see also Medin and Shoben 1988). First, however, we should consider a series of recent studies that independently raise questions about the adequacy of representing word meanings merely as collections of characteristic features.

Problems with Prototypes

In a provocative challenge to prototype semantics Armstrong, Gleitman, and Gleitman (1983) questioned the appropriateness of conclusions drawn from the empirical research on prototype theory. In particular, they focused on the two measures commonly used by Rosch and her colleagues: (1) ratings of typicality of category examples and (2) reaction times to identify legitimate instances. They asked whether data that showed a strong correlation between degree of typicality and reaction time should necessarily imply that the meaning of the term involved was a probabilistic concept organized as a prototype. To assess this possibility, they used the concept of "odd number" and showed that subjects did indeed rate some odd numbers as more typical of the category (for instance, 7 and 3) than others (for instance, 109 and 2003) and that they did take longer to identify the atypical members than the typical ones. Of course, 7 and 3 are not really any more odd than 2003 and 109 and indeed, if subjects are asked directly whether typical odd numbers are or can be more odd than atypical ones, they will flatly deny it.

Armstrong, Gleitman, and Gleitman's study is therefore an existence proof that well-defined concepts can yield an array of empirical results very much like those that purportedly were evidence for a prototype semantics for other terms. Smith and Medin's (1981) review of research on concepts and categories, for example, refers extensively to the sort of data that Armstrong, Gleitman, and Gleitman were able to collect for odd numbers and other well-defined concepts. It is therefore not at all obvious how those data should be interpreted for less well defined concepts. What follows about the nature of concept structure from reaction times and typicality ratings? The most negative conclusion might be that nothing follows and that the data are purely epiphenomenal and have nothing to do with the real nature of concepts.

It might be argued that Armstrong, Gleitman, and Gleitman's results show just the opposite of what they say—that is, that even the most apparently well defined concepts have some parts that are probabilistic. This is a complex claim, since it depends on what we mean by saying that something is "part of a concept." If there are probabilistic relations that are part of the concept "odd number," they do not in any way affect membership in the category "odd number." Consequently, it must be claimed that parts of a concept's meaning bear no relation to picking out its instances. There may be merit to such claims, and one account developed in this book provides a way for making sense of them.

A second objection to Armstrong, Gleitman, and Gleitman's argument has been made by Lakoff (1987), who argues that they and many other cognitive psychologists (such as those whose work is summarized in Smith and Medin 1981) have mistakenly made the Effects = Structure assumption, an assumption that, according to Lakoff, Rosch never made. The Effects = Structure assumption is the belief that the various prototype effects produced in the experiments described above imply that concepts must be structured as prototypes. Lakoff is correct in suggesting that Rosch is careful to caution the reader not to assume that prototypicality judgments imply a particular type of representation (see, for example, Rosch 1978). What Rosch does claim, however, is that prototypicality effects must constrain our models of representation in such a way that they can account for the phenomena uncovered. Moreover, she interprets the patterns of prototypicality judgments as arguing against a particular theory of representations, namely, the classical view.

> A representation of categories in terms of conjoined necessary and sufficient attributes alone would probably be incapable of handling all of the presently known facts, but there are many representations other than necessary and sufficient attributes that are possible. (1978, 40–41)

These subtleties and clarifications do not reduce the importance of Armstrong, Gleitman, and Gleitman's paper, for it not only demonstrates that prototype effects do not entail prototype representations but also strongly suggests that concepts whose major aspects of meaning are classically organized can nonetheless produce these effects. Lakoff would disagree with the claim that integers, for example, are for the most part classically organized. He suggests that there must be a rich underlying cognitive structure in the forms of various cognitive models that produces these prototype effects. Lakoff argues that we use various models to comprehend numbers (and for that matter most any other concept) and that, within each model, some numbers will have a privileged status. One model, for example, might have to do with how we generate numbers in counting, another might have to do with computation, and yet another with the odd/even distinction. It is the composite of all these models that produces the prototype effects. By this account there is still no list of necessary and sufficient features, but merely different models being applied to the domain of numbers with different numbers fitting into each model to varying extents.

Lakoff emphasizes that concepts derive their meanings as a function of their embedding in cognitive models. Although at one level Lakoff's contention is compatible with proposals that theories and concepts are interwoven, there are two problems with his application of this notion to Armstrong, Gleitman, and Gleitman's study.

First, it is certainly not necessary that all prototype effects be produced by cognitive models or, as Lakoff claims more broadly, that categories must have rich internal structures for such effects to be produced. In fact, elsewhere in his monograph (p. 47) he acknowledges that a variety of different mechanisms can produce prototype effects. One such mechanism is the simple recording of typicality information and similarity among exemplars. Thus, in Posner and Keele's (1968) pioneering study on the abstraction of prototypes from sets of related meaningless dot patterns, there is no evidence that subjects developed models of those dot patterns or that any rich internal structure was involved. Consequently, it is not clear what constraints, if any, typicality judgments should place on the internal structure of cognitive categories. We may well have several models for integers (different mathematical models, for example), but the typicality effects associated with those integers may bear little relation to those models and may reflect mere exposure to certain classes of exemplars for reasons unrelated or only faintly related to the models (a model may cause some numbers to be more frequently used, but many model-independent factors can also influence such frequencies). In fact, Armstrong, Gleitman, and Gleitman's results can be construed as demonstrating just such a lack of contact. Since Lakoff does not provide any detailed mechanisms for how such a model might be used to predict prototypicality effects, it is difficult to know how to tell whether such an account would work beyond a general descriptive level.

A second problem with Lakoff's account is that some models might well result in attributing necessary and sufficient features to applicable concepts in the relevant domain. Without a principled account of models and their structure, it is not clear in what ways they should constrain attributions of features to concepts. Thus, simply arguing that concepts are embedded in models does not entail in itself that their structure is constrained in any particular way or that any particular account is automatically excluded.

Several others have also raised questions about how to interpret prototype effects and about the adequacy of representations that might be organized as prototypes (as assumed by many cognitive psychologists). Thus, Bourne (1982) also shows that well-defined categories can yield typicality effects, and Osherson and Smith (1981) challenge prototypes and other views of representations as fuzzy sets on the grounds that they fail to provide adequate accounts of conceptual combination.

The problem of predicting the structure of conceptual combinations from the structure of their constituent concepts has proven to be subtle and elusive. Some of the most impressive work in the area has been a series of studies by Hampton (1987, 1988a, b, c), in which he demonstrates a surprising extent to which the structure of combinations can be predicted from the typicality structure of the constituents. Rejecting older fuzzy set models of conceptual combination (see Osherson and Smith 1981), Hampton develops a new model based on a union of attributes from component concepts but subject to the following constraints: (1) attributes of low importance are excluded, (2) necessity and impossibility relations among attributes must be respected and (3) attributes of "dominant" constituent concepts (those with greater numbers of important attributes) have more influence on the combination than equally important attributes of nondominant constituent concepts. These striking results stand out strongly against somewhat more informal examples of conceptual combinations that clearly cannot be predictable from the typicality structure of their constituents. (Murphy (1987), for example, argues that no model based on typicality could predict the structures of "ocean road," "ocean view," "ocean bird," "ocean voyage," or "ocean plate.") Hampton is fully aware of such examples and discusses how aspects of his data show noncompositionality and inheritance failures; but the primary finding is how well his model works for a wide range of concepts.

Taken as a whole, the work on conceptual combination suggests that, although concepts may well have vital parts that go beyond typicality and that can be responsible for making combinations unpredictable from typicality, in most cases of everyday discourse where such combinations must be comprehended rapidly and effortlessly, typicality relations subject to constraints of the sort that Hampton proposes may be the predominant structuring influence on the combination. This work, then, may support the heterogeneous view of concepts presented in chapters 1 and 2 in which both typicality structure and some deeper set of coherent beliefs are essential for understanding concept structure.

Perhaps the most relevant concern about concept structure is raised by Murphy and Medin (1985), who document limitations of probabilistic accounts in explaining the coherence of conceptual structures. The crucial point of their overview of the field is that concepts are not merely bundles of features or attributes caused by frequencies of occurrence and cooccurrence. The elements in a concept and the members of a category exhibit a coherence that goes far beyond such accounts. Moreover, the existence of illusory correlations between features reveals fundamental problems with accounts based purely on typicality. Murphy and Medin conclude by arguing that we must have a theory-based account of conceptual structure that deals with the theoretical contexts in which concepts are embedded. By appealing to the importance of theory, we may now be able to consider a model of how the child's concepts of natural kinds develop and change.

Natural Kinds, Theories, and Conceptual Change

In a series of important papers on natural kinds, Quine (1963, 1974, 1977) makes a proposal that bears importantly on thinking about concepts and conceptual change. His paper "Natural Kinds" (Quine 1977) is particularly revealing. He focuses on the famous Goodman riddle of induction (Goodman 1955), which asks what predicates are "projectible" in various settings. If all emeralds we examine are green, we are likely to expect that the next one we encounter will also be green. And yet it is also true that all emeralds we have examined are "grue," where "grue" means "green if examined today or earlier and blue if examined after today." We do not, however, assume that emeralds examined tomorrow will be grue and, therefore, blue. Why is it that green is "projectible" when making inductions about emeralds, whereas "grue" is not? Quine argues that the intuitive reason why we expect the next emerald to be green rather than grue is that green emeralds are generally more similar to each other than grue ones (where one may be green and the other blue). This "answer" hides the real reason in the issue of similarity, an issue that Quine sees as essential to understanding what a natural kind is and how we come to know it. Quine argues that similarity is initially an innate set of preferences that guide inductions (see also Quine 1960). It is here that his nativist remnants become most evident.

> For me then the problem of induction is a problem about the world: a problem of how we, as we now are (by our present scientific lights), in a world we never made, should stand better than random or coin-tossing chances of coming out right when we predict by inductions which are based on our innate scientifically unjustified similarity standard. Darwin's natural selection is a plausible partial explanation. (1977, 166)

But Quine sees a dilemma in evolution's endowing us with an innate quality space that is slanted to see certain properties and relations, such as color, as most relevant to the classification of kinds; for such biases may work against the construction of scientific theories about kinds.

> Evidently natural selection has dealt with the conflict by endowing man doubly with both a color-slanted similarity space and the ingenuity to rise above it....He has risen above it by developing modified systems of kinds, hence modified similarity standards for scientific purposes. By the trial and error process of theorizing he has regrouped things into new kinds which prove to lend themselves to many inductions better than old. (1977, 166–167)

We could not make any progress at all in making sense of our world if we were not endowed with some sort of quality space that gives us similarity metrics that have some concordance with meaningful (for us) cuts in the world. But Quine argues that such cuts may be meaningful only in certain spheres of activity (as with learning basic food preferences) and that they are thereby limited. Consequently, we use their first approximation of how to cut the world as a point of departure for developing theoretically more important cuts. Quine illustrates his point with a marine example, wherein the initial classification of whales and porpoises with fish is superseded by classification of them as a separate kind. All of this leads to a developmental hypothesis, which once again is best described by Quine himself.

> Between an innate similarity notion or spacing of qualities and a scientifically sophisticated one, there are all gradations. Science, after all, differs from common sense only in degree of methodological sophistication. Our experiences from early infancy are bound to have overlaid our innate spacing of qualities by modifying and supplementing our grouping habits little by little, inclining us more and more to an appreciation of theoretical kinds and similarities, long before we reach the point of studying science systematically as such. Moreover the latter phases do not wholly supersede the earlier; we retain different similarity standards, different systems of kinds, for use in different contexts. We all still say that a marsupial mouse is more like an ordinary mouse than a kangaroo, except when we are concerned with genetic matters. Something like our innate quality spaces continues to function alongside the more sophisticated regroupings that have been found by scientific experience to facilitate induction. (1977, 167–168)

> This development is a development away from the immediate, the subjective, animal sense of similarity to the remoter sense of similarity determined by scientific hypotheses and posits and constructs. Things are similar in the later or theoretical sense to the degree that they are interchangeable parts of the cosmic machine revealed by science. (1977, 171)

There is a great deal more of interest in Quine's essay on natural kinds, including arguments that ultimately similarity may dissolve altogether as a guiding principle for organizing kinds. But here I focus on the thesis pertaining to conceptual change, for it suggests that concepts undergo a characteristic-to-theory-based shift (where "characteristic" is construed as immediate, subjective similarity), perhaps analogous to the characteristic-to-defining shift for nominal kinds. There is also a suggestion that the early classifications are more perceptual, whereas the latter are more conceptual. Later-emerging theory may not be completely unconstrained in structure or arise purely out of inductions building up out of the innate quality space. Theories as well as percepts may have innate biases on them, but more groundwork often must be laid for the theoretical biases to become evident. (It is interesting that elsewhere in this essay

(p. 173), Quine indirectly refers to an innate essentialist reductionistic tendency that seems to be a bias on theories, a point considered in more detail later in this chapter.)

In one other respect Quine's proposal will bear significantly on the arguments made here. The notion that the old and new similarity spaces can coexist in adults may be critical for helping us better understand many current conflicts about the nature of concepts, including the interpretation of the Armstrong, Gleitman, and Gleitman study discussed earlier.

Before attempting to tackle Quine's developmental speculation in an empirical manner, we must consider more carefully the nature of the knowledge that we do seem to have about natural kinds and the ways in which it might go beyond characteristic features, or Quine's "immediate and subjective" ones. To understand better what sorts of knowledge structures guide our understanding of natural kinds, let us turn to some more recent literature on the subject, as well as related discussions of possible contrasts with nominal kinds and artifacts.

The Underlying Structure: Natural Kinds and Other Kinds

Almost everyone has had the intuition that things are not always what they seem and that there is something deeper and more basic to a kind than what is immediately apparent. One way to capture this intuition is to argue that things have essences that are often difficult to discern immediately. The notion of essences is a very old one that has pervaded philosophical discussions since Aristotle, partly because it helps capture the common intuition that many natural kinds exhibit a kind of duality between essences and more immediate properties. Several questions arise that are relevant to concepts, theories, and cognitive development. Do natural kinds have underlying structures that are essences or that can at least be construed as corresponding to what we think of as essences? Do essences "cause" surface features, much as genotypes cause phenotypes? Are these underlying structures qualitatively different from those at the "surface"? Are they different for other kinds such as artifacts? What is the role of causal theory and scientific discovery in determining the nature of these structures or, more accurately, in coming to believe in such essences? Are there more detailed developmental hypotheses than Quine has suggested? These are hardly the sorts of questions that can be fully resolved in the next few pages, but by at least raising the issues and pointing out some of their ramifications, I hope to illustrate why these philosophical issues have an important bearing on the study of conceptual development.

Locke (1690/1964) drew an important contrast between nominal and real essences that has led to the distinction between nominal and natural kinds now common in the literature (see, for example, Schwartz 1978; Boyd 1979). Locke felt that all natural kinds had real essences but that these were undiscoverable (since they could not be perceived) and that we might only have access to their "nominal" essences or conventionally fixed definitions. Nominal essences would then reflect little that is intrinsic about the kind but would instead reflect the intentions of the language users, who have decided by convention or fiat that all things having properties a-n will be called "x." These properties might be deemed necessary and sufficient for the label and thus become defining features. Dupré (1981) suggests that it is also possible for nominal essences to be specified by a more characteristic set of features. Under such an account, when a kind has both a prototype and a simple definition associated with it (as with kinship terms), it would be unclear whether the nominal essence corresponded to the defining features, the characteristic ones, or possibly even both.

Locke (1690/1964) seems to have adopted a "defining features" view of the nominal essence. His descriptions of nominal essences seem to consist of necessary and sufficient features. Nominal essences are

> those precise abstract ideas we have in our minds....And what are the alterations that may or may not be made in a *horse* or *lead*, without making either of them another species? In determining the species of things by *our* abstract ideas this is easy to resolve; but, if anyone will regulate himself herein by supposed real essences, he will, I suppose, be at a loss: and he will never be able to know when anything precisely ceases to be a species of horse or lead. (p. 269)

When Locke discusses the nominal essence of gold, he lists what seem to be necessary and sufficient features. In the following passage he illustrates how natural kinds like gold differ from what he calls "simple ideas" and "modes."

> Essences being thus distinguished into nominal and real, we may further observe that, in the species of simple ideas and modes, they are always the same, but in substances always quite different. Thus, a figure including a space between three lines is the real as well as nominal essence of a triangle, it being not only the abstract idea to which the general name is annexed, but the very essentia or being of the thing itself....But it is far otherwise concerning...[gold]....For, it is the real constitution of its insensible parts, on which depend all those properties of colour, weight, fusibility, fixedness, &c., which makes it to be gold, or gives it a right to that name, which is therefore its nominal essence. (p. 217)

Note that Locke would not want other characteristic properties of triangles (such as the most typically shaped ones) to be included in the nominal essence and that other typical qualities of gold are not included. In a different passage (p. 260) he proposes a developmental account of how "gold" would be learned, which consists of gradual addition of more and more necessary and sufficient features with necessary overextensions of use in earlier ages, an account that is strikingly similar to Clark's (1973) original semantic feature hypothesis of word meaning acquisition.

Others have also suggested that Locke's notion of nominal essence appears to be the same as what Smith and Medin call the "classical view." Woozley (1964), for example, argues that Locke sees nominal essences as containing analytic truths of the form "gold is yellow" and not synthetic truths of the form "a quantity of gold can be increased by admixture with red earth" (p. 22).

Locke's view of the contrast between nominal and real essences thus seems to imply a two-fold distinction: one between the epistemological and the metaphysical (see also Rey 1983), and another between pure definitions and other less precise property relations. What, then, are nominal kinds? Schwartz (1980) defines nominal kinds as just those kinds that have no real essence and only a nominal essence. Since the nominal essence of such kinds is in no way causally connected to a real essence, it is solely the product of human conventions and/or stipulations in the form of simple definitions. In the strongest form, nominal kinds might be defined as Putnam's (1975) "one-criterion" concepts, whose instances are fully specified by one and only one if-and-only-if statement.

Are triangles nominal kinds in such an account? Schwartz claims that nominal kinds have no real essences, yet Locke asserts that for triangles, the nominal and real essences are the same. Moreover, many would argue that the concept "triangle" is not merely created by human convention or agreement but is in fact a preexisting abstract form. So as not to proliferate distinctions until necessary, I will assume such things as triangles to be nominal kinds as well, albeit possibly a special subset.

Schwartz may not be correct in assuming that nominal kinds have only pure definitions as their meanings. Perhaps a more probabilistic notion will eventually be needed to deal with current criticisms of the classical view; this would certainly be the case for the nominal essences of natural kinds. Nonetheless, the pure definition version will be the working understanding of "nominal kind" for several of the studies that follow. Moreover, Schwartz's emphasis on nominal kinds having nominal essences that are not causally linked to a real essence (this would also hold for triangles, since a thing cannot be causally linked to itself) entails that they would not figure in stable generalizations or contain projectible predicates.

It is not necessary that the meanings of nominal kinds should be definitional and analytic because they have no real essence; it just seems to be so for most terms of this sort. Thus, as an empirical matter, it is suggested that some concepts, perhaps a relatively small set, do in fact seem to be organized in terms of fairly clean contrasts of characteristic and defining features, where only the defining features figure in the meanings of such concepts and in the identification of true instances.

The question remains whether it is even legitimate to talk of things having essences of either sort (nominal or real), and if not, what is it about kinds that gives rise to our intuitions about such differences. Putnam (1975) quite clearly feels that all kinds have essences. As part of his argument against simple necessary and sufficient definitions for natural kinds, he holds that meaning cannot be given either by a set of Boolean relations among features or by a more probabilistic cluster of features. Rather, those features, in the most optimistic cases, are merely diagnostic of and result from a real essence that is the true basis for deciding whether something is a member of a given natural kind. He is not alone among current thinkers in advocating essentialism (see also Kripke 1972b; Copi 1954), but he has taken one of the strongest positions, suggesting that such things as artifacts have real essences, just like such traditional natural kinds as animals, plants, and minerals. On this view, pencils and chairs have essences, just like tigers and gold. The details of their essences might be different, but they are not the result of conventions or in other ways like Locke's observable essences; they are supposedly potentially discoverable underlying principles of pencil- and chairhood.

Schwartz (1978) takes exception to such a claim, however, arguing that there are several important differences between natural kinds and artifacts that revolve around the concept of essence. Schwartz argues that only terms of natural kinds can be "indexical," which in Putnam's sense means that the referents of such terms possess underlying real essences; the terms of artifacts cannot, because, for Schwartz, artifacts are nominal kinds. Schwartz claims that

> if "pencil" were indexical, then it would also be the case that the term could be extended to things that did not superficially resemble the paradigm pencils, so long as they had the same nature or underlying trait...there is no underlying nature of pencils, nor is there a presumption of such a nature. What makes something a pencil are superficial characteristics such as a certain form and function. There is nothing underlying about these features. They are analytically associated with the the term "pencil," not disclosed by scientific investigation. (p. 571)

Since terms like "chair", "pencil", and "lamp" are not indexical and it is not analytic that chairs, pencils, and lamps are artifacts, I call them nominal kinds to distinguish them from natural kinds. Members of a nominal kind do not share a common hidden nature, and we can give an analytic specification in terms of form and function of what it is to be a member of a nominal kind. (p. 572)

One consequence of this difference, Schwartz claims, is that nominal kinds do not support inductions in the same way that natural kinds do. Thus, the observed fact that several chairs have some property, such as having four legs, does not support the contention that all chairs have four legs. Few predicates are projectible over nominal kinds, whereas several are projectible over natural ones. Schwartz considers this difference relevant to explaining why there can be no science of nominal kinds.

If a scientist were interested in chairs as a subject of scientific study and got himself a good specimen and started to examine it closely in order to discover the nature of chairs, we would think he was crazy. Compare this with the zoologist interested in snakes, who obtains a fine specimen and begins to dissect it....I am not sure if terms for kinds of artifacts like "pencil," or "chair," or "lamp" are one-criterion terms, but they are like "bachelor" in that they name synthetic classes. In order to see what is meant by synthetic class, consider the difference between "dog" and "cat" on the one hand, and "pet" on the other. "Dog" and "cat" are natural kind terms, but "pet" is a nominal kind term. Something is a pet if it satisfies certain descriptions. We do not presume that pets share a common under-lying nature, other than being animals, perhaps. Something is a pet not because of this nature but because of this relationship to other things, its function or role, and so on. "Pet" is not the name of a natural kind, rather, pets form a synthetic class. (p. 573)

In this passage Schwartz describes an important set of intuitions all of us seem to have about some of the contrasts between natural kinds and artifacts. His interpretation of them, however, may not be quite right and may need further elaboration. Two potential problems converge to form a new account both of what underlies the surface for natural kinds and of what makes them different from other kinds: the issue of whether natural kinds really have essences and the issue of whether nominal kinds, and artifacts in particular, are merely synthetic classes defined by certain descriptions. Recent papers in both the philosophy of science and the philosophy of language provide insight into a more systematic way of handling the phenomena that Schwartz describes.

Perhaps even the most widely accepted natural kinds, such as species, do not have real, fixed essences of the sort that have been assumed for so long by philosophers including Putnam. If not, then one wonders about what else exists beyond the characteristic features of natural kinds and about how scientific discovery could change our concepts in the way Quine describes. Several papers have questioned the validity of essentialist assumptions about natural kinds (see, for example, Mellor 1977), though it is not possible to discuss each of them here. Dupré (1981) offers one of the most detailed critiques in the context of biological kinds. Dupré wonders whether Locke's contrast between real and nominal essences is warranted and is concerned that current thinkers have gone even beyond Locke. Emboldened by progress in the more reductionistic aspects of twentieth-century science, they now hold that Locke was prematurely pessimistic and that real essences might be very close to things like genetic structure and atomic numbers. Dupré questions whether Putnam's distinction between a stereotype (much like Rosch's prototype) and an extension determined by theoretical (and often microstructural) truth is correct, and whether it can be equated with the nominal and real essences for natural kinds. The crux of his objection concerns the notion that no unique or privileged set of "sameness relations" can be found for uniting sets of things into biological kinds.

Dupré holds that experts differ from laypeople not qualitatively but in degree. Accordingly, the only change that occurs with increasing conceptual sophistication is increasing knowledge of characteristic features and development of richer stereotypes. Dupré (p. 73) bases much of his argument on the observation that preanalytic, lay uses of terms for biological kinds correspond poorly with scientific distinctions. Thus, contrary to Putnam's views, there is no obvious tendency for common natural language categories for biological entities to converge on the same classes uncovered by the most current scientific theories. Dupré mentions many examples, particularly from the plant kingdom, of things that look and perhaps function very similarly (that is, have common stereotypes) and have the same common name but in fact are members of very divergent species (see also Gould 1983 for many other examples). He also describes the converse: plants that differ from each other in appearance and function and have different common names but are members of closely related species. For example, all those things we normally call "trees" belong to very different species. Thus, pine trees are conifers, whereas oaks and maples are angiosperms (flowering plants). This might be reasonable if conifers and angiosperms were both simple subsets of trees; but they are not, for a great many other nontrees count as angiosperms, including daisies, cacti, and roses.

Dupré advocates what he calls a "promiscuous realism," a view that favors the existence of indefinitely many sameness relations that can be used to distinguish classes of organisms (hence the realism) but also claims that none of these relations is privileged (hence the promiscuity). For Dupré, "The class of trees, for example, is just as real as the class of angiosperms; it is just that we have different reasons for distinguishing them" (p. 82). Dupré doubts the existence of any set of essential properties that can be based on genetic material or other microstructural features and notes that these can be as variable as other more surface-based morphological features.

> If one examines the trees or birds in a particular area, it is apparent that these fall into a number of classes that differ from one another in numerous respects. But the essentialist conclusion that one might be tempted to draw from this fact is dissipated first by more careful study, which reveals that these distinguishing characteristics are by no means constant within classes, and second by extending the scope of the investigation in both space and time, whereupon the limitations both of intraspecific similarity and interspecific differences will become increasingly apparent. (p. 89)

In sum, Dupré's account suggests that natural kinds may not be so different from any other kinds and that the notion of an underlying essence may be illusory. It is not immediately clear what the psychological consequences of this view are, but at the least it raises questions about whether a qualitative shift might take place in the way concepts for natural kinds are represented. Qualitative shifts might only remain tenable if one were to reinterpret the nature of what underlies the stereotype or characteristic features of a natural kind. In fact, there are hints of such a reinterpretation even in Dupré's words; for when he states that "we have different *reasons* for distinguishing them," he is relying on something beyond the stereotype for organizing conceptual space. The best suggestion about what such a reinterpretation would look like is in a paper by Boyd (1984) entitled "Natural Kinds, Homeostasis, and the Limits of Essentialism."

Boyd's Causal Homeostasis

Boyd is concerned with the revival of essentialism brought about by "the new semantic naturalism" of Putnam and Kripke. He suggests that the traditional views of essentialism may not be correct, but that there are underlying aspects of entities that demarcate natural kinds and to which scientists refer. He argues that

> kinds, properties, relations, etc. are natural if they reflect important features of the causal structure of the world. (p. 9)

Naturalness in this sense is not a property of kinds, but also of properties (solubility in water), magnitude (mass), and relations (exert a force on). ...Theoretical considerations determine which complex predicates formulated from natural kind, property, or relation terms we should consider projectible; the role of the terms themselves is to refer to causally significant features of the world....Finally...both explanations and scientifically important laws and generalizations may be merely statistical or reflect trends rather than exceptionless regularities, and finding such generalizations or explanations is no less dependent upon theory-determined identification of causally important kinds, properties or relations than is the identification of exceptionless laws. Indeed, to decide otherwise would be to exclude the paradigm of natural kinds—those of biology. (pp. 10–11)

Boyd thus argues against the account of essences as being some simple fixed set of necessary and sufficient principles and instead argues for more probabilistic patterns as well. The crucial point, however, is the notion of a set of causally important properties that are "contingently clustered." Boyd sees the clustering of such terms as being not merely chance coincidences but rather the result of what he calls a causal "homeostasis" where the presence of some properties tends to favor the presence of others or where there are common underlying properties that tend to maintain the presence of the clusters. These homeostatic clusters can be loose or tight and will demarcate natural kinds to the extent that they are in fact tight (that is, to the extent that they exhibit higher intercorrelations of features); and those kinds will be natural to the extent that they are causally important in explaining phenomena associated with the kinds picked out by the cluster. The notion that many natural kind terms are homeostatic cluster terms has several consequences. They can be extensionally vague (that is, unclear cases of reference) and yet still describe excellent natural kinds. There might be several different homeostatic clusters for the same set of entities. The contrasts with other kinds may have less to do with the presence of an essence per se and more to do with the kind of theoretical domain that the causal relations evoke. Note further the difference between Dupré's account and Boyd's. The causal homeostasis notion easily allows for multiple causal clusters underlying roughly the same things. Thus, in addition to the complex causal relations that have created the distinction in kind between angiosperms and conifers, other ecological causal clusters have caused trees to be a kind different from other sorts of plants. Thus, a different stable set of causal relations is responsible for the rigid trunks, sap, patterns of branching, and so on, that set trees apart as a natural kind. In contrast to

Dupré's account, however, the causal homeostasis view does not predict unbridled promiscuous realism, where what are called kinds is largely arbitrary. Though there may be multiple causal clusters forming several kinds over the same instances, they are hardly arbitrary or indefinitely many. Realism thus has some sense of propriety and is not totally promiscuous; it is merely polygamous, and like most forms of polygamy, frowns on true promiscuity.

Boyd takes pains to maintain a distinction between the natural definitions that emerge out of homeostatic cluster concepts and the other features that may be highly correlated with a kind. Even when some features may be extremely useful and diagnostic for identifying a kind, they may not figure prominently in its underlying essence.

> The adoption of a homeostatic property cluster conception of the natural definitions of biological species does not entail abandoning the naturalistic distinction between definitional features and mere symptoms, even where morphological characteristics are at issue....It is by no means the case however that all of the morphological characteristics by which species are typically distinguished in taxonomic practice will meet this condition [of entering into biological laws] it is highly doubtful, for example, that the differences in scale counts by which closely related reptile species are traditionally distinguished are evolutionarily significant differences in morphology. Scale counts are, on the homeostatic cluster conception of natural definitions, mere symptoms not constituents of the definitional cluster. (pp. 50–51) We should not think of such properties as constituents of natural definitions even when they may be extremely reliable indicators of kind membership. (p. 59)

One of the most important points in Boyd's argument is that the features that are united in a homeostatic cluster are not and should not be taken as the "natural definitions." Rather, the underlying homeostatic mechanism responsible for the cooccurrence of those features is equally if not much more important to the true meaning of a natural kind. This emphasis on a network of causal relations illustrates the limitations of merely representing concepts by probabilistic arrays of features as is done in so many "prototype semantics" approaches; such accounts miss some of the most important ingredients in meaning and may erroneously stress some features that are highly intercorrelated but causally much less important in the underlying homeostatic mechanism. Boyd sees the presence of a property cluster as evidence that an underlying homeostatic mechanism is present—and, therefore, a natural kind—but this strategy can be fallible. In some cases a correlation might arise by pure chance, or by causal relations that are isolated, transient, or central to another cluster. It is the underlying mechanism that is most crucial to our understanding of what the kind is and of how we can make inductions about it. Boyd suspects that, for many natural kinds, the underlying causal mechanisms can be exceedingly complex and that we may often operate, at least as laypeople, with much cruder approximate knowledge of these mechanisms. I suspect that it is rare, however, that we do not develop any such causal structure at all.

Boyd makes an additional point that—although used in the service of a philosophical argument about essences—carries within it a potentially important psychological claim.

> There is an extremely well entrenched philosophical expectation about the definitions or "essences" of kinds—an expectation shared, for instance, by empiricists and "essentialists"—that the essence or definition of any kind will be provided by non-relational properties *internal* to the objects which fall under the kind....Roughly speaking, we don't expect the defining features of the members of a kind to include complex causal relations to, or interactions with, other objects or substances. (p. 45)

Boyd's point in this context is that this expectation is usually wrong—that the "essences" of natural kinds often are described in terms of external relations to other objects—and he cites species concepts as one example, where patterns of interbreeding are such external factors. Though this may be true in many instances for natural kinds, an equally if not more interesting point for psychological purposes is the presence of what seems to be an irrational assumption that, if there is an essence, it must be internal to the natural kind. (Incidentally, Locke was quite explicit on this assumption: "By this *real essence* I mean that real constitution of anything, which is the foundation of all those properties that are combined in, and are constantly found to co-exist with, the nominal essence: that particular constitution which everything has within itself, without any relation to anything without it" (1690/1964, 286).) In empirical studies described in subsequent chapters I will examine whether such assumptions seem to exist and how they develop.

By Boyd's account, the "natural definitions" of kinds, or their essences, are intrinsically causal in nature, and the features and properties in those causal accounts are only part of the essence. Because the features are only important to the extent that they are deeply embedded in this causal structure, we see why the dichotomy between mere symptoms, or characteristic features, and "defining" ones is preserved, thus allowing us to distinguish between a pure prototype representation and "essence." At the same time Boyd's account allows with a vengeance for the defining features themselves to be probabilistic, largely because the laws they enter into can be probabilistic. Thus, we begin to see a dissociation between representations being probabilistic and having a prototype-based semantics, a distinction that has frequently been blurred in the literature. Under Boyd's analysis, the notion that prototype semantics and its variants (exemplar-based and dimensional views) are the only alternatives to necessary and sufficient feature lists disintegrates.

Boyd's ideas may shed some light on the nature of nominal essences as well, although his account is considerably more complicated than the fragments presented here. Boyd refers back to Locke's phrase that nominal essences are the "workmanship of the understanding" rather than of nature: "They are, in some sense, *arbitrary* relative to the causal structures in nature" (1984, 54). This arbitrariness makes them unnatural and likely to be poor bases for scientific induction. This insight made Locke very pessimistic about the success of some sciences, because if the nominal essences were all one could know in those sciences, useful inductive generalizations could never be made. Boyd partly shares Locke's pessimism and feels that there have been cases in the history of science where nominal essences provided little help in making inductions about the underlying natural kinds (as in nominal essences for chemistry prior to recognition of the molecular level), but he suggests that, on at least some occasions, the nominal essence may give some insight into the real essence.

I doubt that the elements in a nominal essence are fully arbitrary relative to the causal structures in nature and suspect that they are often systematically connected to a set of real, or at least supposed, causal relations—not those of biology or physics, however, but those governing human interactions. Moreover, it may be crucial to understand the senses in which they are not arbitrary if we are to understand how natural kinds contrast with artifacts. When a class of artifacts is created and a label is attached, it seems likely that the properties shared by that class of artifacts are not fully arbitrary with respect to causal theory. Chairs have a number of properties, features, and functions that are normally used to identify them, and although there may not be internal causal homeostatic mechanisms of chairs that lead them to have these properties, there may well be external mechanisms having to do with the form and functions of the human body and with typical social and cultural activities of humans. For example, certain dimensions of chairs are determined by the normal length of human limbs and torsos.

Artifacts are different from natural kinds and should not be equated with them; but the difference is more subtle than saying that the features of artifacts are fully arbitrary and fixed by intention. Nominal kinds as well as artifacts seem to be heavily dependent on human intentions for their meanings. Human intentions, however, are not in themselves arbitrary. They reflect responses that are at least partly due to physical regularities in the world. Perhaps the clearest way to distinguish artifacts from natural kinds is to argue that the causal homeostatic mechanisms for natural kinds are closely related to various domains of science, such as biology, chemistry, and physics, whereas those for artifacts and nominal kinds involve more social and psychological domains of causality. Some of the features of some nominal kinds can be truly arbitrary, but I doubt that this could be the case for all their features. Like other conventionally agreed-upon structures or systems, the arbitrariness only exists up to a certain level. Consider, for example, the rules of traffic, such as driving on the right side of the road in the United States. It is exceedingly unlikely that driving on the right or the left side of the road is related to any set of natural laws. Instead, that rule was merely chosen arbitrarily because one of the two possibilities must be consistently honored; at that level the features are arbitrary. But there are properties of traffic rules at a slightly more abstract level for which good causal reasons do exist. Thus, it is not arbitrary that a rule about which side of the road to drive on would become part of the rules of traffic. There are many good causal mechanisms having to do with the consequences of collisions, the frailty of humans in such collisions at sufficient velocities, and the difficulties in responding quickly enough without such rules at those velocities. Social conventions may include details that are arbitrary, but the development of the conventions themselves is usually very heavily motivated by rich networks of causal factors.

It may be easier to envision the likely role of causal mechanisms in determining the nature of artifact property clusters if we consider the reasons why an anthill is a natural kind rather than an artifact. It is a natural kind because the ant has no conscious intention to construct such a hill and because its behaviors are presumably describable in terms of biological laws having to do with survival in various ecological niches. The formal argument would probably be no different for anthills than for various morphological properties of ants. Intentions present an interesting difference (to be further described below), but there may well be coherent sets of natural psychological laws describing the generation of intentions and their translation into action.

What, then, are the best ways of describing the differences between artifacts and natural kinds? The following intuitive distinctions need to be explained. (Some of these are to be found in the above-mentioned papers; others are my own intuitions developed for this argument.)

1. *Internal/external.* One recurrent distinction in much of the literature involves external and internal features and/or properties intrinsic to a kind, on the one hand, and relations between a kind and other objects, on the other hand. Boyd's remarks should make us worry about the validity

of this contrast; yet the intuition is very strong, and, as we shall see later in examining empirical work, it is a pervasive one in children and adults (see also S. Gelman 1984).

2. *Characteristic patterns of change.* This criterion, proposed by Schwartz, suggests that each natural kind has patterns of change that are typical of that kind and unique to it. Thus, the life-cycle patterns of animals and plants tend to provide excellent means of distinguishing them; the corrosion and erosion patterns of minerals are also distinctive and are often felt to be causally related to their essence. This seems less true for most artifacts such as chairs, hairbrushes, and toasters. For these artifacts, any typical patterns of change over time, such as rusting of their component metals or fatiguing of parts, is unique not to them but to their constituent natural kinds. Since all artifacts are ultimately fabricated out of natural kind constituents, natural-kind-like laws still apply to them when they are about the natural kind constituents themselves. The artifact kinds should not be identified with these patterns of change, however, and indeed the same artifact can usually be made of other natural kind constituents that do not have those specific properties of change (consider, for example, a fiberglass car or a ceramic toaster). Further thought reveals possible complications here as well. Complex artifacts such as cars, computers, and televisions do tend to have characteristic patterns of aging and deterioration that may be a consequence of their functional architecture. Even different types of cars can have different patterns of decay reflecting different design principles.

3. *The relevance of science.* Schwartz remarks that there can be no real science of artifacts, whereas there are certainly sciences for natural kinds. Here again the intuition is very strong, and the idea of meaningful discoveries about the underlying essences of chairs, toasters, or hairbrushes is bizarre. It does not seem so bizarre, however, to have a science of how artifacts would optimally fit in with design properties of humans (ergonomics) or a science of the reasons why humans create certain artifact kinds and how those kinds reflect aspects of their needs and beliefs (archaeology). But it is true that we regard it as absurd to have a science that studies the nature of artifacts in isolation from a human or social context. This distinction is, of course, closely related to the relative ease with which natural kinds (as compared to artifacts) promote inductions about their properties. Again, I think this may oversimplify; rich inductions may be possible about many artifact properties as well, though they are not in the realm of the traditional natural sciences. Though it may be true that the properties that all hitherto examined chairs are made of wood or have four legs are not projectible to new instances, what about the properties that they are usually comfortable, transportable, and stable, that they provide support to the back, and so on?

4. *The relevance of substance to identity.* Related to these distinctions is the notion that determining the true nature of a substance will be of little or no relevance to the kind of an artifact. Thus, if in doubt about the status of an artifact, one is unlikely to perform chemical assays to make a determination. Of course, chemical analyses may be performed to determine the authenticity of a work of art or an antique; but such analyses play a very different role from those performed for natural kinds.

5. *Richness of homeostatic clusters.* Using Boyd's terminology, it appears at least that the network of causal interconnections that are homeostatically stable and form a cluster is much more rich and dense for natural kinds than for artifacts. That is, the causal mechanisms responsible for the feature clusters are much richer, as are the features themselves. Artifacts seem to be less multifaceted in terms of the causal connections that are responsible for their features. Perhaps this is because of the role of intention in the construction of artifacts, where there are limits on the sorts of functional properties that humans normally build into an artifact kind.

6. *The Need for Intention.* It seems that a true artifact presupposes some degree of intentionality in its creator. By this criterion, the esthetically pleasing object created by tenants randomly tossing things out an apartment window is not an artifact; nor is the entity created in figure 3.1; nor is the easily recognizable caricature of Winston Churchill traced by an ant crawling on the sand (Putnam 1981). Such a thing does not have any sort of homeostatic cluster that can explain its properties; it is truly a product of random processes. Conversely, to the extent that intention intrudes into the creation of natural kinds (for instance, hunting dogs), they become strange hybrids that take on the properties of artifacts as well. Nominal kinds may be more fully determined by intentions than artifacts, which also are governed by a number of real-world constraints (such as physical mechanical principles).

7. *Preservation of kind across transformations.* Natural kinds seem to have a striking resistance to change of kind type across transformations of almost any of their observable properties, whereas artifacts do not. Though the intuition here is strong, again it is difficult to describe in detail how this criterion would work. Because instances of some natural kinds might have their memberships changed by transformations on genetic structure, the major contrast with artifacts relies on the observability of features. Observability, however, is a slippery notion that can lead to many indeterminate cases. The real question is why we view some of these property changes as more important or basic than others. I suspect again that the answer lies in our intuitive notions of natural sciences and natural domains of explanation.

8. *Origins and kind.* The origin of a natural kind seems more basic to its kindhood than does the origin of an artifact. We tend to think that an

Figure 3.1
An entity created by humans, but which is not an artifact because its creation was
unintentional. (Reprinted with permission of *The New Yorker*)

entity is a legitimate member of a natural kind only if it can claim a specific detailed causal chain explaining how it came into being that is appropriately similar to the causal chain claimed by other members of the kind. Thus, we experience conflicting intuitions about whether a thing that is constructed in a laboratory by nonbiological means to be molecule for molecule the same as a real dog is in fact a dog, whereas we feel no such discomfort in deciding that something is a chair, regardless of how it was manufactured, as long as the correct intentions are present. Parfit (1984) discusses at length such a discomfort about physically identical "replica" persons constructed by "deviant causes." (Parfit's case is not strictly analogous, however, because we must distinguish between preserving individual identity and preserving membership in a kind.) Origins are not irrelevant to artifacts, but they relate in a less determinate, less richly causally structured manner. Only for "pure" nominal kinds would they be irrelevant.

9. *Symptoms and causation.* Although the characteristic features of artifacts may have causal mechanisms that help explain their clustering, those mechanisms—which are usually intrinsic to the natural kind— tend to be external to the artifact. The causal mechanisms explaining why chairs have certain structural and functional properties do not arise from chairs themselves. We cannot point to something inside or about chairs that is responsible for their having the properties they do. (Again, however, such accounts are more plausible with more complex artifacts.) Similarly, although the characteristic features of bachelors might—in some subtle and indirect manner having to do with social norms and culture—be connected to the defining features of being an unmarried male adult, one could not, by examining bachelors more closely, discover a mechanism that explained their behavioral symptoms without considering the broader social context. With respect to animals, plants, and minerals, however, most laypeople at least assume that each kind possesses an underlying mechanism that explains why it has many of the morphological and behavioral properties that it has. Again, this assumption may not be entirely correct in light of Boyd's comments, but the intuition is a strong one.

The Importance of Fuzzy Cases and Complex Artifacts

Highly complex artifacts like computers and even televisions, as well as artifacts like plastics whose identity seems to depend wholly on reference to their internal structure, are also difficult to classify. Such examples serve to clarify both the differences between most artifacts and natural kinds and the continuum nature of the distinction. As we construct artifacts in the form of increasingly complex machines with increasingly complex functions to perform, they seem to approximate more and more closely the natural kinds. Computers are perhaps the best example. Over the last two decades they have evolved into extremely complex devices with a vast array of underlying causal mechanisms responsible for their easily observable behaviors. A field of inquiry known as computer science has developed and it no longer seems quite so bizarre to state that someone is studying computers in detail to try to understand what they are. As these machines have become more complex and as the problems they try to solve have become more difficult, many have argued that only certain kinds of architectures will be capable of efficiently solving such problems and that all successful machines will naturally converge on these design principles. (A Turing machine might theoretically be able to engage in such computations, but not practically in terms of computational demands.) Though this account is certainly controversial, it at least illustrates in principle that there might be a unique set of complex causal principles that can underlie certain complex functions for machines due to formal computational considerations and the like. In such cases we might wish to conclude that these devices have essences in the same way animals or plants do.

Consider the difficulty of classifying complex machines, especially computers according to the criteria listed in the previous section.

1. The internal/external feature contrast is less useful with machines like computers since their internal parts are intimately related to their function and may help identify it.

2. Various brands of computers may have characteristic patterns of change that occur as they age and start to fail, such that certain patterns of decay are most common and reflect properties of the computer's internal architecture that are not easily reducible to its constituents. Similarly, certain makes of cars have favorite rust spots and other highly characteristic patterns of decay.

3. The relevance of science has already been discussed. It does not seem strange to attempt to discover principles that explain how computers work.

4. Substance still seems to be less relevant to the identities of computers, however. Thus, no one would think that computers were no longer computers because, for example, their chips were now made out of exotic ceramics rather than silicon. This criterion, then, seems to preserve some of the distinction between natural kinds and artifacts.

5. Are the causal homeostatic clusters for computers less well developed and less complex than those for biological kinds? At present the answer is almost certainly yes, though the usefulness of this distinction seems to decrease as the complexity of such machines increases.

6. Building a computer of course requires intention, but intention may be less involved than we might think in determining its final architecture

and method of operation. If a certain computational problem has only a small class of stable solutions, then the architecture of a computer designed to solve it may be determined as much by the problem as by the plans of its creators, whose intentions tend to operate at the broader level of solving a functional problem.

7. Questions of kindhood preservation across transformations on computers are not easy to assess, but intuitions about whether computer kind changes as a result of transforming surface properties are not nearly as clear-cut as they are for things like chairs and toothbrushes.

8. Origins do still seem to distinguish computers from natural kinds. How a computer was built doesn't seem to matter; if it functions appropriately, it's a computer.

9. Finally, much like the features of natural kinds, many of the characteristic features of computers (say, those of an Apple Macintosh) seem to be consequences of a set of internal mechanisms. This is more true for behavioral characteristics (such as the operating system and disc access speeds) than for morphological ones, since the latter reflect more ergonomic considerations and are not directly caused by the machine's internal structure (except possibly external properties related to heat dissipation and the like).

This analysis of complex machines suggests that the dividing line between artifacts and natural kinds can be fuzzy in many cases. As machines become more and more complex and evolve over several "generations" to serve more and more sophisticated functions in various "ecological niches," they take on many of the properties that supposedly distinguish natural kinds from artifacts. This is also true, albeit to a lesser extent, for machines that are considerably simpler than computers, such as televisions and perhaps automobiles. I do not think the two categories ever become fully equivalent, but it is clear that many of the dimensions on which simple artifacts and biological kinds can vary are markedly reduced in the more complex cases.

There are many other fascinating, difficult cases that further illustrate the nuances of artifacts and natural kinds as categories. Plastics seem to be artifacts since they are man-made, yet they are defined totally by their molecular structure; and the principles by which this molecular structure translates into clusters of features are the natural laws of chemistry. I suspect that plastics are only marginally artifacts, since it could be argued that they are "discovered" or "synthetic" natural kinds. If their essences can be fully described independently of human intentions and in terms of natural chemical laws, it seems that the role of humans in their creation is one of bringing into existence an entity for which a set of coherent natural causal laws accounting for all its properties already exists. The same is true for elements such as lawrencium and californium, which follow the laws of chemistry and physics but do not occur in nature.

Natural by-products of animals and plants are also natural kinds even if, in at least some cases, substance seems much less relevant to their identity. Thus, a pearl is a pearl no matter which of several different chemical compounds is used to make it. What counts for it to be a pearl is its method of creation. It clearly is still a natural kind, however, since it follows a coherent set of natural laws. Coral may be a similar case; and even birds' nests could be argued to form a natural kind, given some of the mechanistic accounts biologists have offered of how they are created. Dilger (1962), for example, describes how various cross-breedings among lovebirds can selectively knock out discrete parts of the nest-building routine. Obviously, birds' nests have no essential substance, underlying internal structure, or unique patterns of change, and yet they are arguably fine natural kinds.

In all of this, one important fact must be remembered. "Natural kind" is a technical term developed by philosophers to answer certain questions about projectability of predicates, the nature of scientific investigation, and the like. For that reason it is a bit strange to ask exactly what it means or to explore it as if it were itself a natural kind. We should view it as a way of understanding why we have the beliefs we do about the categories of things there are in the world.

Conclusions and Developmental Speculations

The purpose of this chapter has been to consider how concepts for natural kinds might be represented and acquired and the implications of these considerations for prior work suggesting a characteristic-to-defining shift for nominal kinds. It seems clear that most natural kinds do not have any simple small set of features, properties, or relations that we can point to as defining their meanings or constituting their essences. At first glance this seems to suggest that perhaps the characteristic-to-defining shift is a relatively narrow phenomenon confined to a small set of terms. A closer look at the arguments in the philosophical literature, however, reveals that it would be a serious mistake to equate the meanings of natural kinds with prototype-like concepts or with other merely probabilistic accounts of representations. Prototypes in themselves are surprisingly atheoretical entities that provide no explanation of a natural kind's structure and of the correlations among its various properties. It would seem that part of our understanding of natural kinds consists of an appreciation of a rich causal, mechanistic structure that underlies them and is responsible for their overt features. Though it may be inaccurate to see such a causal homeostatic system as fully internal to each member of a kind, the emphasis on such a causal system is critical.

As shown in the passages cited earlier, several authors have independently attempted to preserve something akin to a characteristic/defining contrast for natural kinds. Not only does this view suggest that there is more to natural kinds than characteristic features, it also suggests a new way of viewing the nominal kind concepts so common in older studies on concept development. As the contrasts between natural kinds and artifacts demonstrate, almost all kinds may have some set of causal mechanisms that are at least partly responsible for the correlations among their properties. Except for the purest nominal kinds, definitions may not be as fully arbitrary as they seem. They may be arbitrary relative to the laws of a particular natural science, but not relative to the laws governing human interactions, intentions, and culture (see Putnam 1983). Thus, it may even be inaccurate to use the term "defining features" for many nominal kind concepts if there is a theory about why their features cooccur and about why that kind exists. These theories may often be greatly oversimplified and sufficiently unidimensional that they appear merely to be a list of necessary and sufficient features; but this is an illusion that can be exposed with more careful inspection of our intuitions about many nominal kinds. (The case of "lie" may be one such example.)

This is not to merge completely the distinctions among natural kinds, nominal kinds, and artifacts. They do differ from one another in several important ways, but these differences seem to be more a matter of dimensional continua than of the presence or absence of specific features. Perhaps all concepts for such kinds tend to be at least partly embedded within intuitive theories, and the differences among them concern differences among the natures of these causal theories. The continuum notion is illustrated in figure 3.2.

The studies reviewed in chapter 2 and the ideas developed in this chapter suggest a more detailed version of Quine's developmental speculation. What may develop is an increasing appreciation of the network of causal relations and mechanisms that are responsible for making natural kinds cohere as distinguishable classes of things. Younger children may have a much cruder grasp of the theoretical principles that are fundamental for organizing objects in a domain and explaining their properties and relations to other objects. They may also hold a different theory that, for a variety of possible reasons, comes to mind more easily at that developmental point. In addition, we may rarely, if ever, attain a complete understanding of the extremely rich set of causal connections that become homeostatically stable and yield meaningful categories of things. Consequently, we form only approximate impressions of these causal systems, and our approximations seem to be distorted in systematic ways.

We tend to believe that most concepts have relatively simple definitions, much like necessary and sufficient features (a bias that has been

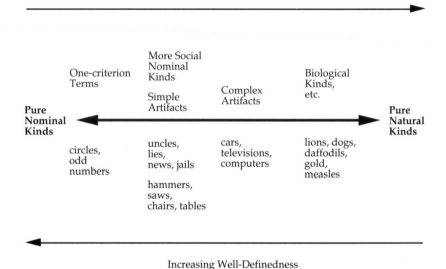

Figure 3.2
Illustration of the continuum nature of the contrast between natural and nominal kinds.

empirically supported by McNamara and Sternberg (1983)). A perhaps even more important bias repeatedly surfaces in the philosophical literature, namely, a tendency toward essentialism. Philosophers such as Quine, biologists such as Mayr (1982) and Gould (1983), and historians of science such as Hull (1965) have deplored this tendency as an unfortunate impediment to the nonessential truth about natural kinds such as animals. (This viewpoint is perhaps best summed up by the title of Hull's paper: "The Effect of Essentialism on Taxonomy: 2000 Years of Stasis.") We will want to examine evidence for this tendency in the empirical studies to be presented in later chapters and explore its possible significance. I will argue that, for all its faults, this essentialism has a fundamental value in learning about natural kinds and making sense of them (see also Medin and Ortony, in press).

Throughout this chapter another aspect of concepts quite different from clusters of causal relations has also been implicated, namely, atheoretical tabulations of correlations and feature frequencies. Although nearly all concepts may be partially structured by causal beliefs, we can never have full knowledge of all such relations and therefore must have an alternative means for storing information that lies beyond explanation. For children, especially, it is vital to be able to store patterns of characteristic feature distributions as a framework upon which to lay increasingly elaborate causal interpretations. All theories and causal beliefs eventually "run dry" in their ability to explain feature patterns; when they do, these more associative aspects of concept representations take over. Of course, these associative relations must always be constrained so that not all logically possible associations are made. For Quine, the young child's "animal sense of similarity" and a general set of associative relations provide adequate constraints for the development of all later theory. The following chapters will empirically assess whether there is such a shift from a purely atheoretical "original sim." to a causally interpreted, theoretically coherent conceptual structure.

Chapter 4
The Development of Nominal Kind Concepts:
A Preliminary Model

Explicit assumptions about the nature of concepts are needed for viable models of qualitative change.[1] In chapters 2 and 3 attempts to deal with Fodor's concerns about qualitative change led to the proposal that concepts should be viewed as internally heterogeneous and that shifts in the distribution of the sorts of elements within concepts may provide a way of modeling qualitative change. The first concepts subjected to empirical inquiry should therefore be those for which claims about qualitatively different constituents are easiest to make. Nominal kinds are such a case in that their theoretical organization is sufficiently degenerate that they are often construed to be more like classical definitions. At the same time many nominal kinds may be associated with vivid stereotypes that seem clearly distinct from their definition-like components. Thus, as we reach the leftmost parts of the continuum shown in figure 3.2, it becomes easier to talk about concepts as having simple analytic cores surrounded by a more probabilistic typicality structure. Whether this is ever strictly correct even for the supposedly "one-criterion" terms is clearly a hotly contested issue, but at the least it offers a convenient fiction within which to begin to explore conceptual change.

One way of representing this contrast puts to use a distinction made by Smith, Shoben, and Rips (1974) between characteristic and defining features. This distinction, which has venerable predecessors in the philosophy of language, seems simple enough in principle. Defining features are a relatively small set of properties that are necessary and sufficient for describing an instance of a concept. By contrast, characteristic features are not necessary for describing instances but are highly characteristic of most familiar ones; that is, they are symptoms that are typically, though not necessarily, associated with most instances.

The characteristic/defining distinction faces many of the problems of the classical view discussed in chapter 3. Moreover, the whole notion of decomposing meaning into lists of features, whether defining or not, has been under attack for some time (see, for example, Bolinger 1965; Fodor

---

1. This chapter draws heavily on material presented in Keil and Batterman 1984.

et al. 1980). I do not wish to defend the distinction at the principled level, and I have already argued for a more subtle distinction in chapter 3. Nonetheless, at a pragmatic level the distinction is a useful point of departure for investigating changes in conceptual structure, especially for that restricted class of lexicalized concepts known as nominal kind terms.

For nominal kinds, characteristic features may predominate early on in concept acquisition but give way to defining features with increasing knowledge and conceptual sophistication. This shift from characteristic to defining features resonates strongly with several of the traditional developmental patterns discussed in chapter 2. Consider, for example, Vygotsky's claim that in early stages "new phenomena or objects are named after inessential attributes, so that the name does not truly express the nature of the thing named." Only later is the child able to uncover the "essential" attributes. Inessential attributes could easily be construed as characteristic features. Though often intimately associated with a phenomenon or object, they are not necessary or essential to its meaning. Similarly, the "essential" attributes would be the defining ones.

Werner's holistic-to-analytic shift is less concerned with the essential/inessential distinction; he stresses instead a shift from globally attending to all features or dimensions associated with a concept to emphasizing each of these features or dimensions individually in its own right. Nonetheless, if a child initially treated all features as being characteristic and identified an instance of a concept as anything with a sufficiently large subset of the characteristic features, such behavior would appear to be holistic. If the child later focused on just a few dimensions and evaluated each one in its own right, the concepts so organized would then seem to be more analytic.

More generally, if early representations are heavily instance bound, one reasonable way to model such representations is to assume that the concept consists of those features most commonly shared among the most typical instances. No one feature is ever necessary; it need only be frequently observed in common instances. Such features would be characteristic features. If later representations are more instance independent and principled, they might well be modeled in terms of a set of necessary and sufficient conditions.

Of course, the characteristic-to-defining shift may never occur. Perhaps most concepts are composed of characteristic features throughout all stages of their acquisition. Certainly one way of construing Rosch's pioneering work on the nature of natural concepts in adults (see, for example, Rosch and Mervis 1975) is to assume that characteristic features can do all the conceptual work necessary. As described in chapters 1 and 3, several approaches have sprung up in reaction to what Smith and Medin (1981) called the "classical view." If such approaches are correct, then no shift to defining features would be expected, since concepts based on defining features are in essence examples of the classical view. If a qualitative shift is uncovered, however, it places a burden on the anticlassical views to explain it without reference to such things as defining features. The studies described here and in chapters 5 and 6 represent an initial attempt to understand possible qualitative change by focusing on a special subclass of concepts that are closest to being well defined: nominal kinds.

Spontaneous Definitions: An Informal Study with Preschoolers

Most dictionary definitions are not simply lists of defining features. Instead, they frequently—and often only—contain characteristic features. Thus, dictionary "definitions" are very different from lists of "defining" features. Not surprisingly, then, adults who are asked to define concepts frequently list characteristic features in addition to, or even in place of, defining ones. Despite this mingling of the two types of features in definitions, there may still be a developmental change in the degree to which, and the manner in which, children refer to the two kinds of features. Perhaps the easiest way to assess the usefulness of the characteristic/defining contrast as a developmental model is simply to ask children to give definitions for various concepts.

Asking children for such definitions is one of the oldest techniques used in cognitive development research. Anglin (1984) reviews much of the literature based on this technique and comes to the following conclusion:

> Thus many studies have supported the notion that there is a qualitative change in the structure of definitions with development which has been described as a transition from definitions in terms of use to definitions superior to use, or from concrete definitions based on personal experience to abstract definitions in terms of genus and differentia. (p. 11)

This pattern is somewhat like the putative characteristic-to-defining shift; but it is not a conclusive example. A significant limitation of most studies on children's definitions is that the words used have most often *not* been ones that have both clear defining features and a large set of characteristic features. Thus, natural kind terms such as "tiger" and "gold" have no simple definitions, whereas other terms such as "prime number" have clear definitions but only weak associated characteristic features.

It seemed reasonable, therefore, to conduct yet another study on children's definitions, focusing this time on nominal kinds having both clear defining features and several salient characteristic features. One such set of words, the kinship terms, has also been used in other studies, but several other words such as "island" and "advertisement" have rarely been studied in this manner. An informal exploratory study was conducted with 36 preschoolers ranging in age from 3 1/2 to 5 1/2 years, using the terms shown in table 4.1. The terms were selected on the basis of three criteria: (1) they should be familiar to all children at all ages in the study; (2) they should have clear defining features as well as salient characteristic features; and (3) they should cover as wide a range of phenomena as possible. Selection of terms meeting these criteria was simply decided by consensus among several adult judges.

Children were asked what each term meant, and their responses were followed up with simple probes that attempted to assess their understanding (examples of the probes are shown in the transcripts below). Though not fully systematic, the probe questions were highly similar across children and focused on potential contrasts between characteristic and defining features. As I will discuss shortly, this sort of study has severe methodological limitations; the one described here was conducted under the assumption that suggestive patterns might emerge that would aid in devising a more informative method.

The results provided tentative support for a characteristic-to-defining shift in that the preschoolers almost always mentioned only characteristic features in their definitions. The following excerpts from the transcripts illustrate the sorts of responses given:

Island
C: You dance.
E: What kind of dance? Can you show me?
C: I can't...I mean you can watch people dance like you put on a song.
E: So whenever you put on a song and dance, that's an island?
C: Uhuh...people watch.
E: What does an island look like?
C: It looks like a jungle...but not Indians live in islands. Indians live in jungles.
E: Who lives on an island?
C: People...yup, people without clothes on—you can't.
E: You can't have clothes on an island?
C: No, but you can watch.
E: Is there an island in Ithaca?
C: No.
E: Why not?
C: 'Cause it's not summertime yet.
E: You mean there can only be islands during the summer?

Table 4.1
Terms used in exploratory study on nominal kinds

Term	Approximate defining features	Salient characteristic feature
Advertisement	Information that one pays to publicize for purposes of financial gain	Music, songs, numbers, smiling people, interrupts thematic content
Check (as in "checking account")	An authorized, hard-copy commitment of a stipulated part of one's funds to another	Has a pattern, is roughly 3"x7", comes in a booklet, is used in stores a lot
Credit card	Imprinted card enabling one to be billed for goods & services and requiring interest payments on outstanding balances	Has brightly colored graphic designs, owner's name & long numbers are imprinted on it, small wallet size
Crook	Person given to fraudulent practices	Mean looking, wears a face mask, has a gun, wears dark clothing
Election	Act of selecting something by vote	Speeches, commercials, candidate banners & buttons, polls
Island	Body of land surrounded by water on all sides	Palm trees, sandy beaches, sea shells, warm weather, sunshine
Lake	Large, freshwater body of water	Boats, docks, fish, pretty, swimming
Mail	Items conveyed to an address for a fee	Envelope shape & size, stamps to lick, delivered to a box, cards & letters
Money	Generally accepted medium of exchange	U.S. coins & bills

Table 4.1 (continued)

Moon	A natural satellite	Reflects light from the sun, has craters, has "man in the moon," changes shape, causes tides
Princess	Daughter or granddaughter of a sovereign	Beautiful, long, golden hair & blue eyes, wears lovely dresses & a crown, sweet disposition, young
Taxi	Vehicle that may be hired to transport one from place to place	Bright yellow color, black & white checkered sign with phone number, has adult driver, has lighted sign on roof, meter
Uncle	One's father's brother	Approximately same age as father, fun, brings presents, visits on holidays, kids you a lot
Wine	Fermented grape juice containing alcohol	Dark red color, clear, usually drunk at dinner or on special occasions, often imported, comes in a tall, slim, green-tinted glass bottle with a cork

C: Yeah.

E: But it's summertime now.

C: Yeah.

E: So is there an island?

C: No.

E: Why not?

C: Because people are not there.

E: Where?

C: At the island.

E: Is an island near water?

C: Yeah.

E: But Ithaca is near water. What's the difference?

C: You know what? We went to Danny's house and swimmed there.

E: Great. Is that an island?

C: No.

(No reference to being surrounded by water, but ample reference to other typical properties of islands.

Taxi

C: You go in a car.

E: You mean I can just go into my car and it's a taxi?

C: Yeah.

E: Any car is a taxi?

C: Yeah...taxi car!

E: What's a taxi car look like?

C: It's yellow.

E: Does it have to be yellow?

C: Yeah...and there are some more colors but I don't know what the colors are.

E: If I have a yellow car, is that a taxi?

C: Yeah.

E: Do people do anything special in taxis?

C: No, you just take a ride.

E: So could my yellow car be a taxi? Is it one?

C: No.

E: Why not?

C: Because it don't have the thing on top of your car.

E: What do people do in taxis?

C: You take a ride.

E: But I take a ride in my yellow car. What's the difference?

C: A taxi!

E: So it must be a taxi?

C: Yeah.
E: Could you drive a taxi?
C: No—because I'm not big...
(Age of the driver cited as one of the characteristics of taxi.)

Princess
E: Princess?
C: In a castle!
E: If I live in a castle, am I a princess?
C: And kings live in castles!
E: What does a princess look like?
C: Looks like an Indian.
E: Can a princess be ugly?
C: No.
E: Can a princess be old like a grandmother?
C: No.
E: If she doesn't live in a castle, is she still a princess?
C: No.
E: Are there any princesses in Ithaca?
C: No.
E: Why not?
C: Because this is not a castle.
E: If there was a castle in Ithaca, could there be a princess here?
C: Yeah.

Mail
C: What you put letters.
E: How do I get some?
C: Make some and then put it in the mail, and then you see a mailwoman.
E: Could this card be mail?
C: Yup.
E: Could I just put this in the mailbox and it'll be mail?
C: Yup.
E: I just put it in and it'll get to you?
C: Yup.
E: I don't have to do anything to it?
C: No...and then...
E: Could a toy be mail?
C: No.
E: Why not?
C: Because it's not a letter.
E: Only letters can be mail?

C: Uhuh...and then you can send it.
E: Who do you get mail from?
C: People.
E: Can a newspaper or magazine be mail?
C: No...just paper.
(Characteristic features of letters dominate whereas the more functional role of mail is ignored.)

Uncle
C: I think I have two uncles.
E: So what's an uncle?
C: A friend.
E: Oh, I have a friend Doug. Is he my uncle?
C: I don't know...My two uncles are Uncle Johnny and Uncle Mike.
E: And they're just your friends?
C: Yeah.
E: Oh, can my friend Mary be an uncle?
C: No.
E: Why not?
C: Is she a girl?
E: Yes.
C: Then she's an aunt.
E: Oh, so all my girl friends are aunts and all my boy friends are uncles?
C: Yes.
E: Can an uncle be seven years old?
C: No...because he would be too small.
E: Can an uncle be 80 years old?
C: Yes.
E: Does an uncle have to be handsome?
C: Yes.
E: Can an uncle be ugly?
C: No.
(Age, sex, handsomeness seem to organize the concept with no reference to kinship relations.)

Advertisement
E: Advertisement?
C: You put shows on for people.
E: Where?
C: Tonight for real I have to go on stage and I get to wear a blue, red, or white ribbon.
E: What for?
C: A dance.

E: What's an advertisement?
C: A show.
E: So if I get up and dance, that's an advertisement?
C: Yes.
E: Do they have advertisements on TV?
C: Sometimes there're parades for people on TV.
E: Parades are advertisements?
C: Yeah.
E: Is "Sesame Street" an advertisement?
C: No.
E: Well, that's a show. What's the difference?
C: An advertisement is for parades and when you dance.
E: Could there be an advertisement in the newspaper?
C: Yeah...my picture was in the newspaper.
E: But that's not a parade and dancing. You can't have a parade in the newspaper.
C: Yes, you can...because you take pictures of it...The newspaper does and puts it in the newspaper.
E: Oh, so a picture of a parade and a picture of a show in the newspaper is an advertisement?
C: Yes.
E: Can there be an advertisement on the radio?
C: Yes...because the people never hear of it before they would get to see it and if they'd never saw it before, they could see it...
E: I see—can there be an advertisement on the radio?
C: Yes.
E: What is it like?
C: That is like someone singing and announcing a number.
(Attributes of public performers, especially musical ones, and the presence of numbers are mentioned.)

Island
C: Sometimes an island is in Hawaii.
E: What does it look like?
C: I don't know because I never seen it before.
E: What do you think it looks like?
C: I don't know.
E: There are only islands in Hawaii?
C: Yes.
E: They can't be any place else?
C: No...I think in Florida, too.
E: And you don't know what they look like?
C: No.

E: Are they near to the water?
C: Some islands are near to the water.
(Necessary feature of being near water is treated only as characteristic.)

The excerpts illustrate a prevalent pattern in which the younger children seem to focus heavily on instance-bound information and in which various characteristic features consequently dominate the definitions, often at the expense of defining ones. Every one of the 36 children showed an excessive reliance on characteristic features on at least some of the words given. Even though this study, using a special set of terms with clear defining and characteristic features, offers a clearer view of a qualitative characteristic-to-defining shift than other studies using a broader array of concepts, it is not fruitful to conduct a more detailed analysis of the results because of two major problems common to all studies on spontaneous definitions.

1. Quantitative reporting of children's definitions is difficult because of the wide range of definition types that children give. Some give very episodic definitions ("It's when you do X"), others highly idiosyncratic ones ("It's like that place I was this summer"), and still others very terse ones; some do not respond at all. Thus, any scoring system sufficiently general to cover such a range of responses tends to miss the finer points.

2. The task of giving definitions places unusual demands on children, and the younger ones may have little experience with it. Consequently, such definitions may distort their true knowledge of word meaning. A characteristic-to-defining shift may reflect more an increased understanding of the task and less a change in representation. Perhaps the youngest children also see the terms as having defining features and simply fail to realize that the task is asking them to focus on such features. The definition task is at least partly a metalinguistic skill; a different task that more closely approximated natural language understanding might be more sensitive.

If there is a shift in emphasis from characteristic to defining features, a better experimental technique would be to manipulate the relative importance of the two kinds of features, to see whether such manipulations affect children's understanding of the terms.

This informal study is therefore offered as an illustration with concrete examples of the sorts of spontaneous behavior that for over a century have led observers to posit qualitative shifts along the lines discussed in chapter 2.

The Characteristic-to-Defining Shift Study

In light of the two considerations just described, Nancy Batterman and I (Keil and Batterman 1984) devised a set of stimuli consisting of brief pairs of descriptions of things, events, or situations corresponding to lexicalized concepts. All of the concepts had (1) corresponding linguistic labels that were judged to be in most kindergartner's vocabularies and (2) both relatively clear definitions and salient characteristic features. The list of terms used is shown in table 4.2.

These terms are far from a random sampling of words that are likely to be in the vocabularies of young children and clearly refer to nominal kinds near the left end of the continuum in figure 3.2.

In addition to being familiar to most kindergartners and having reliable defining and characteristic features, each term in this study had to be such that two descriptions could be constructed for it, one that included the most salient, highly characteristic features associated with the concept but had an incorrect defining feature (the +c/-d case) and one that included several uncharacteristic features but had a correct set of defining features (the -c/+d case). Examples of the descriptions, which were approximately 20 seconds in length, are shown in table 4.3; the full set of descriptions is given in appendix 1.

There is no algorithm that generates characteristic and defining features for each term, but it is evident from the two description types and from the common examples described in table 4.1 what they were meant to be in each case. An important principle used in constructing each description was to put the defining features toward the end. This was done in response to other studies on moral reasoning (for example, Kun, Parsons, and Ruble 1974) and narrative recall (for example, Brown 1976) suggesting that the order of presentation of elements in a story can dramatically influence comprehension and recall. Younger children show a strong tendency to notice and remember mainly the last elements in a story or description. This order effect could have resulted in an artifactual characteristic-to-defining shift if the definitions had tended to be at the beginning of descriptions. Putting defining features at the end—

Table 4.2
List of terms used in characteristic-to-defining shift study

Lie	Sign	Factory	Church
Robber	Taxi	Island	Uncle
Menu	Hat	Lunch	Museum
Jail	Mailman	Vacation	News
Twins			

Table 4.3
Examples of +c/-d and -c/+d descriptions used in the characteristic-to-defining study

Lie

(+c/-d) This girl hated a boy in her class because he was so mean and did really nasty things to her. She wanted to get him into trouble, so she told the teacher all the nasty things the boy had really done. Could that be a lie?

(-c/+d) This little boy always got good grades in school and prizes for being so smart. The other children were jealous of him because of it, and he didn't want to make them feel bad and wanted them to be his friends. So, one time, when he really got a good mark on a test, he told them that he got a bad mark so they'd be his friends. Could that be a lie?

Robber

(+c/-d) This smelly, mean old man with a gun in his pocket came to your house one day and took your colored television set because your parents didn't want it anymore and told him that he could have it. Could he be a robber?

(-c/+d) This very friendly and cheerful woman came up to you and gave you a hug, but then she disconnected your toilet bowl and took it away without permission and never returned it. Could she be a robber?

Island

(+c/-d) There is this place that sticks out of the land like a finger. Coconut trees and palm trees grow there, and the girls sometimes wear flowers in their hair because it's so warm all the time. There is water on all sides except one. Could that be an island?

(-c/+d) On this piece of land, there are apartment buildings, snow, and no green things growing. This piece of land is surrounded by water on all sides. Could that be an island?

Uncle

(+c/-d) This man your daddy's age loves you and your parents and loves to visit and bring presents, but he's not related to your parents at all. He's not your mommy or daddy's brother or sister or anything like that. Could that be an uncle?

(-c/+d) Suppose your mommy has all sorts of brothers, some very old and some very, very young. One of your mommy's brothers is so young he's only 2 years old. Could that be an uncle?

Museum

(+c/-d) There is this beautiful building with columns. Mr. Johnson lives there, but he has a big problem. There are all these cracks in his floors and his walls. So, he covers them with paintings and statues, and he never lets anyone inside to see them. Could that be a museum?

Table 4.3 (continued)

(-c/+d) There is this small, wooden shack in the countryside. People come from all over and pay 50 cents to get inside and see the interesting display of dirty shirts with rings around the collar and spots and stains. Could that be a museum?

News
(+c/-d) You turn on the radio and there is this man talking very seriously about foreign countries, wars, fires, and robberies. He is reading from a book that was written last year. Could that be news?

(-c/+d) You turn on the TV and these children are singing and dancing to loud rock and roll music—and they're singing everything that happened in the world that day—the weather, the fires, the robberies. They even sometimes hold up crayon drawings to show what they were talking about. Could that be news?

---

the most conservative test of the developmental hypothesis, since it would bias children toward focusing on those features—would therefore provide a more compelling demonstration of a genuine shift. Occasionally the defining features appeared earlier in the description so that the effects of order could be examined as well.

Sixteen children in each of three grades (K, 2, and 4) in the Ithaca, New York, area participated as subjects. (Average ages were 5:7, 7:11, and 9:9 years, respectively.) Each child was seen individually for approximately one half hour. With the younger children, two half-hour sessions on successive school days were frequently required. The descriptions were presented in a semirandom order, the nonrandom component being a restriction that the +c/-d and -c/+d descriptions for any given term should be at least eight items apart in the stimulus set. The experimenter read a description to the child and then asked, "Could that be a(n) x?", where x was the term for which the description was constructed. Answers were often followed up by probe questions to clarify ambiguous responses, to ensure focusing on the task, and more generally to get a more detailed picture of the child's understanding of the particular term. All questions and answers were tape-recorded and transcribed. Finally, the descriptions were usually repeated several times for the children to further reduce order-of-presentation effects.

The transcripts were scored independently by two judges according to a three-point system:

1. A score of 1 was given to children who seemed to rely solely on characteristic features in making their judgments, including those who treated the defining features as merely characteristic. Thus, a score of 1 would be given to a child who judged a +c/-d description to refer to an instance of the queried term and also to one who judged a -c/+d description to refer to a noninstance.

2. A score of 2 was given for three types of responses: (a) (the most frequent type) a judgment that both the defining and the characteristic features were necessary for a story to describe an instance (thus, in the -c/+d case a child might state that in addition to the defining features given, certain characteristic features were also required for it to be judged an instance); (b) judgments in which the child relied on defining features, but incorrect ones (for instance, defining an uncle as one's father's father); and (c) judgments that vacillated between a defining features response and a characteristic feature response.

3. A score of 3 was given for responses in which defining features predominated, in other words, in which the child judged that the -c/+d stories referred to instances and the +c/-d stories did not.

This scoring system worked quite well, and the two scorers agreed on 91% of all scores. The remaining disagreements were resolved through discussion between the scorers. In all cases there was agreement on the final score. Missing or unscorable responses were handled by a repeated measures analysis of variance (ANOVA) that took into account incomplete cells (Dixon and Brown 1979). The results showed a clear increase in use of defining features with age ($F(2,30) = 16.86$, $p < .001$): children shifted from judging that the +c/-d descriptions referred to an instance and the -c/+d stories to a noninstance, to the reverse. There was also a significant main effect of description type: children generally used more defining features (received higher scores) with the +c/-d descriptions ($F(1,30) = 39.01$, $p < .001$). Finally, there was no significant interaction between description type and age. Of the 17 descriptions, 15 showed overall increases in scores with age at the .06 level (13 at the .05 level). There were significant main effects for 14 of the concepts and only 3 cases of significant age-by-story-type interactions.

These overall results, though clearly showing a general shift from accepting instances on the basis of characteristic features to doing so on the basis of defining ones, are only a crude reflection of the developmental patterns for each individual concept. One important finding was that the children did not seem to shift at the same time for all concepts. Thus, almost all kindergartners relied on defining features for both the +c/-d and -c/+d descriptions of "lie" and "robber"; yet several fourth graders still relied on exclusively characteristic features for the "news" and "museum" stories. The terms are ordered according to mean overall scores in table 4.4, which can be construed as a rough indication of the relative order in which the shift occurred for each concept.

If the scores are transformed, there is an intuitively natural way to present the results graphically. Instead of assigning a score of 1 to 3 based on the extent to which a child made use of defining features, a score of 1 to 3 can be assigned based on the extent to which the child judged each

Table 4.4
Mean overall scores in characteristic-to-defining shift study

Term	Mean overall score	Term	Mean overall score
Lie	2.90	Factory	2.23
Robber	2.71	Island	2.17
Menu	2.53	Lunch	2.17
Jail	2.40	Vacation	2.12
Twins	2.39	Church	2.10
Sign	2.39	Uncle	1.98
Taxi	2.33	Museum	1.91
Hat	2.30	News	1.86
Mailman	2.27		

description type to describe an instance of a concept. For the -c/+d descriptions, the scores remain the same, since relying on defining features amounts to judging the text as describing an instance. For the +c/-d descriptions, however, the scores are inverted, each 3 becoming a 1 and each 1 becoming a 3 (2's stay the same). Figure 4.1 shows the graphic representations of these new scores for all of the concepts studied. The graphs allow us to observe the shift by noting crossover patterns of the two lines. Where the two lines cross over, or where they would cross over if projected to younger or older ages, can be construed to represent roughly the age at which the shift occurs. Reading the graphs in the order shown in table 4.4, this point tends to shift to the right. Thus, the crossover presumably occurs during the preschool period for such terms as "lie" and "robber" and a little after the second grade for "news" and "museum." The graphs in figure 4.1 vividly show that the shift occurs at different times for different concepts.

These patterns clearly illustrate that some degree of characteristic-to-defining shift was occurring for most of the terms used in the study. Above and beyond these numerical patterns, however, a few excerpts from the transcripts provide a more concrete picture of how the responses change with increasing age.

The following responses by kindergartners illustrate a heavy reliance on characteristic features:

Uncle (-c/+d)
E: Could he be an uncle?
C: No...because he's little and two years old.
E: How old does an uncle have to be?

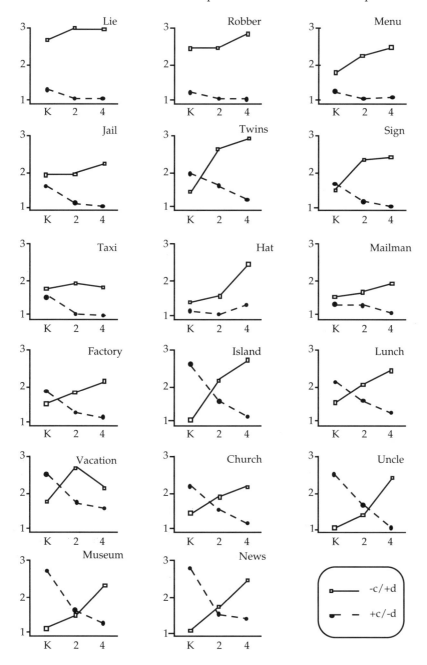

Figure 4.1
Mean scores for each of the concepts in the characteristic-to-defining shift study. The actual or extrapolated crossover points of the solid and dashed lines correspond roughly to when a shift occurs for a specific concept.

C: About 24 or 25.
E: If he's 2 years old, can he be an uncle?
C: No...he can be a cousin.

Robber (-c/+d)
E: Could she be a robber?
C: No...'cause robbers, they have guns and they do stickups, and this woman didn't do that, and she didn't have a gun. She didn't do a stickup.
E: Does a robber have to have a gun?
C: Yes...'cause robbers kill sometimes.
E: (Repeats story) Could she be a robber?
C: No.

Uncle (+c/-d)
E: Could that be an uncle?
C: Yes.
E: What is an uncle?
C: An uncle is that he brings you presents at Christmas.
E: What else?
C: An uncle is that he lets you come over to his house.
E: Could I be your uncle?
C: No...because I don't know you.
E: If I got to know you and brought you presents, could I be your uncle?
C: Yes.

Island (+c/-d)
E: Is that an island?
C: Yes.
E: Why is that an island?
C: Because it has coconut trees and palm trees.

Museum (-c/+d)
E: Could that be a museum?
C: No...a museum is something with dinosaur bones.
E: Well, suppose (repeats story). Could that be a museum...can they have dirty shirts?
C: No, that's a laundromat!

Children did not always progress directly to adult-like responses. Some responses (scores of 2) showed an intermediate level of understanding at which the child either used somewhat unusual defining features or required both characteristic and defining features in order to evaluate an instance. The following examples from the transcripts of second graders illustrate these sorts of responses:

Factory   (-c/+d)
E: Is that a factory?
C: No...because you have to make things.
E: They're making buttons. Is that a factory?
C: No...it's a house. Factories have to make all sorts of things.
E: More than buttons?
C: Yes.

Lunch (-c/+d)
E: Could that be lunch?
C: No...because lunch you have to have sandwiches and stuff like that.
E: Can you have cereal for lunch?
C: No.
E: Can you have pancakes for lunch?
C: No.
E: Well, how do you know if something is lunch or not?
C: If the time says 12:00.
E: This was 12:00.
C: Well, I don't think so.
E: (Repeats story) Is that lunch?
C: I know...that one is not lunch...you have to eat sandwiches in lunch.
E: Can you have anything else?
C: You can have drinks, but not breakfast.

In the most mature responses the children seemed to attend primarily to defining features, as these fourth graders' responses demonstrate:

Uncle (-c/+d)
E: Is he an uncle?
C: Yes...because he's still my mother's brother? *(response ended with a question intonation)*
E: Can an uncle be any age?
C: Yes.

Island (-c/+d)
E: Could that be an island?
C: Yes...because it's surrounded by water...An island's just a piece of land surrounded by water.

Church (-c/+d)
E: Could that be a church?
C: Yeah...I guess so 'cause they're talking about God and stuff like that and they pray.

E: Could a church be a red and white tent in the middle of the ocean?
C: I don't know.
E: But this place is (repeats story). Is it a church?
C: Sort of...but it's not on ground.
E: Does a church have to be on ground?
C: I guess it doesn't have to be...it could be out in the ocean.
E: (Repeats story once more) So is this place a church or not?
C: Yeah, it's a church.

News (+c/-d)
E: Could that be news?
C: No...because the news would be happening that year and that day, not from a book or from last year.

Uncle (+c/-d)
E: Could he be your uncle?
C: No...because an uncle would be related to you...an uncle is your aunt's wife *(sic)*!

These children seem to represent these concepts in different ways at different ages, shifting from early reliance on a broad spectrum of characteristic features to a sharp focus on a small number of critical properties, relations, and/or dimensions. Moreover, they seem to go through a kind of transitional period with, perhaps, an intermediate form of representation. Equally important, however, is the finding that for some items the kindergartners seem to know exactly what the defining features are, whereas for other items even the fourth graders experience difficulty. Consider these two brief examples:

K(1) Robber (+c/-d)
E: Is that a robber?
C: No...'cause robbers steal stuff, but if someone says they don't want it anymore or you ask, 'cause they don't want it any more, they could give it to you.
E: That's not a robber?
C: No.
E: Even though he's a mean old man with a gun in his pocket?
C: No.

4(1) Museum (-c/+d)
E: Could that be a museum?
C: No...because in a museum there are things old in it, but not dirty things and all. And seeing shirts is not a museum because you can just throw that away. A shirt doesn't mean anything, you just wear it. It doesn't go in a museum.

This first study on the characteristic-to-defining shift suggests several possible patterns for how the shift occurs that should be pursued in follow-up studies. In addition, several alternative explanations for the data arise that should be addressed. First consider the patterns that emerge above and beyond the shift itself:

1. Most significant, the shifts do not seem to occur at the same time for all concepts, suggesting that additional factors (for instance, the conceptual complexity of the domain) may influence when a shift occurs.

2. Scores on the +c/-d judgments were generally higher. This might indicate a particular type of transition stage in which both the defining and the characteristic features are believed to be essential for a word's meaning. Children in such a transition stage would show just such a pattern of responses. Alternatively, the pattern could simply represent a general response bias to give more "no" than "yes" responses.

A Follow-up Study with Preschoolers

Given that for at least some items even kindergartners were able to override characteristic features correctly with defining ones, it seemed appropriate to study still younger children to see whether they exhibited an even higher reliance on characteristic features. Consequently, a follow-up study was undertaken with 22 preschoolers at a day-care center in the Ithaca, New York, area. The children ranged in age from 3:0 years to 5:8 years, with a mean age of 4:5 years. The same stimuli and stories were used as in the main study, the only difference being that frequently the task was broken down into several brief sessions, and responses were not probed as extensively. In addition, there were more cases of missing and unscorable responses.

A final group of 16 children was able to complete enough of the responses (more than 75%) so as to be included as subjects. Overall, these children gave 86% scorable responses for all items, with a few items, such as "factory" and "menu," accounting for most of the missing values. Spot-check reliabilities between the two judges averaged 94%, and differences were resolved through discussion.

Means for each of the terms were calculated and compared to those for kindergartners. In general, the means for preschoolers were lower than those for kindergartners, indicating a greater reliance on characteristic features. (The overall mean for all scores for the preschoolers was 1.72, whereas the overall mean for the kindergartners was 1.86.) The single sample t-test of difference scores against a population mean of 0 was significant at the .005 level. Averaging across +c/-d and -c/+d cases, the largest age changes, in descending order, were found for "robber," "factory," "vacation," and "taxi." In general, however, the relative performances on the terms were quite similar across the two age groups, with a .70 correlation between the scores of the two ages. The preschool findings thus suggest a natural continuity with the kindergarten findings and show (1) that the tendency to rely on characteristic features is even more marked in preschoolers than in kindergartners and (2) that for some of the terms studied by Keil and Batterman, a shift from characteristic to defining terms may occur even before a child reaches kindergarten age. Even the preschoolers, however, showed more attention to defining features for some terms than others. They relied on defining features the most for "hat," "lie," "menu," "mailman," and "jail," and the least for "news," "museum," "island," and "vacation." Thus, even preschoolers do not seem to completely give in to characteristic features for all concepts.

New Questions

The general shift and the subsidiary patterns described above also raise a number of questions about how to interpret the data and point out the many limitations of this study and its preschool follow-up.

1. Could the shift reflect a change in response bias or strategy? Perhaps the children were merely shifting in terms of what they thought the experimenter wanted and, if they had been probed differently, would have shown an understanding of defining features for all concepts at all ages. Other investigators (for example, Kossan 1978; Landau 1982) have shown that strategic considerations can influence the extent to which children will gave more analytic, definition-like judgments—perhaps that is what occurred in these studies.

There are good reasons for doubting that the shift merely reflects a general strategy change. First, the shift apparently occurs at different times for different concepts; if it were a general strategy shift, it should instead occur at roughly the same time for all concepts. Second, the transcripts are rich enough and involve enough interactions that any simple strategy changes should have been observable. Third, the simplest strategy changes would not account for the shift. For example, a change in yes/no biases, though creating a main effect of description type, would not be able to account for the shift itself across both types of descriptions; nor would it be able to account for the crossover patterns shown in the graphs in figure 4.1. Nonetheless, the main study described here cannot strongly rule out possible strategy effects, and future research should attempt to address this issue more directly. As will be seen in ensuing chapters, other relevant published studies using different methods should help resolve this issue.

2. A venerable theme in developmental psychology is that children tend to shift from perceptually based representations to conceptually based ones (see Anglin 1984). In many cases the characteristic features used in this study were more perceptual than the corresponding defining ones. To what extent is that distinction a major factor driving the shift? It still might occur at different times for different concepts but it could be proceeding from the perceptual to the conceptual (rather than from characteristic to defining). Although there are some indications that this may not be the best explanation for the shift, since it is still observed when both types of features are either perceptual or conceptual (as with "island"), for the most part the characteristic and defining features used in this study are highly correlated with the perceptual/conceptual distinction. Is the shift really one from characteristic to defining?

3. An alternative account is that the child always operates on the basis of defining features, but that early in the acquisition of a concept those features tend to be so idiosyncratic that they never are brought out in the experimental sessions, with the result that the child appears to be relying on characteristic features. For example, suppose a child felt that the necessary and sufficient features of islands were palm trees and sandy beaches. Unless this came out during the questioning, such a child would give the same pattern of responses as the child who genuinely represented the concept in terms of characteristic features. Parents tell anecdotes about children who insist that an object absolutely must have certain features in order to be labeled an instance. If so, how common is this pattern?

4. Perhaps representations at all ages consist of characteristic features, and developing children are changing the weights they attach to the centrality of various features in the typicality space for a concept. If so, then there may not be a real shift from a holistic, probabilistic representational format to a more well defined, analytic format.

5. To what extent is the shift merely a reflection of changing parental input? Considerable research in the last few years has shown that parents and other adults change the nature of their speech as a function of the age of the child they are addressing. Do parents tend to include many more characteristic features in explaining concepts to younger children, and do the children therefore merely reflect what they hear in parental explanations?

6. To what extent is the shift a consequence of the child's adopting cultural values for the way to express and use concepts?

These questions are addressed by a series of studies described in the next two chapters. Though such studies will not resolve every issue, they will provide a much finer-grained picture of what develops and why.

Conclusions

The notion of characteristic and defining features put forth in the semantic memory literature has proved useful as a first approximation toward describing what appears to be a shift in conceptual structure for a special set of natural language concepts. These concepts, sometimes known as "nominal kind concepts" because their meanings are purportedly conventionally defined via their names, are a useful tool in starting to develop a broader theory of the nature of conceptual development.

Many questions were raised by the study described in this chapter, some pertaining to alternative interpretations of the data, and others to the nature and generality of the observed shift and the reasons for it. Let us now turn to these issues.

Chapter 5
Nominal Kinds and Domain Specificity

Concepts rarely, if ever, exist or develop in isolation. They are almost always enmeshed in a relational structure with other concepts. This relational structure usually forms a conceptual domain, which may be unified by a theory or coherent set of beliefs about the relations among the members of that domain. If concepts are embedded within relational structures, most structural changes in development will not be restricted to a single concept. Thus, when a concept undergoes a shift, that shift may involve not so much a reorganization of the structure of that particular concept as a reorganization of the conceptual domain and of how the concept fits into the structure of that domain. The study described in this chapter examines the relation between domain structure and qualitative changes in the representation of nominal kind concepts. Nominal kinds are used for several reasons: (1) the domains are often easily demarcated by a few general principles, (2) the characteristic/defining paradigm is easy to use, and (3) the studies in chapter 4 suggest that nominal kind concepts shift at different times, perhaps reflecting a domain-by-domain course of acquisition.

By examining how concepts develop in relation to domains of knowledge, it is possible to understand better some of the issues that were raised at the end of chapter 4. The questions about strategies and general response biases are particularly relevant. If it is shown that shifts occur on a domain by domain basis and often at very different ages across domains, the notion of a general strategy shift becomes much less tenable.

An independent reason for investigating domains and conceptual change came from two studies that Michael Kelly and I conducted on metaphor. The first study (Keil 1986b) examined the emergence of children's ability to comprehend metaphor and strongly suggested that part of coming to understand a term is knowing how it opposes or contrasts with other terms in the same conceptual domain. More specifically, the study suggested that once a child understands one metaphorical relation between two domains (such as "The man is slippery," which expresses a relation between the domains of texture terms and personality types), that child is very likely to understand other metaphorical relations between the two domains ("She is scratchy," "The boy is sticky," and so on). Thus, metaphorical understanding seemed to emerge as a unified whole for sets of relations between two coherent domains. For different pairs of domains, this process could occur at different ages, but in each case the ability tended to emerge all at once within a pair of domains. The results were interpreted as indicating that understanding a metaphor usually requires juxtaposition of two complete domains, not just the isolated concepts in any specific metaphor. Consequently, the ability to understand any metaphor between two domains entails a knowledge of the structural relations between many of the concepts in each domain. Without such knowledge, a successful juxtaposition would not be possible (see Lehrer 1978; Tourangeau and Sternberg 1982).

Kelly and Keil (1987) followed up on this notion of juxtaposition of conceptual domains in metaphor by examining the influence of domains on the comprehension of metaphor in adults. The act of comprehending one metaphor between domains not only made the terms used in metaphors move closer together in a multidimensional conceptual space but also made other terms that were never mentioned, but would make good metaphors between those domains, move closer together. Moreover, comprehension made terms that would form inappropriate metaphors move farther apart. Thus, the two concepts explicitly involved in the comprehension of any one metaphor would seem to require the realignment of each of the systematic domains in which they are embedded.

Five Conceptual Domains

The five conceptual domains used in the study of nominal kinds and domain specificity were selected according to several criteria. It was decided that:

1. The domains should not all be ones where the shift occurs at roughly the same time. Since one of the major purposes of the study was to examine how the occurrence of the shift is linked to developing knowledge in specific domains, it was thought preferable to include at least some domains that follow different developmental time courses.

2. The terms in each domain should be familiar to most kindergartners. The child certainly did not have to know the defining features, but it was necessary that some concept or set of concepts should come to mind when the child heard the term.

3. The domains should be sufficiently coherent that knowledge of one term involves understanding its relation to contrasting terms in the same

domain. That is, some concepts might be so loosely associated in a "domain" that changes in the understanding of one might have minimal impact on the others. Thus, highly superordinate "domains" (such as vehicles) and "ad hoc" (Barsalou 1987) nominal kind categories (such as household belongings) were not used.

4. As in the study described in chapter 4, all terms must have relatively clear defining features as well as a number of salient characteristic features.

5. The terms must lend themselves to the construction of easily comprehensible +c/-d and -c/+d descriptions. This often proved to be a stumbling block for a domain as one member of a description pair became too convoluted or implausible. (As was the case in chapter 4, the descriptions must not be rejected by the children as simply too outlandish. They must accept the premise of the described entity as really existing and then evaluate what sort of thing it is.)

Five domains were selected: moral act terms, meal terms, hand tool terms, kinship terms, and cooking terms. The data from the Keil and Batterman study suggested that moral acts form a domain that shifts early and that meal and kinship terms shift somewhat later. Even though hand tool terms do not form as coherent a domain as other terms, they were included so as to have a class of artifacts and also because their characteristic features are especially salient. Cooking terms were selected because, like kinship terms, they have been traditionally studied as "semantic fields," which are sets of lexical items closely related at the conceptual level (Lehrer 1974).

These terms were pretested on kindergartners for familiarity and were all found to be known to most of them. The terms are shown in table 5.1, examples of the descriptions in table 5.2, and the drawings used for the tool terms in figure 5.1; the full set of descriptions is given in appendix 2. The descriptions were constructed according to the same guidelines as those used in the first characteristic-to-defining study: the defining features tended to occur toward the end of the description, and the overall descriptions were brief. Two adult experimenters decided on the characteristic and defining features for each term largely by generating both many atypical instances and many noninstances possessing the largest number of typical features possible. There is no algorithm that one can simply apply to decompose a concept into the two feature types; instead, one must resort to heuristics of this sort, keeping in mind the continuum discussed in chapter 3.

The procedure was modified somewhat in light of the first study. Because the stimulus set was so large, children were seen on successive school days, in some cases as many as four times, so as to reduce fatigue in any one session. One especially important change made assessments

Table 5.1
Terms used in the nominal kinds and domain specificity study

Moral Act	Meal	Tool	Kinship	Cooking
Lie	Breakfast	Screwdriver	Aunt	Boil
Steal	Lunch	Hammer	Uncle	Fry
Cheat	Dinner	Saw	Cousin	Bake
Tease		Scissors	Grandmother	
		Drill	Grandfather	

Table 5.2
Examples of descriptions used in the nominal kinds and domain specificity study

MORAL ACT TERMS

Lie
(+c/-d) This girl hated a boy in her class because he was so mean and did really nasty things to her. She wanted to get him into trouble, so she told the teacher all the nasty things the boy had really done....Did she lie to the teacher?

(-c/+d) This little boy always got good grades in school and prizes for being so smart. The other children were jealous of him because of it, and he didn't want to make them feel bad and wanted them to be his friends. So, one time, when he really got a good mark on a test, he told them that he got a bad mark so they'd be his friends. Did he lie to them?

MEAL TERMS

Breakfast
(+c/-d) One evening at six o'clock when the sun was going down, it was time to eat. Everyone got their PJs on and came to the table. You had scrambled eggs and bacon and toast and orange juice. Your parents had a cup of coffee and read the newspaper. Were you having breakfast?

(-c/+d) One morning when your family woke up, you all put on your best clothes...mommy wore a fancy dress and daddy wore a suit. You had company coming over. When they arrived at 8 o'clock in the morning, you all sat down at the table. The meal was steak and potatoes and a salad. Your parents drank wine, and you got to have chocolate milk. For dessert you had apple pie and ice cream. Were you having breakfast?

Table 5.2 (continued)

TOOL TERMS (see figure 5.1, which shows drawings that accompanied these descriptions)

Screwdriver

(+c/-d) There's this thing that has a long flat metal bar and it has a wooden handle. It's used for cleaning out the grooves in the top of screws and it looks like this (see drawings). Could this be a screwdriver?

(-c/+d) There's this round pink plastic ball and it's shaped like this (see drawings). And it has this little edge sticking out that will fit into screws to turn them. Could this be a screwdriver?

KINSHIP TERMS

Aunt

(+c/-d) There's a lady who's the same age as your mommy. You see her a few times a year. She loves you very much. She likes to buy you clothes and take you shopping. And sometimes she lets you sleep over at her house. She's not your mommy's or daddy's sister (and she's not married to your mommy's or daddy's brother). Could she be your aunt?

(-c/+d) There's this little girl that you've met once before. She wears her hair in braids and goes to school in California every day like you. She's your father's sister. Could she be your aunt?

COOKING TERMS

Boil

(+c/-d) Your mother was cooking some eggs to make egg salad for lunch. So she took a pot and put a little bit of water in the the bottom. Then she put a rack in the pot to hold the eggs above the water like this (show pic.) so that they would not roll around and break each other. She put a flame on under the pot to heat the water. Was she boiling the eggs?

(-c/+d) Michael brought a big bathtub in a truck out to a field. He filled it with water and built a fire around it...He wanted to wash his shirts out in the fresh air. When the water started bubbling, he added the soap and bleach. Was Michael boiling his shirts?

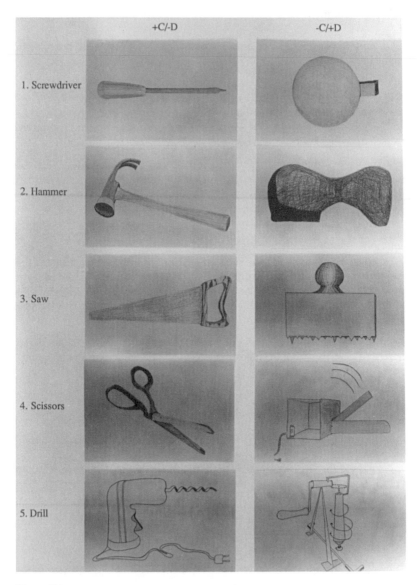

Figure 5.1
Drawings used for tool term descriptions in the study on nominal kinds and domain specificity.

of the shift more conservative. To ensure that children were aware of and had carefully considered both sets of features (characteristic vs. defining) before responding, they were asked about the features they had not relied on. Thus, whichever set of features a child relied on, the experimenters reminded the child explicitly of the other set of features and asked whether they mattered, often repeating the story in the process. The sample transcripts included later in this chapter illustrate the nature of this procedure in detail.

Sixteen children in each of three grades (K, 2, and 4) participated as subjects. (Average ages were 5:8, 7:9, and 10:2 years, respectively.) The children were from schools in the Ithaca, New York, area. In addition, 18 adults (Cornell University undergraduates) also participated. The adults were included to assess whether the descriptions for some terms elicited a bias for characteristic features at all ages.

All sessions were tape-recorded and then transcribed. The transcripts were scored by two independent judges according to principles similar to those described in chapter 4. A score of 1 was given for responses indicating that the story described a noninstance of the concept and a score of 3 for responses indicating that the story described an instance. A score of 2 was given when the child (a) vacillated between the type 1 and type 3 responses, (b) insisted that both sorts of features were necessary, or (c) specifically used an incorrect defining feature (12% of all responses received a score of 2). The scorers agreed approximately 95% of the time, and the remaining disagreements were resolved through discussion. For various reasons ranging from subject fatigue to equipment malfunctions, a small number of values were missing. The tape recorder completely malfunctioned for one second grader, who was replaced by an additional subject.

These studies yielded considerable information, which can be summarized in a variety of ways. The first overall summary is shown in figure 5.2, which illustrates the crossover patterns for the five conceptual domains. These graphs represent the average values across all children in each age group as well as across all items in each domain. In each case the characteristic-to-defining shifts are significant as tested by two-factor, repeated measures ANOVAs. (That is, in each domain both main effect due to age and main effect due to description type are significant, as well as the age-by-type interaction.) The most obvious result is that the shift occurs at a different time for each domain and that the shifts occurred in a clearly defined order: moral act terms, meal terms, tool terms, kinship terms, cooking terms. In the case of moral act terms it is not clear when, if ever, the lines would cross; as soon as the child can speak and be adequately tested, the defining features may be at least partly available. Nonetheless, even in the moral act terms case, the age-

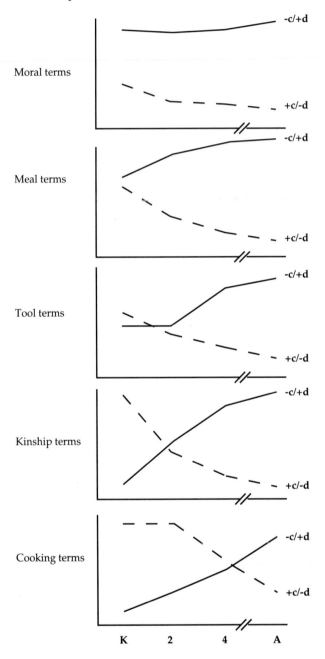

Figure 5.2
Mean scores across all concepts in each of five conceptual domains in the study on nominal kinds and domain specificity.

by-type interactions were significant, indicating an increasing clarification of the characteristic/defining contrast.

Within each domain the shifts look roughly the same for all the terms used. This is shown in figure 5.3, which illustrates the shift pattern for each term. All are significant with respect to both main effects and interaction, except for "tease," which had no significant main effect for age. With only a few exceptions, the shifts seem to occur in a similar way for each term in a given domain; moreover, the patterns can vary substantially across fields. These intra- vs. interdomain relations are explored more quantitatively in tables 5.3 through 5.6, which show the average correlations within and across fields at each grade level. Correlations with asterisks are significant at the $p < .10$ level. Because the range of scores for some items is often small (as in the case of moral act terms), these patterns of correlations can only be taken as suggestive. Nonetheless, whenever they approach significance, the average correlations between terms within any domain are higher than those between terms across domains.

The correlation matrices shown in tables 5.3 through 5.6 also suggest that some of the conceptual domains are more coherent and tightly interrelated than others. Excluding the moral act terms, since children at all ages seemed to attend to their defining features, the correlations do seem to reflect the coherence of the domains. The most coherent domains were kinship and meal terms—a sensible result, since mastery of just one of the terms in those domains reveals almost all the relevant dimensions along which to look for defining features for other terms in the same domain. Moreover, the domains are well bounded, so that it is very clear whether a new instance should be evaluated within the context of one of those domains. The least coherent domain, at all ages, was tool terms. Again this result is sensible since knowledge of the defining features of one tool term does not provide easy access to the defining features for another. (Simply knowing that function counts is not enough, since that is true for all artifacts. One would only be aided by the more precise knowledge that hand tools have some common function that distinguishes them as a class from other kinds of tools.) This lack of coherence can also be seen in the curves in figure 5.3, where it is clear that the developmental patterns are the most variable among the tool terms not only with respect to the overall shape of the curves for each tool term but also with respect to the location of the crossover point, which varies from slightly before kindergarten for "drill" to somewhere between the second and fourth grades for "saw."

A more revealing measure of domain coherence can be seen in figure 5.4, which shows the numbers of children at all three ages (adults were excluded because they show so little variation) who based their judg-

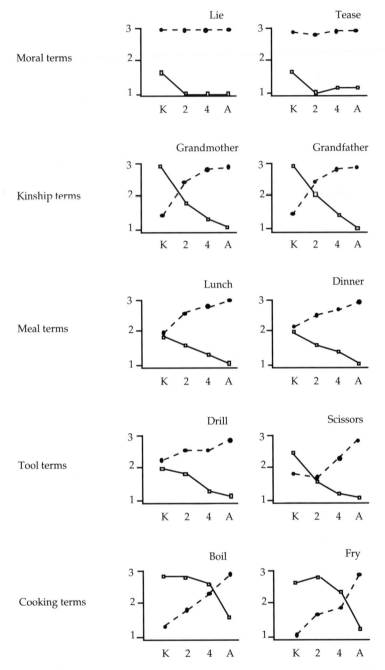

Figure 5.3
Mean scores for each of the concepts in the study on nominal kinds and domain specificity.

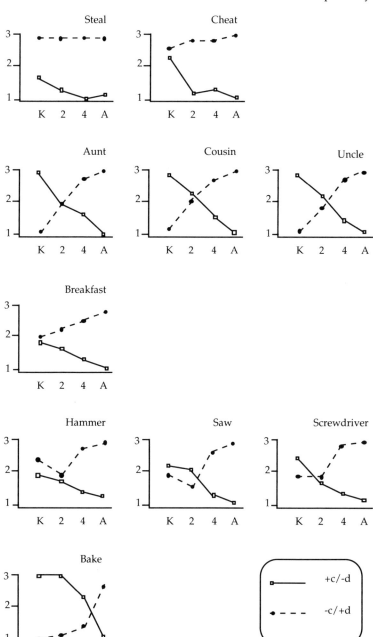

Table 5.3
Average correlations within and across fields. Kindergartners (n=16)

	Moral	Meal	Tool	Kinship	Cooking
Moral	.17	.20	.06	.01	.02
Meal		.89*	-.12	.34	.01
Tool			.22	-.18	-.06
Kinship				.75*	.04
Cooking					.10

Table 5.4
Average correlations within and across fields. Second graders (n=16)

	Moral	Meal	Tool	Kinship	Cooking
Moral	.30	.02	.09	.22	.07
Meal		.76*	-.02	.20	-.42
Tool			.38	.20	-.16
Kinship				.63*	-.05
Cooking					.30

Table 5.5
Average correlations within and across fields. Fourth graders (n=16)

	Moral	Meal	Tool	Kinship	Cooking
Moral	-.02	.08	-.04	-.05	.04
Meal		.91*	.25	.25	.19
Tool			.42	-.05	.01
Kinship				.92*	.35
Cooking					.31

Table 5.6
Average correlations within and across fields. Overall (excluding adults, n=48)

	Moral	Meal	Tool	Kinship	Cooking
Moral	.40*	.28*	.23*	.35*	.24*
Meal		.87*	.28*	.48*	.32*
Tool			.60*	.51*	.48*
Kinship				.89*	.61*
Cooking					.77*

ments on defining features for either 0–20%, 20.1–40%, 40.1–60%, 60.1–80%, or 80.1–100% of the terms in each of the five conceptual domains. This measure is meant to show how likely it is that a child who has shifted for one term in a domain has also shifted for other terms in the same domain. If the shift tends to be an all-or-none process reflecting the child's insight into the fundamental organizing dimensions for a domain, out of which defining features originate, then the patterns shown by such a measure should be primarily bimodal in nature. Alternatively, if each term is acquired in a more isolated fashion, the number of children in each percentage range should be roughly the same, indicating a gradual term-by-term shift to defining features.

The five graphs in figure 5.4 do show a general bimodal pattern, wherever adequate interage variation allowed it to be observed. Once children shifted to defining features for one concept in a domain, they tended to do so for all the other concepts in the domain. Thus, for all domains there are very few children in the 40–60% range and relatively few in the 20–40% and 60–80% ranges, in contrast to the number in the 0–20% and 80–100% ranges. The bimodal effect is particularly clear for the kinship terms and strongly indicated by the meal and cooking terms. It is weakest for the tool terms, which follows directly from the correlational analysis and from the patterns observed in figure 5.3.

The clearest way to understand how these shifts occur in each domain is to examine them on a domain-by-domain basis with examples taken from the transcripts. This analysis reveals several patterns that are suggestive of the underlying mechanisms.

Moral act terms

It is clear that even the vast majority of kindergartners are attending to the defining features for the morally evaluable acts of lying, stealing, cheating, and teasing. No kindergartner, for example, was attending to characteristic features more than 50% of the time. This is not to say that children's understanding of morally evaluable human acts does not develop after age five; one certainly hopes that it does. But at least in this simple setting the children were rarely fooled by the characteristic features.   Moreover, their responses were frequently surprisingly sophisticated. This was particularly impressive since the main manipulation of characteristic features was to equate the characteristic features with overt consequences and behavioral actions and the defining features with intentions. The Piagetian account of the development of moral reasoning (Piaget 1932) would suggest that these children should have attended almost exclusively to the characteristic features. Consider the following transcripts (at each grade level children are distinguished by a number in parentheses following the grade):

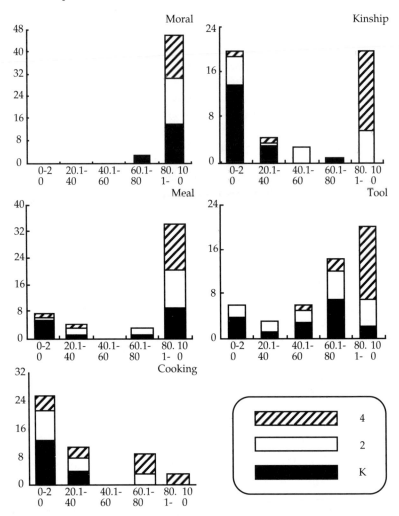

Figure 5.4
Numbers of children at grades K, 2, and 4 who based their judgments on defining features for either 0–20%, 20.1–40%, 40.1–60%, 60.1–80%, or 80.1–100% of the terms in each of the five conceptual domains.

K(1) Tease (+c/-d)
C: No.
E: Why not?
C: He thought they were pointing at his haircut but it was really the spider on his back and he doesn't know.
E: Even though he ran inside and told the teacher, they weren't teasing him?
C: No.

K(2) Steal (-c/+d)
C: Yes.
E: Why do you think so?
C: She took it away without permission and didn't return it...and that is like a robber.
E: Even though she was friendly and nice...she stole your toilet bowl?
C: Yes.

No excerpts are included from the transcripts of older children and adults because they did not differ significantly and because the kindergartners performed in such a mature fashion.

Several other interesting patterns emerged in the judgments about morally evaluable acts. Perhaps most significant was that even when children did judge a +c/-d description as referring to an instance or a -c/+d description as referring to a noninstance, they often did so by distorting the description in such a way that it was either +c/+d or -c/-d, thus making the features internally consistent. To use a more specific example, one kindergartner judged the +c/-d description for "cheating" as describing a legitimate instance of cheating and, when asked why, insisted that the protagonist "always wanted to cheat every time." When the experimenter repeated the description twice and asked if there was "anything in the story that says that she cheated," the kindergartner still responded that the protagonist always wanted to cheat although she didn't know why. Such cases suggest that these children know something about the defining features of the concept and the special role that such features play, but they cannot bear to have them be inconsistent with the characteristic ones.

It should also be noted that although the overwhelmingly predominant response pattern among kindergartners was to attend to defining features for the morally evaluable terms, on a few occasions kindergartners did seem to be genuinely relying on characteristic features with no distortions of consistency. These cases are useful because they indicate that the stimulus descriptions were at least in principle capable of getting children to rely on characteristic rather than defining features. Looking at those stimulus descriptions in more detail, it is difficult to know how one could have developed a richer set of characteristic features in each of the +c/-d stories to pit against the defining ones. Virtually all the typical features associated with scenarios for lying, cheating, stealing, and teasing were included and yet the vast majority of kindergartners were not taken in by such features. By contrast, the same children were easily swayed by the characteristic features associated with various kinship terms even though they seem to be no more salient or frequent.

In sum, for the domain of morally evaluable acts, kindergartners are surprisingly sophisticated in knowing the relevant defining features and in distinguishing them from highly salient characteristic features. In many of the descriptions the perceivable scene may have all the characteristic features of the act; only an unseen intention clashes at the defining level. Even so, the children were rarely confused.

Recent studies on moral development and in particular on the child's concept of a lie help us to better understand the incompatibility of these results with the Piagetian account (Piaget 1932). Wimmer, Gruber, and Perner (1984), for example, have demonstrated that preschoolers know a good deal more about the concept of lying than was previously thought. That study and several others in the moral development literature indicate that preschoolers are quite able to take intentions into account in evaluating moral acts. For example, the Piagetian study on judgments of culpability suggested that even six-year-olds will predominantly take only consequences of an action into account and tend to ignore the intention. More recent studies, however, suggest that various task-specific difficulties, rather than a neglect of intentions, were responsible for the children's performance; thus, videotaping the event, presenting the intention at the end, equating consequences, and varying the intention all result in preschoolers' evaluating intentions (see, for example, Parsons et al. 1976).

Meal terms
When tested on meal terms, 8 kindergarten children gave responses that clearly indicated attention to defining features, 7 gave responses that clearly relied on characteristic features, and 1 seemed to vacillate between the two. As figure 5.4 indicates, the results were strongly bimodal, with 13 children receiving the same score on all six of their meal term responses. The meal terms also showed the highest intercorrelations at all ages in comparison to the four other conceptual domains. The reasons for the all-or-none nature of the shift become apparent upon consideration of the nature of the conceptual domain and the types of responses the children offered.

As a rough approximation, the domain of meal terms can be construed as varying along three dimensions: time of day, type of food, and level of formality. This is undoubtedly an oversimplification of the real adult concept, but it serves to illustrate the phenomenon. Initially, children weigh all three dimensions equally and see no single one as being critical. Consequently, if a described event shares values on two out of three dimensions with a highly typical exemplar, children judge it to be an instance regardless of which two dimensions are shared. Later, when they realize the primacy of the time dimension, that realization immediately applies to all three meal terms, and all three shift at the same time. The meal terms domain is special in this respect. Though all the terms in other domains can be defined by a small set of relations, the adult definition of those terms does not reduce so neatly to one linear dimension. For instance, although the definitions of moral terms all have to do with certain patterns of intentions and other mental states, they share no simple common ingredient. Meal terms, on the other hand, do share a single defining dimension (time of day) and vary only in their values along that dimension. It is possible to select one of the other dimensions as the critical one along which to organize meal terms, and in some contexts this might make sense (for instance, formality in a social-pragmatic theoretical system). The children in this study, however, showed little variability along these lines.

A few excerpts from the transcripts illustrate the occurrence of the shift. The following kindergartners are quite typical of those who still relied exclusively on characteristic features:

K(4) Dinner (-c/+d)
C: No.
E: Why not?
C: Because we were having mostly morning and lunch stuff.
E: So was it dinner?
C: No.
E: When were you eating it?
C: Night.
E: So wasn't it dinner?
C: No...my father eats waffles for dinner once in a long time...
E: So if you are at your friend's house and (repeats story) were you and your friend having dinner?
C: No.

K(5) Breakfast (+c/-d)
E: Do you think that they are having breakfast?
C: Yeah.

E: Why do you still think so?
C: Because bacon you usually have for breakfast.
E: And if you had bacon and the other stuff at 6 o'clock at night would it still be breakfast?
C: No.
E: Why not?
C: Because it's not time to eat breakfast.
E: Well, what time are you eating in this story?
C: Six in the night.
E: And what do you have to eat?
C: Bacon and eggs.
E: And what do you have to drink?
C: OJ.
E: And what do your parents have?
C: Coffee.
E: And what are they doing?
C: Reading the paper.
E: And while all of this is going on, are you having breakfast?
C: No....
E: Why not?
C: I mean yes.
E: Why?
C: Because that sounds like you're having breakfast.
E: And what time are you having it?
C: Six o'clock at night.
E: So if you have (repeats story) and it's at 6 in the evening, that's breakfast?
C: Yes.

K(6) Breakfast (-c/+d)
C: No.
E: Why not?
C: It didn't look like breakfast...it didn't look like breakfast...it didn't have toast or cereal or anything. *(This was the first meal term description for the child.)*
E: And what did you have? Was it steak and potatoes?
C: Yeah.
E: And what did you have for dessert?
C: Ice cream and pie.
E: And what time of day did you have it?
C: Monday?
E: And what time of the day did you have it?
C: Eight.

E: In the morning or in the evening?
C: In the morning.
E: And what did you wear?
C: My best clothes.
E: (Repeats story again) So it was or wasn't breakfast?
C: It was like supper.
E: So if you have (repeats food) at 8 in the morning in your best clothes...that is supper?
C: Yes.

K(6) Lunch (-c/+d)
C: No.
E: Why not?
C: Because lunch is sandwich...(gives several examples).
E: At what time of day do you eat (repeats food) in this story?
C: In the morning.
E: And the story says (repeats story, stressing time of day (noon)). So you think that is or isn't lunch?
C: It isn't.
E: And what time is it when you eat the stuff?
C: Twelve o'clock.
E: And if you eat (repeats food) at 12 o'clock it is or isn't lunch?
C: It isn't.

K(6) Dinner (+c/-d)
C: Yes.
E: Why not breakfast?
C: Because you don't go to breakfast in restaurants, you go to breakfast at home and you eat cheerios or regular oatmeal.
E: And what time do you go to the restaurant?
C: Morning.
E: And what do you eat?
C: Chicken and corn on the cob...
E: So that is or isn't dinner?
C: It is.

K(7) Breakfast (-c/+d)
C: No.
E: Why not?
C: Because you usually don't have steak for breakfast.
E: So what else did you have with this meal?
C: (pause)
E: Potatoes and what did you drink and have for dessert?
C: Wine and chocolate milk and apple pie and ice cream.

E: And what time of day was it?
C: Eight o'clock in the morning.
E: So if you have (repeats food) at 8 o'clock in the morning and you have company coming, it is or it isn't breakfast?
C: It isn't...'cause how could you wake up in the morning and get your clothes on and have the company come at 8 o'clock in the morning!
E: If they *get* up by 6:30 and got dressed and fixed the food and sat down with the company at 8, would that be breakfast? And if they ate (food), do you think it is or isn't breakfast?
C: No, it is NOT breakfast!

These transcripts illustrate several points concerning both the method and the results of this experiment. Perhaps most obvious is the extent to which the experimenter, in this case Lianne Ritter, went to heroic lengths to ensure that the children understood and remembered all parts of the story. Moreover, the experimenters almost always challenged the children's answers with competing features and then asked the children to justify their responses.

More substantively, these excerpts, and the transcripts as a whole, indicate that most children who had not yet made the shift were nonetheless fully aware of the time-of-day feature in the story and clearly did take this to be a highly characteristic feature of each meal type. However, they failed to see it as a defining feature and thus allowed it to be overruled if all the characteristic features were "pushing" in the opposite direction. Several children even distorted the story in their memory so that the antidefining feature (which for them was only atypical) was changed into a defining (for them, highly typical) one. This is an important pattern, because it shows that, at least for one domain, the child can be fully aware of the defining features but may treat them as merely equivalent to all other highly characteristic features.

Several kindergartners, and almost all of the older children, did shift to defining meal terms by time of day. The following excerpts illustrate such a shift at different ages:

K(8) Breakfast (-c/+d)
C: Yes.
E: Why do you think so?
C: Because it was morning out and you eat breakfast in the morning.
E: And what did you have to eat...what kind of meat was it?
C: (Pause)
E: It was steak and potatoes and salad...and what did your

parents drink?
C: Wine.
E: And what did you drink?
C: Chocolate milk.
E: And what did you have for dessert?
C: Apple pie.
E: And that was breakfast?
C: Yeah.

2(1) Lunch (+c/-d)
C: No.
E: Why not?
C: Because you have lunch at the noon time and you have breakfast in the morning.
E: Even though you have (repeats food), it isn't lunch?
C: No.

2(1) Breakfast (-c/+d)
C: Yeah.
E: Why?
C: It was in the morning; but it doesn't seem like a good break-fast.
E: So do you think it was or wasn't a breakfast?
C: Was.

4(1) Lunch (-c/+d)
C: Yes...you could have practically anything for lunch...and maybe people would look at you like a weirdo, but that doesn't mean that you couldn't have it for lunch.
E: So if it is (repeats food), it is lunch?
C: It could be, it could be brunch or something.
E: Why would it be brunch?
C: Because you didn't have breakfast.
E: If you had something to eat earlier in the day?
C: Then it would probably be considered a lunch.

Though the scores suggest that children shift in an almost all-or-none fashion, these transcripts illustrate that they can still have some doubts even while favoring the time-of-day dimension. By the time they grow up, however, they very rarely have any doubts, as was clear from the adult transcripts. (Some new subtleties can emerge, however, such as the notion that "second regular meal of the day" is more critical to the definition of "lunch" than the precise time at which the meal is eaten—again illustrating the difficulty of giving fully adequate definitions for even nominal kinds.)

To summarize, the meal terms undergo a shift that seems to occur simultaneously for all the terms in the field; this all-or-none nature of the shift seems to be a consequence of the simplicity of the defining dimension and its commonality to all three terms.

Tool terms
The next domain to show a shift, hand tool terms, contrasts in several ways with the meal term domain. Though meal terms vary in definitional meaning roughly along one simple dimension, hand tool terms vary in many ways, sharing clearly only the notions of intended function, "portable," and "usable by hand" as their common definitional component. Hand tools were included largely because they are an excellent example of a physical artifact class, in contrast to the other, more standard nominal kind domains used in this study. With respect to both characteristic and defining features, overt perceptual properties played a major role in this domain. The drawings illustrated a host of characteristic features. The defining or antidefining features were usually also salient in the drawing and were emphasized in the verbal description.

As shown by the drawings in figure 5.1 and the descriptions themselves in table 5.2 and appendix 2, at the same time that the +c/-d description stressed many of the characteristic features of a tool, it also stressed and illustrated the antidefining features. Since the functions of its members vary considerably, it seemed likely that this domain would display lower interterm correlations than the meal term domain; and indeed this was true. Though the mean correlations between hand tool terms were higher than the correlations between hand tool terms and terms from any other domains, the overall correlation was not nearly as strong as it was for meal terms, averaging roughly half the meal term intercorrelations. This means that the insight into which sorts of properties were defining did not as automatically render the other hand tool definitions apparent. The following transcripts illustrate where characteristic features seem to dominate and where the defining features are interpreted as merely characteristic.

(K1) Drill (+c/-d)
C: Yes.
E: Why do you think so?
C: My dad uses these and he suck (starts to say "sucks up sawdust" as in the story, but then stops and says)...he goes and drills and calls them drills.
E: (Repeats story) Do you think it could be a drill?
C: Yes.

K(2) Scissors (+c/-d)
C: Yes.
E: Why do you think so?
C: Because it has handles and it is flat in the front, and then it cuts paper.
E: Can you tell me what *I* said it does to paper?
C: It flattens it.
E: So could it be scissors?
C: Yeah.
(This child attempts to change the tool's function but, even when reminded of the antidefining function, still judges it a pair of scissors.)

K(3) Scissors (-c/+d)
C: No.
E: Why not?
C: Because scissors you put on your fingers and you don't have to plug it in...
E: And what does this thing do?
C: You plug it in and there is a motor inside and these things go up and down.
E: And what do these things do when they go up and down?
C: They cut.
E: And do you remember what they are made out of?
C: ?(questioning look)
E: The whole thing is made out of plastic (repeats story). So do you think it is or isn't scissors?
C: It isn't.
(Here the child explicitly remembers the function (and even the scissor-like function) of the blades but apparently treats these defining features as merely characteristic and overlooks them because of the atypical features of having no handles to grasp, being plugged in, and so on.)

K(3) Saw (-c/+d)
C: No.
E: Why not?
C: Because if you drop it, it can break easily...and when you drop saws they don't.
E: (Repeats story) So is it or isn't it a saw?
C: It isn't.

K(4) Drill (-c/+d)
C: No.
E: Why not?

C: Because drills have plugs and they have special levers to push it on and off and it drills a hole.
E: What does this do?
C: It has a handle and you turn it around and around and you use this green thing and that puts a hole in it.
E: So is it or isn't it a drill?
C: It isn't.
(The child specifically lists defining feature of drilling, but again seems to construe it as a characteristic feature that is overwhelmed by atypical features and by lack of typical features.)

2(1) Saw (-c/+d)
C: No.
E: Why not?
C: Because it is plastic and a saw is metal and has a wooden handle.
E: So this thing (repeats story and question).
C: No.

2(2) Drill (+c/-d)
C: Yes.
E: Why do you think so?
C: It looks like one, and my dad has one.
E: So this thing (repeats story). Do you think this is a drill?
C: Yes.
E: Do you think you could tell me what I said in the story?
C: It sucks up little bits of sawdust like a straw.
(The child clearly remembers the antidefining function but allows it to be overridden by typical appearance features.)

4(1) Saw (+c/-d)
C: Yeah.
E: Why do you think so?
C: It looks like one...it is made like one.
E: Can you describe more about it to me?
C: It is metal...the handle is wood.
E: And what is on the edge?
C: Ink is on the edge...to mark trees.
E: And how does it mark the trees?
C: Mmmm...can't remember.
E: How do you use it?
C: Rub it back and forth.
E: What happens when you rub it back and forth?
C: Mmmm...(long pause).
E: The blue ink goes onto the wood and marks it...and if you rub

your hands over the edges, they are really smooth...so do you
think it is or isn't a saw?
C: It is.
E: And can you describe to me what you use it for?
C: Marking trees.
E: And how does it mark the trees?
C: With blue ink.
E: Is that the only thing it does?
C: No.
E: What else does it do?
C: It smooths out the bark.
E: How does it do that?
C: If you rub it back and forth.
E: How does it do that?
C: Mmmm...(pause)...It's hard to explain.
E: Did I say it does that?
C: No.
E: If I told you it didn't do that, would it make any difference?
C: Yeah.
E: What difference would it make?
C: Mmmm...(pause)...I don't know.
E: Well, (child's name), why don't you tell me what you really
think! Do you think it is or isn't a saw?
C: It is.
E: So that the only thing that it does is that it marks the wood,
and you rub it back and forth so the ink will mark the wood...and
you think it is a saw?
C: Yeah.

As with the meal terms, the children who identified instances of tools
on the basis of characteristic features occasionally distorted the -d
features in the +c/-d stories by changing them into +d features (for
example, K(1) said the nondrill drilled, and K(2) said the nonscissors cut).
This response pattern shows that they were well aware of the +d features
for the terms; but when reminded that the +d features were not present
and that the -d features were, they nonetheless called the item an
instance. They apparently regarded the +d features as important and
perhaps often highly typical features, but characteristic and nonessential
features nonetheless. More broadly, the children often were aware of the
defining feature and recognized it as being highly correlated with
normal instances of the item, but they failed to realize its special role and
thus treated it like all the other characteristic features.

These repeated patterns in the transcripts illustrate that the children
who have not yet made the shift are not simply perceptually bound and

ignorant of the functional features associated with these items. Occasionally they were, but more often than not they had some knowledge of the function. They simply failed to recognize its fundamental importance in organizing the concept. Use of the defining features to judge an entity as an instance seemed similar at all ages, as the following excerpts illustrate:

K(1) Saw (-c/+d)
C: Yeah.
E: Why?
C: Because it will cut things.
E: Do do you think that it is or isn't a saw?
C: Yeah, it is.
E: Even though it looks like that and it is made out of plastic?
C: I think that it is...

2(1) Scissors (-c/+d)
C: Yes.
E: Why do you think so?
C: Because even the ones you use for foil could be a scissor.
E: Why do you think this one is a scissor?
C: Because it moves up and down and it cuts paper.

4(1) Scissors (+c/-d)
C: No.
E: Why not?
C: Because scissors cut paper, they don't make it stay shut.
E: Even though it looks like that?
C: Yeah.

These transcripts, in conjunction with the quantitative data, clearly illustrate a shift from reliance on characteristic features to reliance on defining features and show a moderate to weak domain effect. This weak effect suggests that hand tools do not really form a tight conceptual domain and may only constitute a domain at all because they tend to occur in the same situation and thus are experienced together. Consequently, differences in experience would tend to make them cluster conceptually in different ways. It is unlikely that kindergartners are in general prone to ignore the special status of defining features for all functional artifacts; hand tools are a special subset that probably takes longer to master than others for which the function is more familiar and intimate to a child, such as perhaps eating utensils. Hand tools form too diverse a class with too many different sorts of defining functions for them to show much of an all-or-none effect where the characteristic-to-defining shift is concerned. Nonetheless, future research should address the extent to which younger children can, with appropriate artifacts, use defining features to overrule characteristic ones.

Kinship terms
Kinship terms form one of the most widely studied conceptual domains; it was in part for this reason that they were selected for this experiment. Developmental psychologists have repeatedly noted apparent developmental changes in the meanings that children have for these terms, and they have proposed a variety of hypotheses to explain them. Nonetheless, no studies have used the characteristic/defining paradigm (Landau's 1982 study comes closest in this respect), and it therefore seemed important to use that paradigm and to compare the results with those of other studies.

Perhaps the most obvious pattern in the results is the greater coherence in the kinship domain than in the hand tools domain; it proved to be almost as coherent as the meal term domain, with an average interterm correlation of about .75. Intuitively this makes sense, since defining relations for kinship terms, though not as simple as the single one for meal terms, are all very similar and easily contrastable with such features as behavioral dispositions. Though the precise bloodline relations differ from term to term, bloodline relations in general are such that comprehending one makes the others much easier to comprehend. Nonetheless, children who recognize the importance of such relations as defining might still fail in the characteristic/defining task if they cannot distinguish one set of blood relations from another, especially when the more complex relations are involved. Thus, a child might have shifted to an understanding of what sorts of relations are defining but nonetheless make mistakes. The following transcript excerpts illustrate some of the patterns.

K(1) Uncle (+c/-d)
C: Yes.
E: And why do you think so?
C: He loves you so much.
E: And what else does the story tell you about him?
C: I can't think of anything else.
E: (Repeats the story) could he be your uncle?
C: YYYeeesss yeah! yeah!
(Reference to highly typical features)

K(2) Aunt (-c/+d)
C: No...she's a little girl.
E: (Repeats story) She is or isn't your aunt?

C: She isn't.
(Reference to highly atypical features)

K(3) Cousin (+c/-d)
C: Yes.
E: Why?
C: Because he doesn't live with me...I have lots and lots of cousins out in Kansas, over a thousand...
E: (Repeats the story) So he could be your cousin?
C: Yes.
E: Can you tell me how much of that story you can tell me? (*sic*)
C: I can't remember things very well.
E: How about if I help you?...How old is he?
C: About six.
E: About the same as you, right? And when do you see him?...(pause)...One of them is a holiday?
C: (Pause)
E: When you eat turkey?...(still no answer)...Thanksgiving...and what about on your birthday...Do you see him?
C: Yeah.
E: Do you play with him?
C: Yeah.
E: And do you know who his mother is?
C: Yes.
E: Who?
C: Your sister.
E: (Repeats story) So could he be your cousin?
C: Yeah.

The quantitative and qualitative data on the kinship term domain reveal a strong effect of field coherence and suggest that the shift is the result of recognizing the sorts of information that are relevant to kinship relations. It may not be the case that young children have no hypotheses about the relevant dimensions, and in fact one set of hypotheses might center around a social theory of what kinship terms mean. In such an account, the behavioral dispositions of the individuals might be deemed to be most crucial. This "psychological" theory about the meaning of kinship terms might then give way to the more biological theory that adults usually use. Indeed, it has been proposed that this sort of transition from psychologically based theories to biologically based ones is responsible for a major shift in the way children understand animate entities (Carey 1985).

The data might be construed as suggesting that kinship term meanings are acquired in an all-or-none fashion. This is an oversimplification, however, and it is contradicted by other results. Consider, for example, a study by Haviland and Clark (1974) that clearly demonstrates a graded acquisition of kinship terms. In that study children were shown to grasp the precise meanings of various kinship terms in an order that was predicted by the complexity of the semantic features required to specify those meanings. Thus, "brother" was correctly understood earlier than "cousin." Though Haviland and Clark did not specifically ask whether the child who erred on one kinship term but succeeded on another was nonetheless paying attention to the same sorts of relations (for instance, biological) in both cases, such an interpretation is certainly compatible with their results. It should be unlikely for a child to use a general distribution of all characteristic features or all social behavioral features for one kinship term and bloodline relations for another. A child might well use the wrong bloodline relations for some of the more complex terms (for instance, use the meaning of "grandmother" for "aunt") but would, for most kinship terms, use bloodline relations as the primary means for differentiating one term from another. The study described here did not pit one set of detailed bloodline relations against another related set and hence would not pick up the developmental differences uncovered by Haviland and Clark. Instead, it documented more broadly a shift in emphasis from characteristic features to the sort of features and relations that adults deem important for structuring the space. It also illustrates that once children uncover the relevant sorts of relations in a domain, there is still room for considerable development as they learn the subtleties concerning values and interactions of those relations.

Cooking terms
The final terms studied, the cooking terms, were considered to form a highly interrelated domain in Lehrer's (1969) discussion of semantic fields. However, they were not tightly intercorrelated in this study. The low intercorrelation may be largely because even the fourth graders frequently relied on characteristic features in making judgments on these terms. Since the adults, by contrast, relied almost exclusively on defining features, there is no age group in which there was enough variance to assess the coherence of the domain per se. It is abundantly clear, however, that the shift from characteristic to defining features occurs later for this domain than for the others in the study and that once it does occur, it occurs completely, adults being highly consistent in their judgments. Future studies with intermediate ages will have to assess whether the shift itself occurs all at once across the domain, and what role experience plays. The data pertinent to this issue—namely, the data for the fourth graders—suggest that the cooking term domain is not as coherent as either the kinship term or meal term domain. Thus, a

number of children relied on characteristic features for some cooking terms but defining ones for others. However, there remained a tendency to give the same response across items. I suspect that the defining features, which are a relatively diverse set of procedural relations, are sufficiently broad in scope that the shift will not be found to be tightly linked across all terms.

A few brief excerpts from the transcripts make the nature of the transition clearer; the adult transcripts are included to illustrate the full shift. The first transcripts demonstrate reliance on characteristic features:

K(1) Bake (+c/-d)
C: Yes.
E: And why do you think so?
C: He was following the directions for a chocolate cake.
E: And what else did I say about this story?
C: They put frosting on it...
E: And how did they make it?
C: They put a pan in it.
E: Where did they put the pan?
C: On the stove and they put it on.
E: And so they baked it?
C: Yeah.

K(2) Fry (-c/+d)
C: No.
E: Why not?
C: Because they put them in a grill.
E: Did they put them in the grill or in a box top that was on the top of the grill?
C: In a box top.
E: And what else was in the box?
C: Grapes and...uh...
E: And there was this much oil (shows about an inch)...(repeats story). So they did or didn't fry the grapes?
C: They didn't.

2(1) Fry (+c/-d)
C: Yes.
E: Why?
C: Because they were crispy.
E: (Repeats story) She fried them?
C: She cooked them.
E: Did she fry them?

C: Well, um...she fried them in the oven.
E: And how do you know that she fried them...what did she do that was frying them?
C: The batter.

2(2) Fry (-c/+d)
C: No.
E: Why not?
C: First thing...you can't fry grapes.
E: Why not?
C: Because...(pause)...grapes can't be fried.
E: So when they take the big metal box about this big (repeats description) and they put the grapes in...they did or didn't fry the grapes?
C: Didn't.

The experimenter had the following exchange with a child in a transitional stage (a score of 2):

4(1) Bake (-c/+d)
C: I don't...I get my fried, boiling, and all that mixed up...so I don't know which one it is.
E: Which do you think this is?
C: I don't know.
E: Do you think it is baking?
C: I guess, yeah.
E: Do you think you could try to explain to me what you think baking, boiling, and frying mean?
C: I only know what one of them means...and that is boil...it's when you can like...boiling means...boiling is when you're boiling eggs you stick them in water and there is no lid and you just leave it there for about 20 minutes.
(Younger children almost never said they didn't know what a cooking term meant. To know that you don't know what a term means implies that you know what sort of information is needed but don't have it; that is, you have rejected characteristic features but have discovered only some of the procedural defining ones.)
E: If you put a lid on it, would it be boiling?
C: Uh...yeah, I guess...

Finally, some fourth graders and most adults relied solely on defining features:

4(2) Boil (+c/-d)
C: No...she was boiling water...were the eggs in the pot?

E: (Repeats story)
C: No.
E: Why not?
C: Because the eggs were above.
E: And so they weren't boiling?
C: No, she was boiling the water.

Adult(1) Fry (+c/-d)
A: No, you can't make them that way, can you? 'Cause she put them in the oven.
E: OK.
A: She baked them.
E: She baked them, OK.
A: Never heard of them done that way.

Adult(2) Bake (+c/-d)
A: No, they, uh, guess that's almost like frying.
E: OK, and why didn't they bake it?
A: They didn't put it in an oven. They put it over a flame.

These excerpts illustrate several patterns that are typical of the cooking term transcripts as a whole. First, it is clear that children frequently mastered one meaning before the others and that this field was not as coherent as the others. There are some suggestions, as with subject 4(1), that children might understand what sorts of features are needed for all terms but only know them for a few. The adult responses had an interesting component that was lacking in the responses of the fourth graders: they explicitly compared and contrasted the given cooking term with other possible terms, many of which the experimenter had not mentioned up to that point or indeed never mentioned at all. Thus, for adults, it was as though the terms constituted a much more unified domain whose meanings were understood more fully by considering how they related to other terms. This would seem to be the hallmark of a fully developed domain: the tight interconnection of concepts such that each one derives its meaning partly from the others.

The cooking term domain raises interesting questions about expertise. Children can have widely varying levels of experience with cooking activities, and one therefore might expect this factor to affect when the shift occurs. Since level of experience was not specifically manipulated in this study, it is not possible be certain whether it indeed had this effect; nonetheless, conversations with some of the younger children who did well on this task suggest that they had a larger than normal amount of experience in cooking environments. One possible way to estimate experience is to assume that stereotyped sex roles might give girls relatively more experience with cooking procedures than boys and perhaps relatively less experience with tools. When children in all relevant age groups with sufficient variances were examined (fourth grade and adult for cooking; second grade, fourth grade, and adult for tools), the sexdifferences were always in the right direction; however, in no cases were the differences significantly different. This might be explored in future studies with larger numbers of children, although it would be hoped that more enlightened patterns of socialization would minimize such sex differences anyway.

Conclusions

Overall, this study of five domains helped answer the questions that motivated it, and it has raised several new ones as well. It is abundantly clear that the characteristic-to-defining shift can occur at very different times for different conceptual domains and at ages ranging from the preschool years to adolescence. This finding argues against any global stage-like change in manner of representation. It also argues against any suggestions that the shift merely represents a changing response bias or strategy shift. If it were the case that both defining and characteristic features were available at all ages and that what develops is merely a recognition of the task's demands (that one use defining features), the shift would again be expected to occur at roughly the same time for all domains. In addition, children occasionally had no access to defining features even when they knew they were needed. Thus, if anything, in some cases children may be aware of the need for defining features but be forced to rely on characteristic features because these are the only ones to which they have access. It is therefore not possible to explain these findings by a model in which all that develops is an increasing understanding of what definitions are in general.

The question of whether the shift merely represents a perceptual-to-conceptual shift is complex and problematic (certainly part of the complexity is in making the distinction at all). One simple way of construing this contrast is to view it as one between "what you can see" and "what you can't see," which is obviously a distortion of the notion "perceptual vs. conceptual" but at least illustrates the flavor of a narrative account of the shift. Such an account operates on the assumption that visible features are developmentally prior to nonvisible features—that is, they are more salient, easier to think about and represent, and so on. Most proposals of this sort claim the perceptual comes before the conceptual, not just the visible before the nonvisible. One can substitute accordingly in what follows, but given the notorious difficulties of making such a contrast, I will continue to refer to visible vs. nonvisible features in this discussion. It is possible to rule out an explanation of the shift along these lines based on analyses of the types of features involved in each of the domains. A visible-to-nonvisible shift predicts certain outcomes: (1) If both defining and characteristic features for a concept happen to be visible, the shift should occur very early, whereas if both are nonvisible, it should occur relatively late. (2) If the defining features are nonvisible and the characteristic features are visible, then presumably the shift should occur after the visible/visible case but before the nonvisible/ nonvisible case. (3) Finally, there should never be a characteristic-to-defining shift where the defining features are visible and the characteristic features nonvisible.

In each domain it is possible to label crudely whether the defining and characteristic features are primarily visible or nonvisible. Thus, in the case of moral act terms both characteristic and defining features often refer to acts and behavioral dispositions and are thereby nonvisible. In the case of meal terms and kinship terms the characteristic features are generally visible and the defining features nonvisible, although the fit is by no means perfect. Finally, in the case of hand tool terms and cooking terms both defining and characteristic features are directly visible. The +c/-d hand tools, for example, always had some easily perceivable feature that was antidefining. To the extent that this classification of feature types by domain is even roughly correct, it is clear that the developmental data do not conform to any predictions that the visible features are more accessible at an early age. If the nonvisible features are important and familiar to a young child and if the child has developed a working theory about them, she will easily be able to access and use them. Later studies in this book will show more dramatically the limitations of the perceptual/conceptual account.

The developmental patterns for the five domains also illustrate another important point about the endstate representations. It is quite clear from the transcripts as well as from simple reflection on the definitions of these concepts that the ways in which defining features are instantiated vary dramatically from domain to domain. One does not attain definitional expertise in the same way for each domain. Thus, definitions for the cooking terms are highly procedural in nature, whereas the procedures most relevant to kinship terms (those of reproduction) do not play a central role in the concept and are certainly not mentioned. A causal set of relations with intentional states at the center seems to be the defining representation for moral acts, whereas for meal terms it is a simple one-dimensional continuum with three points. Finally, for artifacts, the defining element is the function intended by the artifact's creator.

This diversity of end-state representations is a vital point, for it argues against the notion that the acquisition of expertise in every domain is the same psychological process involving the same sorts of representational shifts. The acquisition of expertise can take a different pattern in each domain, depending on the peculiarities of that domain. Of course, there may be parallel patterns for closely related domains, but I suspect that diversity is the rule. To the extent that this diversity exists, the notion of defining features becomes increasingly awkward given the range of phenomena covered. It is less clear whether the initial state representations are so different. Perhaps the most naive conceiver uses roughly similar principles of representation—say, prototype abstraction—across many domains, tabulating frequencies and correlations of features with procedures that are relatively insensitive to the content involved. The data collected so far are compatible with such a view, although the transcripts do contain hints of some specification at earlier ages as well, suggesting, for example, that younger children might have a behaviorally specific theory of kinship terms.

One pattern to be expected in future work on conceptual domains and developmental shifts is that more closely related concepts in a domain should develop in tandem. Thus, clear opposites, which vary only on one feature or relation, would be expected to shift in a closely linked fashion. Some studies on metaphor (Gardner 1974 and Keil 1986b) suggest that children tend to grasp metaphorical relations for terms and their opposites at roughly the same time. Since the domains used here included no clear opposites, no direct test of this idea is possible.

Several questions remain concerning the nature of the shift and how it comes about: (1) Do younger children simply have more idiosyncratic defining features that are not being accessed, or do they perhaps treat some of the characteristic features as defining? (2) What is the role of more knowledgeable people in providing information about concepts to children? (3) How does instruction in a new concept relate to other knowledge in a conceptual domain? (4) Is the shift restricted to certain cultural settings? These issues are addressed in the next chapter.

A final message arising from these developmental patterns—a message that will grow in importance until it becomes the central theme of this book—concerns the whole notion of domain. What "glues" terms together to form a conceptual domain and what is the nature of the "glue"? Do younger children see groups of objects as coherent domains in the same ways that adults do? The answer may lie in understanding the types of intuitive theories children have developed to explain the phenomena associated with these concepts. This notion of changing theories will prove to be a powerful one in understanding the developmental patterns throughout this book. The knowledge that children come to have that unifies a domain and overrides characteristic features may be far too systematic and interconnected among concepts to be considered merely knowledge of definitions. Its relational nature and systematicity, in conjunction with its explanatory role, may be best described as theoretical knowledge. This will become clear as later studies move farther along the continuum from nominal to natural kinds.

Chapter 6
The Nature and Causes of Nominal Kind Shifts

The characteristic/defining features paradigm has provided strong evidence for a shift governing judgment about nominal kind terms. It is not yet clear, however, what the shift represents and how it comes about. This chapter describes four studies that attempt to shed some light on these difficult questions. The first study examines whether the younger child's representations can be legitimately construed as probabilistic representations based on characteristic features, the second examines how adults' input might influence the shift, the third examines how the child's "conceptual readiness" interacts with explicit instruction in the characteristic and defining features of a concept, and the fourth concerns the possible cultural specificity of the shift.

Defining Features throughout Development

Children frequently seem to seize on highly idiosyncratic aspects of a phenomenon and use those aspects to partially "define" it. Parents often swap stories of the child who denies that a newly met doctor can be a doctor because all doctors have to be male. (Our own son made the opposite error in that all the doctors he knew for some time were women; upon meeting his first male doctor he vigorously denied that that person could be a doctor because he was a man.) If these phenomena are widespread and if they represent the child's seizing on one idiosyncratic feature as necessary (and perhaps seizing on several jointly as sufficient), then much of what appears to be a characteristic-to-defining shift may be an idiosyncratic-defining to conventional-defining shift. (It should be noted, however, that almost all anecdotal reports concern a child taking one characteristic or idiosyncratic feature as necessary, not a child taking a full set of abnormal necessary and sufficient features as a definition.) The studies described in chapters 4 and 5 argue against such a tendency in younger children, as we can see by considering some ways in which a child's representation might differ from an adult's.

Assuming that adult concepts consist of a list of characteristic features and a smaller set of defining features, children's concepts might differ from adults' in one of three ways: (1) Children might rely on most of the adult characteristic features and many of the defining ones but treat them all as merely characteristic. (2) They might have a mixture of defining and characteristic features for each concept, like adults; unlike adults, however, they might treat all the defining ones as characteristic and one or more of the characteristic features, or a novel feature, as defining. (3) They might have both defining and characteristic features for each concept, including all the adult characteristic features but only a subset of the adult defining features.

Each of these alternatives should lead to a different type of characteristic-to-defining shift. In case (1) the shift should occur at roughly the same time for the +c/-d and -c/+d descriptions. In case (2) one would expect children to generally shift sooner for the +c/-d descriptions; that is, one would expect children to judge the +c/-d descriptions to refer to noninstances earlier than they judge the -c/+d descriptions to refer to instances. By this account, children should occasionally have idiosyncratic defining features that are neither characteristic nor defining for adults. In such a case a child would reject the +c/-d description as referring to an instance since it does not have the child's own defining feature. If all the children's defining features were idiosyncratic, they would be expected to show near adult-like performance on the +c/-d descriptions and near baseline performance on the -c/+d descriptions. However, they would also often be expected to pick one of the adult characteristic features as defining, and a child who did so would also be incorrect for the +c/-d case. In case (3) children would be expected to perform at a completely adult level for the +c/-d descriptions, since none of them would have members of the subset of defining features, and they would be expected to also correctly accept the -c/+d descriptions to the extent that their defining features were a true subset of the adult set. They would only be mistaken in correctly accepting descriptions that had some, but not all, the necessary features.

From the data collected on the shift in chapters 4 and 5, no simple pattern resembling any of these possibilities emerges. In some cases +c/-d descriptions seem to shift earlier; in other cases the -c/+d descriptions do. If either the idiosyncratic defining feature account or the subset account were correct, one would expect a more consistent pattern in the data. Nonetheless, such a retrospective analysis is clearly not the most straightforward test of the mechanism underlying the shift. To explore the issue more directly, a study was conducted that systematically manipulated clusters of characteristic and defining features.

If, in the early stages of acquiring a concept, the child represents it solely in terms of characteristic features (not necessarily precisely the same set of characteristic features used by adults), then no one feature should be regarded as essential for describing an instance of the concept. Instead, a weighted sum of several features should indicate category membership. This is the sort of representational system argued for by most probabilistic views of conceptual structure (see, for example, Rosch and Mervis 1975). If these accounts are correct and if there are no defining features, whether conventional or idiosyncratic, then children should identify as instances entities that have a sufficiently large number of characteristic features regardless of whether one particular characteristic feature is present.

To assess this possibility, Barbara Bauer and I designed a study in which five different descriptions of an entity were given to different children. Four descriptions (A–D) included three of the four most salient characteristic features that seemed to be associated with a concept, and all had the same antidefining feature. The fifth description (E) included none of the four characteristic features and the same antidefining feature. Five such descriptions were developed for each of six terms: "fireman," "island," "uncle," "twins," "parade," and "basement." In addition, three terms were included as controls: "traffic light," "weed," and "refrigerator." The descriptions for each of these terms contained both correct defining features and highly characteristic features. They were included in the study to ensure both that children were attending to the task and that they had clear "yes" responses available to them. Without these three items they might have adopted a strategy of judging all items to be noninstances. As before, the experimenters independently came up with putative characteristic and defining features for both experimental and control terms, and then conferred and resolved the few differences through discussion.

Stimulus construction proved to be difficult in that candidate concepts had to have four discrete characteristic features that were sufficient in any combination of three to cause a young child to judge the description as valid. In addition, the fifth description had to possess the features that were shared by descriptions A–D and that hopefully were not sufficient in themselves to suggest a real instance. Finally, several of the features had to be pictorially conveyable. The "island" descriptions illustrate the complexity of the task. The four characteristic features were "beautiful palm trees," "starfish and seashells," "warm and the sun shines all the time," and "some people dig for buried treasure there." Stories A, C, E and the accompanying pictures for "island" are shown in figure 6.1 (the full set of stories is given in appendix 3). Descriptions A–D shared the same antidefining feature, which was also pointed out on each illustration: "There is water around three sides of Alboa and land on the other side." The fifth description had none of the four characteristic features and the same antidefining feature. It is important to note, however, that

A. No trees
This is a special place called Alboa where there are beautiful starfish and seashells, and where it's warm and the sun shines all the time. Some people dig for buried treasure there. There is water around three sides of Alboa and land on the other side. Could Alboa be an island?

C. No sun
This is a special place called Alboa where there are beautiful palm trees, and starfish and seashells. Some people dig for buried treasure there. There is water around three sides of Alboa and land on the other side. Could Alboa be an island?

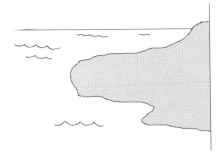

E. Stripped story
This is a special place called Alboa. There is water around three sides of Alboa and land on the other side. Could Alboa be an island?

Figure 6.1
Drawings accompanying some of the descriptions used for "island" in the study on idiosyncratic defining features.

the fifth description was not devoid of features. It did after all have the features of being a piece of land with irregular contours and of being almost surrounded by water. In addition, it had a somewhat exotic "island-sounding" name and was described as being "a special place."

It became clear to us in constructing these stimulus items not only that a fifth description was necessary to correct against "yes" response biases but also that it had to have many properties of the concept. "There is this thing that sits out in the desert and there isn't any water anywhere for thousands of miles...could that thing be an island?" would hardly be a fair test as the fifth description for "island." The characteristic features given in the fifth description for each term should not be sufficient in their own right to make the child think the description refers to an instance, but should be close enough so that any three of the four salient characteristic features could make it seem like an instance. (Incidentally, some of the features in the fifth descriptions may have been not characteristic but necessary (though not sufficient), such as that an island should be a physical place.) This stimulus design also assumed that all four features were equal in salience, weight, and so on, as characteristic features, which is never really the case. The hope was that they were close enough in weight so that they were sufficient in all possible combinations of three.

In summary, the principle motivating the stimulus design was that each of the A–D descriptions should have a set of characteristic features sufficient to cause a pre-shift child to accept that description as an instance. If the children judged A–D to be descriptions of instances but judged E to be a description of a noninstance, they would not be basing their judgments on any fixed set of defining features because no one feature was common across all four descriptions. (Of course, all story types were restricted to the +c/-d form. No -c/+d stories were used since they would much less directly test the issue in question.)

There are two ways to administer these stimulus descriptions to children, each with its own advantages and disadvantages. One technique is to give each child all five descriptions for a concept and ask whether each one describes an instance of the concept. The advantage of this method is that it will show whether the same child will judge all the stories A–D as describing instances even though they share no single feature. The disadvantage is that such repeated adminstrations of essentially the same description with only one feature changed are likely to create all sorts of response biases and other artifactual strategies; for example, the children might easily decide to give the same answer for all items.

An alternative method is to give a different description to each child. Although this approach overcomes the serious problem of repeated administrations of similar descriptions, it does make the interpretation of the results more difficult. Though a pattern of data showing that children identified each of the descriptions A–D as referring to an instance more often than description E would support the hypothesis, it would still be possible that each child was using different characteristic features as defining. In such a case, however, it is likely that most children would select one of the four characteristic features and that such a pattern would be discernible in the data. Overall, this technique, though more difficult to interpret and less efficient in the use of subjects, seemed more methodologically appropriate.

Eighteen children in each of three grades (K, 2, and 4) participated as subjects. These children were divided into six groups with the combinations of stimulus types shown in table 6.1.

These combinations ensured that, for each term, three children in each grade received description A, three received B, three received C, three received D, and six received E. The order of presentation was randomized for each subject. Since each E-description was to be contrasted with four other descriptions for the same term, it was appropriate that more children were tested for those descriptions. Obviously, a larger number of subjects in each group would have been desirable, but considering the time involved in generating transcripts for three groups of 18 children, it was decided to conduct at least a preliminary study with groups of that size.

Results can be summarized quite succinctly given that there were so few children in each condition and because it was necessary to make measures across conditions. The mean scores for descriptions A–D (three-point scale: 1 = judged not an instance, 2 = transitional, 3 = judged an instance), in contrast to mean scores for description E for each term by age, are presented in table 6.2. Since descriptions A–D all have the format +c/-d and E has the format low c/-d (that is, fewer characteristic features and the same antidefining one), we would expect more judgments that A–D are instances, or more scores closer to 3.

Children always scored higher on descriptions A–D than they did on description E, which had three fewer characteristic features. (This was true 18 of 18 times for each of the six items at the three grade levels.) Moreover, there was an apparent shift with increasing age to a reliance on the defining features. Though it was never the case that the children receiving descriptions A–D for a term scored all 3's while the children receiving description E scored all 1's, for some terms ("fireman," "twins," "basement") this was nearly the case in the younger ages, where the effect should be largest. For other terms ("parade," "island") description E contained a sufficient number of characteristic features that several children received scores of 3 for that description. Finally, several chil-

Table 6.1
Stimulus configurations assigned to the six groups of children in the study on idiosyncratic defining features

I	II	III	IV	V	VI
Basement(E)	Basement(D)	Basement(C)	Basement(B)	Basement(A)	Basement(E)
Parade(E)	Parade(E)	Parade(D)	Parade(C)	Parade(B)	Parade(A)
Fireman(D)	Fireman(C)	Fireman(B)	Fireman(E)	Fireman(E)	Fireman(A)
Island(D)	Island(C)	Island(E)	Island(E)	Island(B)	Island(A)
Uncle(D)	Uncle(A)	Uncle(B)	Uncle(C)	Uncle(E)	Uncle(E)
Twins(B)	Twins(C)	Twins(E)	Twins(E)	Twins(D)	Twins(A)
Weed	Weed	Weed	Weed	Weed	Weed
Traffic	Traffic	Traffic	Traffic	Traffic	Traffic
Refrigerator	Refrigerator	Refrigerator	Refrigerator	Refrigerator	Refrigerator

Table 6.2
Mean scores in the study on idiosyncratic defining features

	K (n=18) Mean scores, descriptions A–D	Mean scores, description E	2 (n=18) Mean scores, descriptions A–D	Mean scores, description E	4 (n=18) Mean scores, descriptions A–D	Mean scores, description E
Parade	2.8	2.0	3.0	2.7	2.7	2.3
Uncle	1.8	1.2	2.0	1.3	1.2	1.0
Basement	2.5	1.0	1.9	1.0	2.7	1.0
Twins	2.1	1.0	1.6	1.0	1.7	1.3
Island	3.0	2.7	2.5	1.8	1.6	1.0
Fireman	2.8	1.2	1.9	1.0	1.4	1.0

dren received 1's on descriptions A–D for "uncle." For these terms as well, however, the data were in the appropriate direction.

None of the descriptions A–D for any term ever elicited uniform scores of 1, for either of the two younger groups. Thus, it does not appear that the children were focusing on some particular characteristic feature as defining. Of course, each child could have focused on a different characteristic feature as defining; but it seems unlikely that no common preferences for some characteristic feature would emerge. In short, the data support the notion that early on, for at least some terms, children frequently have true probabilistic representations wherein no one feature seems essential but a weighted sum of several is sufficient for describing an instance. Informal piloting of a within-subject design with six first graders reveals that the same child will often assent for all of descriptions A–D but reject another set of -c/+d descriptions; but a more formal study along these lines still needs to be conducted.

This first study, though not conclusive in its own right, lends additional support to the claim that early on in concept growth children do not merely use idiosyncratic defining features in judging instances of a concept. If they did, one would expect them either to reject all five descriptions because an idiosyncratic defining feature was not present (this rarely happened in the transcripts) or to show a tendency to pick out one characteristic feature as defining (again, no one feature seemed to predominate in this respect). Finally, in the clearest cases, such as "fireman," where 11 of 12 kindergartners scored 3 for descriptions A–D and 5 of 6 kindergartners scored 1 for description E, no alternative interpretation seems remotely plausible. These findings, however, do not necessarily show that later representations are structured by defining features; characteristic features could dominate conceptual structure throughout development but with different weights being attached to them at different points in development. I discuss this alternative in detail in chapter 7.

Changing Patterns of Input

A consistent finding in language acquisition research in the last two decades has been the demonstration that adults, and even young children, often dramatically alter their patterns of speech as a function of the age of the listener. This has been amply demonstrated for the prosodic, morphological, and syntactic aspects of speech (Snow and Ferguson 1977) and to a lesser extent for some of its semantic aspects (Anglin 1970). Sheila Jeyifous and I, with the help of Robert Altman, investigated whether parents change their descriptions of concepts as a function of the child's age. In particular, they might use a higher ratio of characteristic features with younger children and defining features with older children. Such a pattern would raise the possibility that the characteristic-to-defining shift is a function of changing patterns of input. Of course, the question then arises why the parents would change unless they perceived a relevant developmental difference in the children; but, at the least, it seemed important to examine the relations that exist, if any, between parental explanations and developmental change.

It was our intent to make the study as naturalistic as possible by picking terms that most children did not know but that referred to things they were at least somewhat familiar with. In addition, it was of course necessary that the adults be familiar with all the words and be able to give correct definitions. The latter constraint on the stimulus set proved to be particularly vexing in piloting, since the precocious second grader may know a number of words with which the average adult is not familiar. After extensive piloting, we settled on the following 11 terms: "mammal," "appetizer," "harvest," "insulation," "luggage," "catastrophe," "weapon," "fertilizer," "apprentice," "abbreviation," and "barricade." These terms were also selected as ones that had both relatively clear definitions and many highly typical exemplars with rich characteristic features. Again, the decisions on characteristic and defining features were based primarily on discussion among the experimenters and involved using the heuristic of thinking of clear instances that had as many atypical features as possible and of noninstances that had as many typical features as possible. With nominal kinds this strategy usually reveals a small number of features that are approximately necessary and jointly sufficient, and a larger number that are merely characteristic.

The experimenters went into the homes of 24 children ranging in age from 3 to 7 1/2 years and asked one of the parents (in most cases the mother) to explain to the child what each of the concepts meant. The experimenter first went over the terms with the parent to be sure that she (or he) was familiar with them (parents were instructed to leave any unfamiliar terms out). The parent was then instructed to explain each concept to the child in a natural way, as if the child had come up and asked what the word meant. The parents were told that we were interested in how children understood such explanations; only after the session did we add that we were also interested in how parents' explanations varied with the age of the child. After explaining the task to the parent, the experimenter turned on a tape recorder and left the room and the child was brought in. It was felt that both parent and child would be less self-conscious if the experimenter were absent.

When the parent had finished explaining all 11 concepts to the child, the experimenter returned and, in an informal manner, asked the child what each of the terms meant. The questioning assessed whether the children had learned the concepts in terms of characteristic or defining features. Finally, transcripts were made of the entire session with each child (that is, of both parent-child and experimenter-child interactions). The transcripts were often quite long, ranging from approximately 1600 words to approximately 3500 words in length, with most of the words being contributed by the parent. We attempted to quantify the parents' explanations in a variety of ways to see whether patterns of explanations changed in any way as the children grew older. To do this, we divided the children by age into two groups of 12 children each: 3–5 years and 5–7 1/2 years. The first analysis simply involved going through the transcripts and looking for characteristic and defining features in the parents' explanations by matching them with the features we agreed upon when we constructed the stimuli. For the most part this was straightforward, and high spot-check reliabilities between the two judges were achieved.

The percentages of explanations that contained solely defining features, solely characteristic features, or both are shown in table 6.3.

It is clear from this table that there are no differences in the tendency to use characteristic features in explaining concepts to children of different ages. Apparently, the parents did not modify their explanations for the younger children by loading them with more characteristic properties. The predominant pattern of explanation at all ages was to use both defining and characteristic features. The following transcripts illustrate the different patterns:

Characteristic features only: Mammal
M: You know what mammals are? We talked about them. What's a mammal?
C: Mammal.
M: Mammal, what is it? Do you know? Is it a person?
C: No.
M: No, it's a kind of animal. A mammal is a kind of animal. Let's see, what kinds of mammals do we know? A cat is a mammal. A dog is a mammal. I don't think a guinea pig is a mammal. But X (family pet) is a mammal. Right. Can you think of any other mammals? A tiger and a lion...
C: Elephants.
M: What did we say they were? What kind of animals are they?
C: A mammal.

Defining features only: Apprentice
C: Paprentice?
M: Apprentice.

C: Apprentice.

M: OK, an apprentice is someone who learns from someone who knows how to do something, someone who's an expert. So it's kind of like a special kind of student. Apprentice is somebody who learns from somebody who knows how to do something very well.

Both feature types: Insulation

M: OK, insulation, did you ever hear us talk about that word insulation?

C: No.

M: Insulation is some material that keeps you warm. Do you remember when we started talking about putting insulation in our house, in the walls, so the walls would be warmer in the winter? And we have winter coats with insulation in them to keep us warm; insulation are materials to keep warm (pause) or cool in the summer.

Note that in the first example the judges did not count "animal" as a defining feature. It was assumed that the domain of animals was a given, and the question was what sort of features would be used to pick out the appropriate animal type. Thus, there was a certain assumed domain within which the characteristic/defining contrast was evaluated. The same assumption was made for other terms (an apprentice was assumed to be a person, insulation an inanimate physical substance, and so on).

There was also no significant difference betwen the two age groups in the mean number of exemplars mentioned in each explanation. Thus, parents averaged 1.70 exemplars per explanation with younger children and 1.92 exemplars per explanation with older children. The mean number of exemplars varied considerably from term to term, ranging from .07 for "fertilizer" to 3.6 for "mammal"; moreover, there was some

Table 6.3
Types of explanations provided in the study on parental explanations

	Younger children (3 to 5 years)	Older children (5 to 7.5 years)
Characteristic features only	17.6%	17.6%
Defining features only	5.8%	4.0%
Both features	74.6%	72.6%
No parent input (child gave meaning spontaneously)	2.0%	5.8%

degree of consistency across age groups with respect to which words had more exemplars. Thus, the correlation between the number of exemplars for each term for the two groups was .57, which is significant at the .05 level (one-tailed). The lack of a difference in number of exemplars is not an artifact of one age group receiving longer or shorter explanations and thereby canceling out what might be a higher ratio of exemplars to total number of words spoken in the younger children. There were no significant differences between the age groups in the total number of words spoken by the parent, the average sentence length, or the number of sentences used. Again, there was considerable variance in length of explanations across terms, with explanations for "insulation" at one extreme averaging twice as many words as those for "luggage" at the other. The lengths of explanations were also significantly correlated for term pairs across the two age groups ($r = .61$, $p < .05$, one-tailed).

Thus, there is little evidence that parents were modifying their explanations in a manner that took into account a characteristic-to-defining shift on the children's part. We felt that it was important, however, to show some differences in patterns of explanation to avoid conjectures that the task was too formal and therefore did not tap the sorts of natural explanations that parents normally provide. To see whether anything in the transcripts reflected these differences, we removed all children's comments from the transcripts and gave just the parents' explanations to four adult judges, who were asked to sort the transcripts into two piles based on whether they thought the adult was talking to a younger child (around 4 years) or an older child (around 6 1/2 years). The judges were surprisingly good at this task, and they correctly rated the transcripts according to age at a level far beyond chance (judges averaged 80.4% correct against a chance mean of 50%, $p < .01$). When we asked the judges what features they were using, they were not sure but said that it seemed straightforward in many cases. Since some mentioned that patterns of questioning seemed different, we analyzed parents' questions concerning the child's comprehension ("Did you get that?" "OK, now what if...?") and parents' questions and comments about the child's personal experiences ("Remember when we went to the zoo and...?"). Although questions about comprehension did not show any significant difference, questions about personal experience did (1.39 questions per term for younger children compared to .66 questions per term for older children, $p < .06$, two-tailed). Thus, although the incidence of concrete exemplars showed no difference across ages, the exemplars used with younger children were closer to the child's immediate experiences. (For example: With an older child, a parent would say that appetizers are things like cheese and crackers, potato chips and dips, and so on. With a younger child, the parent would mention a specific occasion when a particular kind of appetizer was served.) Finally, it is interesting that a different conceptual measure of parents' explanations, the relative use of basic vs. superordinate categories (Rosch et al. 1976) did not vary with the age of the children. It should be noted, however, that for several terms it was quite difficult to decide whether they referred to basic or superordinate categories.

This study suggests that parents are relatively insensitive to the ages of their children in terms of adjusting the conceptual nature of the explanations. They do alter their speech in various other ways that may well make the communication more effective, but they do not use more characteristic features and/or fewer defining ones with younger children. Apparently the characteristic-to-defining shift is much more of an endogenous process and less a reflection of changing external input.

In addition to data on the parents' explanations, this study contained data on the children's understanding of those explanations. Even though parents' explanations may not differ much overall between age groups, their explanations can differ quite dramatically on a case-by-case basis. Consequently, data on whether the children rely on characteristic features are not as easy to interpret in this study as in the earlier characteristic-to-defining studies. After all, a four-year-old who has just had 11 novel concepts explained to her is likely to have a great deal of difficulty simply keeping them all straight; and indeed there was evidence for this type of confusion in the data.

We informally asked the children about the terms they had just learned by presenting +c/-d and -c/+d cases and asking whether they were instances of the concept. Because the procedure was informal and because several gaps in the data appeared as a consequence of "don't know" responses and fatigue in the younger children, the +c/-d and -c/+d responses were scored on the original scale used in chapter 4 (1 = characteristic features, 2 = transitional, 3 = defining features) and pooled. The mean scores were 1.83 for 3–5-year-olds and 2.30 for 5–7-year-olds, with lower scores on "appetizer," "mammal," and "abbreviation" and higher scores on "insulation," "apprentice," and "barricade." Overall, these scores show a shift with increasing age away from basing answers solely on characteristic features (p < .01, one-way ANOVA). These data are not surprising until one realizes that, in many cases, the child was given a perfect, clear definition by the parent along with several characteristic features suggested by exemplars, and yet the child seemed to misunderstand the meaning. This last finding suggested an additional study to explore how children learn new concepts under explicit instruction.

Explicit Teaching of New Concepts

The study on parent-child explanations suggested that even if a child is exposed to a rich explanation of a concept with a clear statement of the definition, the child may fail to realize the special status of the definition and treat it merely as another characteristic feature or even ignore it entirely. There are a variety of reasons why a child might fail to learn the concept appropriately. Perhaps the defining features have special properties that make them more difficult to acquire than characteristic ones. Although this is possible in some cases, there are other cases where a defining feature for one concept can be a characteristic feature for another (for instance, "unmarried" for bachelors vs. undergraduates). The results of the conceptual domains study reported in chapter 4 make it unlikely that there is a global shift from representations based solely on characteristic features to representations emphasizing defining features; but it also suggests a relevant hypothesis. Perhaps the defining features are only understood as such if the child has a sufficiently well developed and systematic body of knowledge that provides principled reasons why some dimensions or features should be doing most of the conceptual work in the domain. Children and certainly adults might be able to learn a new concept "correctly" from the start if they already have a well-articulated knowledge of the domain in which that concept resides, or if they have already made the shift for more familiar concepts within that domain.

Cindy Hutton and I therefore conducted a study to address two issues. First and most important, we wanted to explore the notion of conceptual readiness; that is, we wanted to follow up on the tentative last finding in the parent explanation study. Is it the case that younger children, when given a perfect explanation with clear defining features, will not realize the importance of those features? Second, can we predict the success they will have at seeing the importance of defining features on the basis of their prior general knowledge of the domains?

We selected three domains: moral acts, agricultural practices, and cooking terms. Moral acts and cooking terms were chosen because more familiar terms from those domains used in the conceptual domains study showed them to be early- and late-shifting domains, respectively. Agricultural practices were chosen as a somewhat unfamiliar domain with many clear examples in the Ithaca area and as a domain with which different children had widely differing degrees of experience. In each case we tried to pick concepts that had relatively clear definitions and highly typical exemplars and for which most children probably had observed at least one exemplar. The sets of terms used were "swindle," "libel," "betray," and "extort"; "sauté," "flambé," "steep," and "baste"; and "irrigate," "fallow" (as a verb), "furrow," and "mulch." The explanations consisted of giving the definition, then several examples, then a somewhat differently worded version of the same definition. By providing the definition twice, at the beginning and the end of the description, we attempted to ensure that the child noticed the defining features and to reduce any order-of-presentation effects. Also, by stating the defining features twice, if children nonetheless ignored them in favor of the characteristic features (presented only once), we would have an especially strong demonstration of their failure to attend to those features.

Again, defining and characteristic features were arrived at through discussion among the experimenters and by having adult subjects generate features of both types for these concepts. Forty-four children participated as subjects (14 kindergartners, 15 second graders, and 15 fourth graders). All were from elementary schools within 30 miles of Ithaca, New York. In the initial teaching phase, the children were asked whether they knew the concept already; if they did, they were asked to define it. If the definition was correct, then no explanation was given; if it was incorrect, the standard explanation was given. All children were asked to repeat the explanation and were informed of any omissions. Immediately after each definition was given and repeated either the +c/-d or the -c/+d description was presented. The other description was given later in the stimulus set, the order of presentation being counterbalanced across subjects. In piloting, we determined that it was necessary to give one description immediately after the definition so as not to overwhelm the children's memories with a nonstop string of 12 definitions. If by the time the second, contrasting description was given the child could not remember the definition, it was repeated. At the end of each session the children were asked to define the concepts as well. Examples of the initial explanations and description pairs in each of the domains are shown in table 6.4 (the full set may be found in appendix 4). The tape recordings were then transcribed (amounting to about 15 single-spaced pages per child) and scored by two judges, who agreed 93% of the time. The scoring procedure was the same as that used in prior characteristic/defining studies (1 = identified as a noninstance, 2 = transitional, 3 = identified as an instance).

Was there indeed a developmental pattern whereby younger children did not understand the special roles that defining features played in the explanations? The data for each of the three domains are presented in figure 6.2. The most obvious pattern is that the children tended to show more adult-like performance at an earlier age on the -c/+d stories than on the +c/-d stories. This pattern was observed for all three sets of terms

Table 6.4
Examples of concept instruction and assessment in the study on explicit teaching of new concepts

MORAL ACT TERMS

Libel

To libel is to say something which is not true about someone that makes him or her look bad to other people. Newspapers and magazines are sometimes in trouble for libel if they say something about an actress or actor that isn't true. Like in *People* magazine they said that the Dukes of Hazzard were bullies and that they beat someone up and it wasn't true, so the Dukes called a lawyer to see what they could do about the paper libeling them. To libel is to say or write something about a person which isn't true.

(+c/-d) A doctor was caught driving when he was drunk one night. The next day when he went to court, a reporter from every paper in the town came. One paper didn't like the doctor and put the story about him driving drunk across the front page, while the other papers just put it in the middle of the paper somewhere. The doctor lost his job when his boss saw the story on the front page of the one paper. Did the paper libel the man?

(-c/+d) Have you ever seen wrestling on TV? Well, one huge wrestler is supposed to be a bad guy and he dresses all in black. People come to watch him because they love to hiss and boo. At Christmastime last year, a radio announcer decided it would be a great story to say this man was really, really nice even though the wrestler was really, really mean. So he made up a story about how the wrestler bought presents for every kid on his block, which is something he would never do. After the story, everybody hated him even more. So even more people went to watch him and he made a lot more money. Did the reporter libel the wrestler?

COOKING TERMS

Baste

To baste is to wet a food with something while it's cooking. For example, at Thanksgiving your mom probably basted your turkey by brushing melted butter and meat juices every half hour so the meat would stay moist. So to baste is to wet something every so often with a liquid while you're cooking it.

(+c/-d) We were having friends for dinner, so we cooked a huge roast beef. We saved the meat juices from the pan the meat was cooking in. And after we took the roast out of the oven and put it on the table, we poured the juices over the roast beef lots and lots of times so it would be nice and wet when we served it to our friends. Did we baste the roast beef?

(-c/+d) One Saturday two friends were making baked apples. They cut out the insides of some apples and poured in cinnamon and sugar. Then they put sugar on top and put the apples in a big black frying pan on top of the stove with a little

Table 6.4 (continued)

bit of water in it. Now and then they would go into the kitchen and pour the sugar which had melted into the pan over the apples. Did they baste the apples?

AGRICULTURAL TERMS

Mulch
To mulch is to put something over the land so that things will grow better on it. I'm sure you've seen people mulch the land in Ithaca. People put lots and lots of wood chips around rose bushes or young plants here in the winter to keep them from freezing and to keep the water in the soil. So mulching is when you cover the ground to help things you've planted there grow better.

(+c/-d) There was a huge rainstorm in Ithaca last year just before a farmer cut his straw, and it got soaking wet. So to dry it off after it was cut, the farmer picked a day when it was hot and sunny and spread the straw out carefully all over a field of carrots and left it there for half a day to get dry. But then he carefully picked it up so the carrots wouldn't get hurt by not getting enough sun. Did the farmer mulch the carrot field?

(-c/+d) Last year a friend of mine put tinfoil all over his garden because he wanted to take extra good care of the garden. He cut little holes out of the foil for the plants so they weren't covered up and could get the sun and rain they needed. The foil looked really pretty when the sun hit it because it sparkled and it also scared the crows away when the sun shining off the foil hit their eyes. Did my friend mulch his garden?

---

as a main effect on a repeated measures ANOVA (p < .01). The reasons for this difference are discussed in a later section of this chapter.

The results also show an overall developmental pattern of increasing attention to defining features with increasing age. With the -c/+d items, performance was generally so near maximum at all ages that ceiling effects prevented any developmental trend. For all the +c/-d items, a main effect of grade was found (one-way ANOVA, p < .02), and for both item types (+c/-d and -c/+d) this pattern was still observed as a grade-related trend (p < .10) and a grade-by-description type interaction (p < .05). This general developmental pattern supports the first hypothesis—namely, that younger children, even when given clear definitions, are less prone to understand the defining features' special status in comparison to characteristic features. The effect is even stronger if one looks at the spontaneous definitions, where there is a strong age trend away from definitions based solely on characteristic features toward those that focus centrally on defining features (K = 1.68, 2 = 2.01, 4 = 2.4, where 1 = characteristic features, 2 = mixture, 3 = defining features, p < .001, one-way ANOVA).

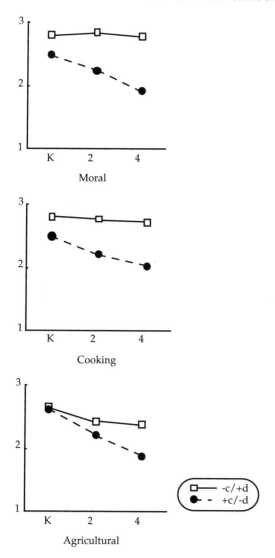

Figure 6.2
Mean scores across all concepts in each of the three conceptual domains in the study on explicit teaching of new concepts.

The second hypothesis for this study was that ability to benefit from the definitions should differ according to the child's level of knowledge in the domain in which the new concept was being taught. Consequently, based on the conceptual domains study, we predicted that children should understand what sorts of relations are defining at an earlier age for the moral act terms than for the cooking terms. No predictions were possible for the agricultural terms, except that as a coherent domain, it might well be expected to develop independently from the other two. The +c/-d lines in the three graphs in figure 6.2 suggest that defining features were attended to first in the domain of moral acts, then in the domain of cooking terms, and finally in the domain of agricultural terms; however, although in the right direction, these interdomain differences were not statistically different from each other.

Overall, the data strongly bore out the prediction that a shift would be found, and there were some suggestions of domain effect. The domain results may have been weakened by aspects of the task and stimulus construction. For example, the kindergartners had more difficulty with the +c/-d moral acts than might be expected from their adult-like performance on more familiar moral act terms in the conceptual domains study. Paradoxically, their difficulty with the novel terms may arise precisely because moral acts are an early emerging domain. Since most kindergartners appear to know the defining features for the most frequent moral act terms, we had to use more obscure ones. In so doing, we may have selected those that are conceptually difficult and hence late in developing. The subtleties of the meanings of "libel" and "swindle" are considerably more complex than those of the meanings of "lie" and "steal." Consequently, it is not surprising that children should have difficulty with these terms. Moreover, of all the terms used, the novel moral act terms were those with which young children were least likely to have had personal experiences and for which concrete instances are difficult for anyone to observe. Fortunately, few young children are swindled, betrayed, or libeled; or if they are, they rarely know about it.

If complexity is the reason for many kindergartners' difficulty with the novel moral act terms, their erroneous responses should have a special property different from those given by children who normally rely on characteristic features: they should still understand what sorts of features or relations tend to be defining and focus on these, but they should pick an oversimplified set and therefore incorrectly accept some +c/-d stories. This conjecture can be assessed by examining the transcripts. Consider the following excerpt in which a kindergartner was scored as judging a +c/-d story to describe an instance:

Betray (+c/-d)

C: Yeah, 'cause she didn't want to tell David that she really liked him and David started laughing at how ugly Susan was.

E: OK, but it says that Suzy wanted to tell David but she was afraid that he might laugh at her...and Suzy said that she hoped someone else would tell him, so Suzy's friend told. But when her friend did, David started to laugh.

C: Well, I guess her friend did do it.

E: Her friend did betray her? Why? Why do you think it was betraying?

C: Well, because she wanted somebody else to tell her, but I think she meant someone else who wasn't her friend or anything.

E: Why do you think she meant that?

C: I don't know.

E: But you think she still betrayed her even though her friend wanted her to tell?

C: Uh huh.

E: Why?

C: Well, because she might not have wanted her friend to do it, I guess.

E: Even though she said she did?

C: Yeah.

E: Should I read the story once more?

C: OK.

E: (Repeats story)

C: Yeah, because Suzy was really mad that her best friend told David.

E: OK, even though she wanted someone to tell him?

C: Uh huh.

The most obvious pattern in this excerpt is that the child repeatedly refers to intentional states of the actors as a way of justifying his judgment that this is an instance of betrayal. It is not that he is merely making the comparison to the characteristic features of the exemplars used in the original description. Rather, it seems that he knows what sorts of relations are relevant to the definition of "betray" but is not sufficiently clear about them to be able to relate them to the story. He exhibits the fairly common pattern noted in other studies of distorting the story so that the intentions become less ambiguous. In contrast, when kindergartners judged +c/-d agricultural or cooking descriptions to refer to instances, their statements were much more suggestive of a simple reliance on characteristic features.

Two additional excerpts from conversations with different kindergartners, discussing different moral act terms, illustrate the generality of this pattern:

Libel (+c/-d)
C: Yes.
E: OK, why was it libeling?
C: I don't remember.
E: (Repeats definition of "libel")
C: I think the doctor wasn't drunk.
E: The doctor *was* drunk. What happened was that one paper that didn't like the doctor put the story on the front page, while the other papers just put it in the middle of the paper. Was that libeling?
C: (Nods)
E: Yes? Why?
C: Because it's not nice to tell about other people.
E: OK, but why was it libeling? Specifically?
C: I don' t know what you just said. I don't know what it means.
E: Yes, you do, you just told me what it meant. To lie.
C: Oh yeah.
E: So do you think the newspaper libeled the doctor?
C: Yes.
E: Why?
C: I don't know why, I just think so.
E: (Repeats story)
C: Yes.
E: Why?
C: Because they made him lose his job and everything.

Swindle (+c/-d)
C: Yes, when John needed a car and he needed a station wagon and he went for a drive with it, so he could listen to the motor, then he bought it. Then he took it back and he wanted to get a station wagon. Then the guy says he only sells new cars.
E: OK, so specifically why was it swindling?
C: By...'cause he can't get another station wagon.
E: He wouldn't let him trade it in?
C: Yeah.
E: And why was that swindling?
C: By being mean.
E: Anything else?
C: No.

In both excerpts the children seem to focus correctly on intentions as the reason for judging the act to be an instance. This general focus on intentions is correct, but incorrect in terms of details, since the children tend to oversimplify the nature of the intentions inherent in the meanings of these terms. To a certain extent, these children's difficulties occur because this set of +c/-d descriptions used a number of negative intentional features as "characteristic features." In the earlier conceptual domains study with more familiar moral act terms, the +c/-d descriptions tended to specify slightly positive or intention-neutral events referring to typical appearance and behavioral patterns. The +c/-d descriptions used for the less familiar moral act terms were much more subtle in that the distractor definitions often were the right sorts of features; they were just wrong in the details. This difference resulted in an unfortunate lack of comparability between the two studies.

Not all kindergartners who made errors on the +c/-d descriptions for moral act terms followed the above patterns. Some seemed to have little or no awareness of even what sorts of features were likely to be defining, instead citing characteristic features common to both the description and the original definition in support of their positive judgment. Thus, for "extortion," some children judged the +c/-d description to identify an instance and then justified their response by pointing out that the passenger said, "If you do that..." Apparently, these children construed any aggressive "if" clause as extortion. Overall, however, most kindergartners who did err on the moral act terms seemed to have some awareness of the sorts of relations that are essential for defining the meaning of those terms, in that they made comments stressing the importance of the protagonist's intentions.

When children judged the descriptions for agricultural and cooking terms, however, the younger ones exhibited less of a constraining theory about the sorts of relations or features that were essential for defining the terms. Consider a few brief excerpts from the transcripts of seven different kindergartners:

Irrigate (+c/-d)
C: I think so.
E: OK, and why?
C: Because they put water through pipes!
E: OK, it wasn't water though, it was stuff that kills mildew.
C: Oh.
E: Is that still irrigating?
C: Yeah.
E: OK, and why?
C: Because it's stuff that's going through pipes. *(Here the child*

seems to focus on the pipes in their own right and not on the function of providing water to plants.)

Irrigate (-c/+d)
C: No.
E: No? Why not?
C: Because they didn't put pipes all around. And they didn't water anything.
E: Well, they made clouds let out the rain.
C: Yeah.
E: But it's still not irrigating?
C: No.
E: Because they didn't put pipes all around?
C: (Nods)
E: OK.

Furrow (+c/-d)
C: Yes.
E: OK, and why do you think it was furrowing?
C: Because he planted seeds?
E: He planted seeds?
C: In the ground.

Flambé (+c/-d)
C: Yes.
E: And why was it flambéing?
C: Because he was, the flame went up and it went out.

Sauté (-c/+d)
C: No.
E: Why not?
C: Because he didn't put it on the stove.

Sauté (+c/-d)
C: Uh huh.
E: And why was it sautéing?
C: Because they had it for a party.
E: Because why?
C: He had it for a party.
E: OK, but why was it sautéing?
C: Because it was fresh.
E: Do you want me to read the story again, or the meaning?
C: The story.
E: (Repeats story)
C: Uh huh, because he...

E: (Repeats definition)
C: No.
E: Why not?
C: Because, yeah they did. Because they were nice and yummy.

Baste (+c/-d)
C: Yes.
E: And why was it basting?
C: Because they got the juice afterwards, it was already cooked
and they put it on there. Be nice and wet.

In several of these excerpts children justify their responses by referring
to elements that are nothing like the defining properties of the terms. This
was a pattern frequently observed in the transcripts, where, for example,
children might use the lack of familiar objects, such as stoves, as justification for their answers. It is almost certainly an oversimplification,
however, to assume that these children had no biases about what sets of
features to select over others and made their judgments solely on the
basis of typicality. Certainly, some of the time they recognized the
importance of more procedural sorts of features over more object-
centered ones. Overall, however, there was a stronger tendency to select
a much wider range of feature types as relevant to the judgment for
agricultural and cooking terms than was the case for moral act terms.

Why were children in general so much more successful on the -c/+d
descriptions when this was not a strong pattern in previous studies?
Though future studies will have to provide a definitive answer, one
strong possibility supported by some of the transcripts is that when
children are given a definition, immediately followed by a test description based on that definition (a -c/+d item), they are able to see the
correspondence even if characteristic features clash. That is, the description repeats some features so accurately from the definition that children
may simply see the match and say it is legitimate. By contrast, if children
used the same strategy for the +c/-d stories and gave assent because of
a match in characteristic features, they would do even worse than normal
as a result of this strategy.

Nominal Kind Shifts in a Different Cultural Setting

One very general mechanism not yet considered as the source of the
nominal kind shift is a variety of informal and formal patterns of
socialization and instruction in Western culture. Perhaps developmental
shifts toward definition-like features are a consequence of formal schooling, literacy, or even the general technical and scientific orientation of
Western culture. Many claims have been made about the cognitive

consequences of a general cultural orientation (see for example, Luria 1976; Olson 1982). Consider, as one example, the following passage from Bruner 1966:

> What differs from culture to culture (and within subcultures) is the extent to which ranges of alternatives are fitted together into superordinate or hierarchical structures, so that a given percept is created as one of only a few alternatives or one of many. The hypothesis I would like to set forth is that there is a greater push toward hierarchical connections in technical cultures than in those that are less technical. The hypothesis is based on the assumption that there are fewer compelling reasons in a less technical society for connecting events to anything beyond their immediate contextual settings, such as money value, abstract cause-and-effect relations, or the intricate uniform timing of work periods. In the sense used by Miller, Pribram, and Galanter (1960), hierarchically organized plans need not be so elaborately formulated in a folk society. All this leads me to suspect that in less complex societies perception is likely to be more ad hoc, more given to filling the magic seven slots (Miller, 1956) with the particularities of a certain object or event than with a domain of the alternative events that might have occurred. (p. 324)

Given these questions about cross-cultural influences, it was fortunate that Sheila Jeyifous chose to conduct the research for her Doctoral dissertation on patterns of conceptual change among the Yoruba people of Nigeria (Jeyifous 1986). In addition to studies on natural kinds, the dissertation contains many accounts of the characteristic-to-defining shift for nominal kind concepts among various subpopulations of the Yoruba. Rather than describe that research in detail here, I refer the reader to the dissertation itself, which is a compelling, insightful analysis of culture and conceptual change.

For the purposes of this book it is adequate to say that Jeyifous found dramatic characteristic-to-defining shifts among rural groups of Yoruba people who had minimal amounts of exposure to Western culture, schooling, and literacy. Of course, culturally appropriate concepts and +c/-d and -c/+d stories had to be constructed, along with culturally appropriate interview methods. Both of these aspects of stimulus design turned out to be monumental tasks, requiring years of intensive work in Nigeria and Ithaca. The following translated examples of a -c/+d story and two interviews (Jeyifous 1986, 110–111) illustrate why interested readers should consult the original work:

Sacrifice
Defining features of sacrifice are (1) that it be done under instruction of a babalawo and (2) that the sacrificial items be placed at a junction

of routes. Characteristic features are the use of such items as dead chickens, raw meat, and palm-oil in a calabash.

(-c/+d)

Baba Segun was a wicked man who wanted to harm Baba Ade. In order to protect himself from Baba Segun's wicked intentions, Baba Ade went to the babalawo, who told him to make an offering to Ogun. As the babalawo instructed, Baba Ade placed a container of beer and tinned fish and biscuits at a nearby junction. Several weeks passed and nothing bad happened to Baba Ade. Was it a sacrifice he placed at the junction?

6-year-old rural child

C: No, it's not a sacrifice.

E: Why do you think so?

C: Because it's biscuits and beer.

E: He obeyed the babalawo's order by making use of biscuits and beer as the ingredients of sacrifice. Can it be a sacrifice?

C: No, it is not a sacrifice.

12-year-old rural child

C: Yes, it's a sacrifice because he went to a babalawo who instructed him to take those things to the crossroad.

There is a great deal more of interest in Jeyifous's research findings, including a strikingly diminished shift among a special subpopulation of Yoruba who were undergoing a highly chaotic and unsettling transition from rural to urban life; but again, I refer the reader to the original account for more details. Most relevant here is the strong suggestion that the characteristic-to-defining shift is a highly pervasive pattern of conceptual change found in otherwise dramatically different cultures. However, although I would guess that the shift is a cultural universal in all but the most deleterious circumstances, one cross-cultural study certainly cannot constitute total verification.

Conclusions

Each of the four studies described in this chapter was designed to provide a better understanding of how the characteristic-to-defining shift for nominal kinds occurs. Perhaps the most obvious findings overall are a recognition of the complexity of the issue and the realization that these studies, though very lengthy and labor intensive, represent only preliminary explorations into their respective areas.

The first study, checking for idiosyncratic defining features, should be followed up by studies exploring under what circumstances children make use of these features and in what domains they might be heavily involved. In addition, providing that perseveration problems can be resolved, studies might be attempted in which each child is asked to respond to all the story permutations.

In following up the second study on parental explanations, more naturalistic settings should be used to ensure that an element of self-consciousness did not influence the results. In addition, some domains might be found for which the conceptual nature of the definitions that parents give to younger children differs from the conceptual nature of the definitions they give to older children.

The effects might have been stronger in the third (teaching) study if a more naturalistic learning situation had been used. Time demands made this a difficult study for the children; possibly too many concepts were taught too rapidly. A more ecologically valid approach would be to teach the children these terms gradually over several weeks, following the method of Carey's "chromium" study (Carey 1978). It may be, however, that except in formal schooling children are rarely, if ever, exposed to formal definitions for concepts. Rather, they may discover the defining properties for a given domain as they develop more sophisticated theories about that domain. This too could be explored by giving children a great deal of experience with a set of novel concepts without ever providing a definition. Presumably, if they have a great deal of experience with the concepts, especially of the sort where they must make predictions and inductions, they might shift endogenously. The parent-child study indicates that this may be the predominant pattern.

Finally, Jeyifous's results suggest that more extensive cross-cultural studies be undertaken that systematically examine the many different ways in which specific cultures could influence the acquisition of concepts in local domains. Jeyifous's work suggests that cultures do not have a domain-general effect of retarding or accelerating a characteristic-to-defining shift for nominal kind terms, but this must remain only a strong suggestion until more cultures are examined.

Despite these drawbacks and the preliminary nature of these studies, they do suggest some of the ways in which we might better explore the mechanisms of conceptual change. In addition, they reveal some of the potential problems of using the characteristic/defining contrast, even for nominal kinds. Difficulties in stimulus creation were often related to subtleties in meaning that resisted description by simple lists of defining features, supporting the idea that even most nominal kind concepts may be at least partly embedded in causal beliefs from the start. At the same time, qualitative shifts also seem to occur in the relative balance of characteristic vs. defining "theory"-driven features. These shifts may do more than help us understand development, however. As we will see in the next chapter, they may also impose constraints on models of concepts in general.

Chapter 7
Semantic and Conceptual Structure and the
Nominal Kind Studies

Two issues have been postponed throughout the discussion of the developmental nominal kind studies: (1) What is the relation between concepts and word meanings in cognitive development? and (2) How do patterns of development constrain models of concepts in general? In light of the nominal kind studies, it is now possible at least to begin a discussion of these issues.[1]

Concepts vs. Word Meanings

Up to this point I have talked about the development of concepts and word meanings somewhat interchangeably, as though development of one automatically entailed development of the other. By at least one account, however, such an entailment is not correct, and it may be appropriate to consider in detail the relations between the two before drawing conclusions about what develops.

Clark (1983) introduces a comprehensive review of research on semantic and conceptual development by stressing the importance of the difference between meanings and concepts. Consider her opening sentences:

> Meanings—that is word, phrase, and sentence meanings—and concepts are as different as apples and oranges. Although they are often discussed as if they were equivalents, the distinctions between them are crucial—not only in talking about development but also in considering the relation between language and thought. (p. 787)

Clark illustrates her point by showing that there are often dramatic differences across languages in the number of distinct lexical items that are attached to a conceptual domain that is well differentiated for individuals from all languages. For example, English has one verb for the general domain of putting on clothes, whereas Japanese has at least four distinct verbs for different parts of the domain (one verb for putting

---

1. Some of the figures in this chapter and their related discussions first appeared in Keil 1987.

on headgear, one for putting clothes on lower body parts, and so on). Though English speakers have only one verb for these actions, they are presumably just as able as Japanese speakers to distinguish them conceptually; hence, the conceptual systems and the lexical ones are hardly isomorphic. Examples such as these are common in almost any detailed comparison between two languages, and although there may be differences between the conceptual structures for two language groups because of cultural differences or possibly some effects of the lexical labels themselves, it is apparent that in many cases the underlying conceptual structures may be roughly equal but the richness of lexical contacts to nodes in those conceptual structures may vary dramatically. Thus, when "word meaning" is equated with coded lexical relations, the relations between semantic and conceptual structure can be complex and indirect. In other contexts "word meaning" has more the sense of referring simply to the subset of concepts that have lexical labels; the structure of such meanings is no different from that for nonlexicalized concepts.

These interlanguage differences in mappings between lexical items and concepts have direct implications for studies of semantic and conceptual development, a point stressed by Clark in her review. Not surprisingly, then, they also have implications for the nominal kind studies described in chapters 4 through 6. At one extreme a characteristic-to-defining shift could reflect changes in the way lexical items are attached to an unchanging fully developed conceptual structure. At the other extreme each change in the lexicon could reflect a corresponding change in underlying conceptual structure. There are undoubtedly clear cases at both extremes. Thus, like adults, children can be taught labels for totally familiar concepts for which they do not currently have lexical items. (William Safire, for example, wrote an essay in which he coined the phrase "sidewalk shuffle" for the highly familiar event, hitherto unnamed in English, that occurs when two people trying to pass on a sidewalk make several false starts before simultaneously moving in opposite directions.) Alternatively, children may be taught new concepts and simultaneously given labels for them. As in most cases with extremes, children are probably somewhere in between. Therefore, it is useful to reconsider the nominal kind studies in terms of the insights they yield into semantic vs. conceptual development.

First, it is important to note that, for all the terms used in the first two characteristic-to-defining shift studies, children at all ages were familiar with the terms and had some meaning associated with them. Thus, it was rarely if ever the case that a younger child simply did not have the label for a concept and then later acquired it. For this reason the relation to the cross-linguistic patterns and the two extremes summarized above is indirect. There might still be a loose link between conceptual and semantic change, however. Perhaps the conceptual structure remains the same throughout development and the semantic change represents the child's changing assignments of the same lexical item to different aspects of that conceptual structure. This possibility can best be illustrated with concrete examples.

Consider kinship terms. The younger child who labels the +c/-d description for "uncle" as being an uncle might also have the adult concept of uncle but might not have attached the word "uncle" to that set of conceptual relations. If so, then development of the meaning of the term "uncle" merely consists in the realignment of that term with a different part of the preexisting conceptual structure.

There are several reasons for suspecting that the young child who seems to have a characteristic representation for "uncle" does not also have a fully developed conceptual representation of the adult meaning. This is not to say that the child might not have some adult-like fragments of that concept before the change in word meaning occurs; but it is unlikely that the younger child who is swayed completely by characteristic features for "uncle" nonetheless has a fully developed conceptual understanding of kinship relations.

One reason for doubting such an account comes from the mere existence and regularity of the characteristic-to-defining shift. Why should the shift exist if the child has the adult conceptual structure as well? Clark suggests that young children can sometimes be construed as casting about in conceptual structure for the right concepts and relations to attach to a word and that they will often seize upon the wrong relations initially. Children surely do sometimes engage in such a process, but this does not explain why some features and not others are likely to be the mistaken ones. In particular, shouldn't a sizeable number of the younger children happen to hit upon the right conceptual features right at the start and thereby have the correct word meaning? This was extremely uncommon for many of the terms studied. Moreover, when the younger children are mistaken, their mistakes are quite systematic in that they reflect a reliance on characteristic features. How can we then explain the systematicity of their mistakes without assuming some differences in their conceptual structures as well?

A related reason for doubting that the shift is merely a remapping of terms onto a static conceptual structure comes from the conceptual domains study described in chapter 5. It was quite clear in that study that the shifts tended to cooccur much more strongly within than across domains, and the transcripts strongly suggested that the children learned new principled dimensions for organizing the relevant domains. If each word becomes attached separately to conceptual structure, the domain effects that were found would be unexpected. Conceivably, the child could learn how a set of terms as a whole should be realigned with different parts of a fully developed conceptual structure; but such an account fails to explain why the child would see those terms as a whole in the first place.

A third reason for thinking that children are not always conceptually ready to acquire new terms can be seen in the results of the teaching study described in chapter 6. Younger children in that study were frequently unable to benefit from explicit definitions of terms because they tended to rely excessively on characteristic features and treated even the defining part of an explanation as merely characteristic. Later, when they had undergone the shift for more familiar terms within that domain, they were more likely to benefit from the same definitions. This is a difficult pattern of results to explain if one assumes that the conceptual structure was unchanging throughout. Conceivably the terms used in the definitions were themselves changing, by becoming attached to different aspects of conceptual structure, and consequently the younger children saw these terms as pointing to different meanings. However, examination of the terms used in the definitions for that study suggests that such an account is improbable and likely to be highly convoluted if specified in detail.

Finally, the transcripts themselves illustrate that the children are not merely selecting some aspects of conceptual structures over others to attach lexical labels to; the children frequently express good reason for why some features are relevant and others are not. Thus, they often have theories or other explanatory systems to justify what features or dimensions are important for organizing a domain and what ones are not. That is to say, their underlying conceptual systems seem to be the driving force behind selecting particular features for inclusion into word meaning. Consequently, only changes in this system that can be responsible for changes in semantic structure.

These four reasons indicate that, at least in some cases, phenomena such as the characteristic-to-defining shift should be taken as diagnostic not only of changing word meanings but also of changing conceptual structures. Nonetheless, in other cases the linkage may not be so tight. Consider the term "island." Many five-year-olds who claim that the +c/ -d description identifies an island and the -c/+d description does not nonetheless have the concept "surrounded by water on all sides." Such children seem to have the necessary adult concept; they merely fail to attach "island" to it—or, for that matter, to any other single feature. Instead, they attach it to the prototype consisting of a large collection of characteristic features. There is a shift from treating a constellation of typical features as roughly equal and forming a prototype, to putting almost total emphasis on the single feature of being surrounded by water. Apparently, the child has decided that this one feature is somehow more principled in terms of organizing the domain. This semantic change must reflect a certain degree of conceptual change as well; although younger children may be able to notice the feature "surrounded by water on all sides," that feature does not do any conceptual work in organizing a domain of geographical things for them; it may be no more important than any other noticeable feature.

Concepts are not merely the same as features or even sets of features; for the most part, they occupy a role in a relational system, a system that is frequently united by explanatory constructs. It is not clear whether the child's shift for "island" represents an emerging awareness of geographical entities as opposed to mere objects, however, such a conjecture seems very reasonable, and, to the extent that it is correct, a conceptual change underlies the characteristic-to-defining shift for "island" as well. Presumably, this could be assessed both by studying other geographical terms and by attempting to teach the correct meaning to young children and observing their patterns of difficulties, if any.

There are undoubtedly cases even more extreme than "island" where a child may learn a new word for a node in a fully developed conceptual system; but for the nominal kind terms studied here, underlying conceptual change may be the primary force behind the semantic change. This will become even more apparent in the studies on natural kind terms presented in later chapters. Of course, the extent to which conceptual change and semantic change are linked will vary considerably across words and across semantic domains. It might seem that the purest nominal kind concepts, which are defined by convention and more or less in isolation from a coherent theory or from other terms, would be closest to pure cases of mapping a word onto an already present conceptual structure. For the nominal kind terms studied here, however, such a dissociation was not evident. Assuming that the characteristic-to-defining shift studies reflect changes in conceptual structure, it therefore is reasonable to ask what implications they have for theories of concepts in general.

Models of Concepts in Adults

The developmental patterns uncovered in the characteristic-to-defining shift studies have an important bearing on how we should construct adult models of cognition. A central question is whether these developmental patterns can be characterized as a shift away from prototype-based or other probabilistic representations to a new sort of conceptual structure. If they cannot, then the label "characteristic-to-defining shift" is somewhat misleading. Perhaps representations at all ages never contain necessary and sufficient features, and perhaps features are always organized around prototypes or exemplars. The developmental shift may simply reflect a change in the significance attached to some features. It is therefore important to consider how the shift might be modeled by simple probabilistic representations throughout development. Several models are possible, of which I will present only one. Nonetheless, within a broad range of such models, similar issues will arise.

Figure 7.1 shows one of the simplest ways in which this shift might be characterized. (In this and many of the following discussions it will seem as though I am assuming that conceptual structures must be specified by constellations of features and certain classes of operations upon them. However, similar arguments can be made for exemplar-based or dimensional views, and I will be focusing on features primarily for expository reasons.) The position of each feature with respect to the outer circle represents the extent to which it cooccurs with instances of the concept (as labeled by adults); features closest to the center of the circle most closely approximate a 1.00 correlation, and features closest to the periphery approximate a 0.00 correlation. The inner circle contains those features that seem to be equated with the concept. This inner circle may have somewhat fuzzy boundaries that can be influenced by such factors as local context. One way to attempt to model the characteristic-to-defining shift is to claim that the inner circle becomes more compact with increasing age, in the sense that the number of features that are likely to be referred to decrease (again, this may all be probabilistic); or, put differently, more importance is attached to those features that are most central. By this account, the most central features (say, f1 and f2 in this

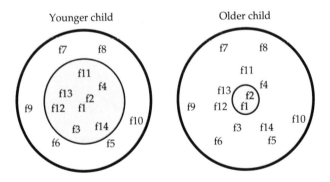

Figure 7.1
A model of the characteristic-to-defining shift in which the only developmental change is an increasing emphasis on central features relative to peripheral ones.

case) are known as "defining" features and the others as "characteristic." No reference is made to necessary and sufficient features and rigid all-or-none boundaries. Moreover, claims of a qualitative characteristic-to-defining change become questionable, since they seem to be based on arbitrary decisions about how close features are to the center of the circle. Figure 7.1 is an nonetheless inadequate portrayal of developmental phenomena, for several reasons.

1. What seem to be equally typical cooccurring features are not treated as equal by older children in terms of how they influence judgments of category membership. Thus, features f1 and f2 might both occur almost 100% of the time with known instances, yet only f1 may guide category judgments for older children and adults. For example, for many children, "is friends with your mom or dad" and "is your dad's or mom's brother" may correlate equally highly with instances of "uncle." That is, for these children, all observed uncles might well be friends with one of the two parents. But only the younger children seem to regard the "friend" feature as important to deciding about category membership. A similar question arises for the younger children in that features such as "wears glasses," "is overweight," "has bad breath," or "is partly bald" might correlate perfectly with all known instances of uncles (especially since young children may only know three or four uncles as such), yet even the youngest children may know that such properties are irrelevant to deciding membership. They apparently believe that the domain of social interactions is especially important to kinship concepts and not arbitrary body parts, odors, or acuity of vision. This first objection is complicated by the observation that many probabilistic models of concepts also stress that occurrence of a highly correlated feature in a contrast can weaken its importance to the target set (see, for example, Rosch and Mervis 1975). The contrast principle, however, raises several new problems as well. It predicts, for example, that "being a friend of one's parents" would not be a feature of "uncle" since many nonuncles are friends of the parents. This prediction works fine for the older children but fails for the younger children, who surely also have encountered many unrelated friends of their parents. The contrast principle also raises the problem of deciding on a relevant contrast set; frequently one's choice of a set can beg the question by implicitly characterizing the relevant conceptual domain.

2. New features are added of which the child was never formerly aware. This is not in principle a problem for a prototype model, but it is not a possibility given the simple model shown in figure 7.1. In practice it may be a serious problem since certain naive theories may guide the child in the search for and successful discovery of new features; and without these theories it is difficult to explain why only some new

features are uncovered and incorporated into the concept and why others that correlate equally well are not.

3. Finally, a child may occasionally use as a defining feature one that is less highly correlated with category members than other features that are not considered defining. This can be a consequence of illusory correlations that fall out of imperfect theories about the world (Murphy and Medin 1985). Our studies contain few explicit examples of illusory correlations because the paradigms were not designed to uncover them.

There are two ways in which one might modify the model to account for the first objection, one of which is intuitively plausible but does not seem to fit the data, the other of which fits the data but does not have any explanatory value. Figure 7.2 shows two variants of the first approach, which assumes that the child's intuitive typicality distributions change with increasing age. In figure 7.2a the features stay the same with respect to overall distribution but change over time with respect to centrality. In figure 7.2b both the centrality of specific features and the degree to which the features as a whole are clustered toward the center change; in this way patterns of sampling of the feature space need not change.

Unfortunately, neither version of this approach seems to capture the facts. Though it is occasionally true that, with more experience, the relative centrality of two features may change, this is not usually the case. An adult might easily judge it to be highly typical of uncles that they are friends of one of the two parents or that they can see and have teeth but nonetheless would not weigh such features at all heavily in deciding who was an uncle.

In the second approach the typicality distributions would remain roughly the same at all ages, but the distributions would be sampled in different ways, with the change taking the form not of the sensible symmetrically shrinking circle but rather of a movement to a seemingly arbitrary and unmotivated sampling, as shown in figure 7.3a. To be more accurate, one should also model the addition of new features, that occurs in conjunction with the change in sampling pattern, as shown in figure 7.3b. This model would of course work, but it seems unmotivated and provides a rather bizarre version of the probabilistic model for adult concepts wherein only some of the most typical features are involved in determining membership and there is no principled, objective way of telling which ones they are. In fact, it only retains the sense of being probabilistic in that no features may be strictly necessary; it cannot explain which features will play more important conceptual roles based on their probabilistic distributions, which is the primary motivation for such approaches.

The developmental patterns of the characteristic-to-defining shift do not require abandonment of category fuzziness or probabilistic repre-

Younger child   Older child

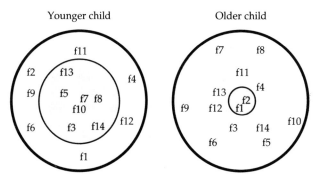

(a) Intuitive typicality distributions change with age, while inner
circle contracts over a constant density of feature
distributions.

Younger child   Older child

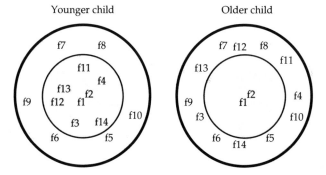

(b) Intuitive typicality distributions and density of feature
distributions both change with age in such a way that only a
few features remain inside an inner circle of constant size.

Figure 7.2
Two models of the characteristic-to-defining shift in which the intuitive typicality distributions change with age.

sentations. Simple tabulations of feature frequencies and correlations,
however, cannot explain the details of the shift in any but the most
arbitrary, ad hoc fashion. Neither typicality, nor patterns of correlation
among features, nor similarity among exemplars can be used to predict
which features will become the "defining" ones. Typicality and correlation cannot be used because highly typical and highly correlated features
are not equally important to definitions. Similarity cannot be used
because it is a theory-laden, nonobjective relation (Quine 1951). All of
this suggests that conceptual structures that are solely prototypes or

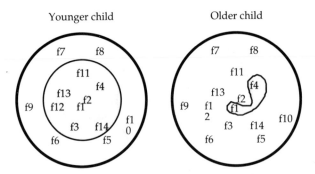

(a) Neither intuitive typicality distributions nor density of feature distributions change with age. As the child grows older, however, the distributions are sampled in an increasingly asymmetric and apparently arbitrary manner.

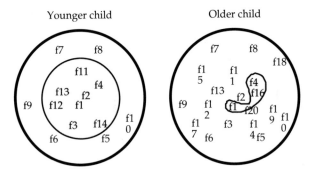

(b) Neither intuitive typicality distributions nor density of feature distributions change with age. As the child grows older, however, the distributions are sampled in an increasingly asymmetric and apparently arbitrary manner. In this version, some new features are learned as well.

Figure 7.3
Two models of the characteristic-to-defining shift in which relatively constant typicality distributions are increasingly sampled in ways that appear to be arbitrary and ad hoc.

other probabilistic representations built up out of "objectively" specifiable feature typicality, exemplar frequencies, or correlational measures cannot explain, except in the most arbitrary and ad hoc way, the very robust developmental patterns seen for nominal kind terms. Something else is needed as well.

Much of the rest of this book is devoted to better understanding what that "something else" is, by expanding the analysis beyond nominal kinds.

Conclusions

Chapters 1 through 7 have demonstrated the following points:

1. Qualitative changes apparently take place in the conceptual and semantic structure of a special subset of relatively well defined natural language terms that we have been calling "nominal kind terms."

2. Such changes are not part of a global representational shift, as suggested by stage theories of cognitive development. Rather, they occur on a domain-by-domain basis, reflecting increasing expertise and increasingly coherent belief systems in each domain.

3. The changes do not merely reflect changing adult input, nor are they consequences of younger children using equally defining but more idiosyncratic features, as compared with older children and adults. Moreover, children cannot easily be taught the defining features for a new concept unless they are conceptually "ready."

4. The shift may be related to the broader range of developmental phenomena described in chapter 2, suggesting the need for new research methods that go beyond the study of nominal kinds.

5. The shift is not merely semantic but also conceptual.

6. The developmental patterns uncovered in the studies seem to pose interesting constraints on models of adult concepts, in particular raising questions about the adequacy of some probabilistic accounts of conceptual structure.

7. Since Chapter 5 it has seemed increasingly necessary to talk about coherent belief systems or "theories." In following chapters I will argue that such notions are even more fundamental to understanding natural kinds.

8. Finally, the studies described so far suggest a view of cognitive development close to some models of novice-to-expert shifts. Such a view would hold that the characteristic-to-defining shift signifies a one-to-many mapping of representational types from domain-general principles of conceptual organization and learning (such as prototype abstraction) to highly domain-specific principles of conceptual organization arising from local areas of expertise. The characteristic-to-defining shift studies described so far would seem to be mostly compatible with such a view (given the seeming diversity of end-state representational types found in different domains, such as kinship terms vs. looking terms). In following chapters, however, I will show that such a view may be an illusion masking a more fundamental and universal pattern of conceptual change. I will argue that this is a fortunate outcome, given some severe conceptual problems posed by novice-to-expert models of cognitive development.

Chapter 8
Discoveries about Natural Kinds and Artifacts

The histories of all natural sciences document the discovery that certain entities that share immediate properties nonetheless belong to different kinds. Biology offers a great many examples, such as the discoveries that dolphins and whales are not fish but mammals, that the bat is not a kind of bird, that the glass "snake" is in fact a kind of lizard with only vestigial limbs beneath its skin. In the plant kingdom it has been found, for example, that some "vegetables" are really fruits and that some "leaves" are not really leaves. From the realm of minerals and elements have come the discoveries, among others, that mercury is a metal and that water is a compound.

In almost all these cases the discovery follows a similar course. Certain entities are initially classified as members of a kind because they share many salient properties with other bona fide members of that kind and because their membership is in accordance with current theories. This classification may be accepted for centuries until some new insight leads to a realization that the entities share other, more fundamentally important properties with a different kind and not with their apparent kind. Sometimes it is discovered that although the fundamental properties of the entities are not those of their apparent kind, they do not seem to be those of any other familiar kind either. In such cases a new theoretical structure must develop that provides a meaningful system of classification. There are many profound questions about when a discovery will have a major impact on a scheme of classification, but certainly a major factor is whether that discovery is made in the context of a coherent causal theory in which the discovered properties are not only meaningful but central.

As described in chapter 3, discoveries about internal essences or underlying causal principles rarely seem to change our minds about the true nature of simple artifacts, presumably because we assume that there is no intrinsic causal homeostatic cluster that binds members of an artifact kind together. This difference between artifacts and natural kinds suggests a developmental study in which children are told about discovered underlying properties or origins of things that appear and behave as though they are members of kinds that have different properties and origins. The contrast between artifacts and natural kinds provides a convenient way of assessing whether any developmental changes are merely consequences of changing response biases, strategies, or demand characteristics. If children show a strong shift in judgments about whether a discovery about properties of natural kinds entails a change in their class membership, but do not show a comparable shift for a similar discovery about artifacts, they are probably not simply exhibiting a general strategic shift.

It should be stressed that there is a separate class of discoveries that might cause both children and adults to change their minds about artifacts as well, but these discoveries would not concern internal properties or principles. Instead, objects that looked like members of one artifact kind and were perhaps even used as members of that artifact kind would be grouped with members of a different artifact kind because it was discovered that they were made to fulfill the purposes and functions of that kind. There are such descriptions in the history of archeology, but note that the nature of the discovery about artifacts is crucially different from the nature of the discovery about natural kinds.

In conjunction with ideas reviewed in chapter 3, these differences between artifacts and natural kinds with respect to discoveries suggest two specific developmental patterns:

1. If children do not have well-developed causal theories about the properties they observe for natural kinds, or if their theories are sufficiently undifferentiated, they are not likely to be impressed by the significance of discoveries about properties central to those theories in adults. Thus, if children do not have much of a theory of biology beyond the simplest characterizations of behavior, they may not gauge discovered properties about blood or internal organs to be of much importance. The development of the relevant theories is a continuing process, and adults who are ignorant of some of the more arcane aspects of biological theory will also mistakenly underestimate the importance of certain discovered properties.

2. Children who are ignorant of relevant theories might show similar response patterns for both artifacts and natural kinds, since in neither case would they judge the discovered properties to be of much importance. As they become more knowledgeable, they should start to give different patterns of answers for the two kinds, answers that may perhaps reflect the emergence of a deeper theory of biology.

Developing Stimuli and a Method

To assess children's developing knowledge of natural kinds through their interpretation of the importance of various discoveries, a method was developed wherein discoveries about natural kinds and artifacts were described to children, who were then questioned systematically about those discoveries. The first steps were to generate pairs of natural kind and artifact terms and to develop descriptions wherein an entity had all the salient perceptual and behavioral characteristics of one member of the pair but the discovered properties of the other. The selection of salient characteristic features was guided by asking undergraduates in several seminars to list the most typical features of the various kinds. These features usually included typical shape, color, texture, and behavior and occasionally included typical smell, habitat, diet, and the like. The features were then reduced to a coherent set that was accessible to most kindergartners.

Selecting the principled, theory-central features was much more difficult, since it presupposed a particular theory of biology. Basing our choices on informal interviews with children and adults, as well as on the issues raised in chapter 3, we decided to use four types of features: (1) internal macroscopic properties such as organs and bones, (2) internal microscopic properties such as blood composition, (3) nature of offspring, and (4) nature of parents (origins). We did not expect either children or adults to know distinguishing internal features at the macroscopic or microscopic level. We did not even expect them to know any more than the most basic organs (brains, hearts, stomachs). Instead, we were concerned with whether they realized the general importance or relevance of those sorts of features to questions concerning the type of natural kind involved. Thus, the stories described scientists discovering that something that looked and acted like one species had all the inside parts of another species as well as offspring and parents of the other species. The inside parts were described simply by saying, for example, "They had the blood of x, the bones of x, and all the other inside parts of x rather than of y." Scientists were mentioned in the descriptions in an attempt to establish the legitimate status of the discovered features. (Scientists were also mentioned in the artifact stories to assess whether children were simply deferring to scientific authority for all stimuli.) Pieces of scientific equipment such as microscopes were also mentioned—again, to make it clear to the children that the discovered properties were bona fide.

The First Discoveries Study

Stimuli
The discoveries paradigm was used in two different studies, which differed primarily in terms of the stimulus sets. In the first study, conducted

Table 8.1
Stimulus pairs used in the first discoveries study

Natural kinds	Artifacts
Horse/cow	Boot/sail
Apple/pear	Nail/screwdriver
Pine/oak	Cup/bowling ball
Dog/cat	Key/penny

Table 8.2
Examples of descriptions used in the first discoveries study

Horse/cow
These are animals that live on a farm. They go "neigh" and people put saddles on their backs and ride them, and these animals like to eat oats and hay and everybody calls them horses. But some scientists went up to this farm and decided to study them really carefully. They did blood tests and X-rays and looked way deep inside with microscopes and found out these animals weren't like most horses. These animals had the inside parts of cows. They had the blood of cows, the bones of cows; and when they looked to see where they came from, they found out their parents were cows. And, when they had babies, their babies were cows. What do you think these animals really are: horses or cows?

Key/penny
There are these things that look just like this (shows key picture). People use these things to open up locked doors, and also to lock up cars and houses to keep them safe. Some scientists just studied a special group of these things that came from a factory in Pennsylvania where they are made for opening locks. They looked at them very closely with a microscope to see what they were like way down inside and to see what they were made out of. They found out that they weren't like most keys; they were made out of exactly the same stuff that pennies are made out of. In fact, when they looked to see where these things came from, they found out that pennies had been melted down in order to make these things; and when they were all done, they melted them down again and made pennies again. What do you think these things are: keys or pennies?

with the help of Lianne Ritter, the items shown in table 8.1 were used. The first item in each pair refers to the characteristic features of the object described, the second to the internal properties, origins, and offspring. The two examples in table 8.2 illustrate the kinds of descriptions that were given for each item (the full set is listed in appendix 5). Several features of these descriptions deserve mention. First and most obvious is the attempt to make the artifact description as parallel as possible to the natural kind description by referring not only to discovered internal properties of another artifact but also to its origins (analogous to parents) and the product made from it (analogous to offspring). Second, the artifact description specifically described the makers' intentions, so that there was no confusion about what the artifact was made to be and what function its creators had in mind. The reasons for this reference to intention should be obvious in light of the issues raised in chapter 3. Third, attempts were made through piloting to ensure that none of the terms in either description was unfamiliar to the children.

All descriptions were accompanied by drawings of both the object itself and the object with which it shared the four types of properties. Both drawings were shown in the course of the description and then left in front of the child during the follow-up question period.

Procedure
Seventeen children in each of three grades (K, 2, and 4) participated as subjects in this experiment. (Average ages were 5:8, 7:9, and 10:1 years, respectively.) All were from public schools in Tompkins County, New York. Sixteen adults, all undergraduates at Cornell University, also participated as subjects.

The descriptions were presented to children in the course of one session ranging in length from roughly one-half hour to an hour. The order of presentation of individual items was randomized. To ensure that the children fully understood the stories, they were frequently asked to repeat them. This would have been desirable for all the items but was generally too tedious for any one child. If a child did seem to have difficulty remembering a description, the experimenter told all succeeding stories more slowly, asking for details as she went along. Sometimes during the question period it became clear that a child misunderstood or misremembered parts of the story. In such cases the story was again repeated, usually in its entirety, and the questions were then repeated as well.

The questions that followed the child's initial judgment of identity were critical and were conducted according to the following guidelines. The child's initial judgment was followed up with a "why" question. (Children who resisted making a choice were again asked which sort of thing the described object really was. On some items a few children did not choose either, and their responses were therefore omitted from the analysis for that item. On rare occasions a child said that the animal was neither an *x* nor a *y* but an *x-y* (for example, neither a horse nor a cow but a horse-cow). Children who did this were told that it really was only one or the other and were asked to choose.) In all cases children's responses to the "why" question were followed by an "even though" question in which the experimenter reminded them that the object in question had certain properties of the category they had *not* chosen as well as the other properties of the category that they did choose. Thus, if a child judged that the animal with the appearance of a horse and the insides, parents, and offspring of a cow was really a horse, the experimenter asked, "So even though this special animal had all the inside parts of cows (such as...) and its mommy and daddy were cows [and bulls if child objected] and its babies were cows, you think it's really a what?" (Occasionally the experimenter put the question differently, by asking, "So how come if it's an *x* it has the *P*'s of a *y*?") This technique of questioning ensured that the children were not neglecting the other features in the description. On many occasions the entire description was repeated almost verbatim if it seemed that the child had not paid attention. The children were also often asked to repeat the entire description themselves so as to maximize their attentiveness to the stories. The same technique was used for the artifacts. Sample transcripts provided in the results section illustrate in more detail the patterns of questioning.

All responses and questions were tape-recorded and transcribed. The transcripts were scored by two independent judges on a three-point scale. A score of 1 meant that the child had judged that identity was not changed by the discovery. A score of 3 meant that the discovery in effect overruled the characteristic features. A score of 2 was less common but was given when the child seemed to be genuinely undecided between the two alternatives. Interjudge reliability was greater than 95% and any differences were resolved through discussion or, if necessary, appealed to a third judge.

Results
Figure 8.1 summarizes the results of the study by showing the mean scores for all artifact terms and for all natural kind terms as a function of age. The main developmental pattern for natural kinds is a shift from judgments that the discovery did not influence kind membership to judgments that it was crucial and overruled characteristic features. For artifacts, the vast majority of subjects at all ages judged that kind membership was not changed as a result of the discovery. Main effects of age and stimulus type were significant at p < .001, and age-by-stimulus-

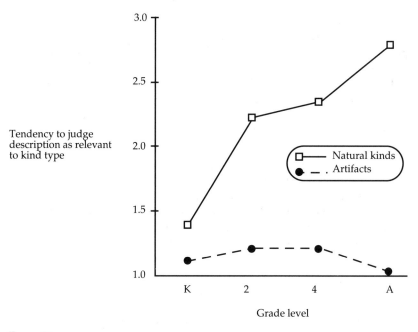

Figure 8.1
Mean scores for natural kind and artifact terms in the first discoveries study. 1 = judgment that discovery did not change kind type, 2 = judgment indicating genuine indecision about whether the discovery changed kind type, 3 = judgment that discovery did change kind type.

type interactions were significant at p < .02. Individual comparisons among grades for the natural kinds showed the kindergartners differed significantly from second graders, fourth graders, and adults (Scheffé test, p < . 05); no other differences were significant (although the second grade/adult difference was marginally significant (p < .10)).

These patterns were consistently found with a more fine-grained item analysis. Thus, essentially the same pattern was found for each of the natural kind and artifact terms, with a significant age effect for all natural kinds and none for any of the artifacts (using one-way ANOVAs). There were also no significant differences among the scores on the various natural kind terms. A few children in each group (2 kindergartners, 2 second graders, 1 fourth grader) responded that the discoveries did in fact change the type of a majority of the artifacts. It should be noted that in all such cases the child said that the discoveries changed the type of all the natural kinds as well. These few children are likely to have employed a general response strategy of saying that the discovery was always relevant, but they were a clear minority. It should also be noted that no child ever said that the natural kind discoveries were irrelevant but that the artifact discoveries were, suggesting again that they would make the positive relevance judgment for artifacts only when they also did so for natural kinds.

In sum, there is a strong developmental effect along the predicted lines. Children at all ages seem to treat artifacts in essentially the same manner with no significant age changes, yet they display a dramatic shift in the way they treat natural kinds. There was no significant difference between the responses for animals and the responses for plants, although the scores for plants generally lagged behind those for animals.

As before, a few excerpts from the transcripts will help to illustrate in more detail how and why the children gave the answers they did. Consider some kindergarten transcripts for natural kinds in which the children tended to deny the importance of the discovery. (All of these responses were assigned scores of 1.)

K(1) (Dog/cat)
C: Dog.
E: And how do you know?
C: They're the same size as dogs and cats don't have long noses like dogs.
E: How come they have the inside parts of cats and cat mommies and cat babies?
C: Their mother was born like a cat and the cat, when the cat comes out it grows into a dog.
E: The cat grows into a dog, that's strange. I have never heard of that before. Is there any way this could be a cat?
C: No.

K(2) Dog/cat
C: Dogs, 'cause cats are a whole lot smaller, 'cause I've seen them and I have one too. I have seen dogs too...you see I don't have one but I've seen them all around the neighborhood...etc. (tangent about dog in neighborhood).
E: How come if this is a dog, the bones and insides and parents are cats?
C: Because (matter-of-factly) they have the same bones as cats.
(Again, a common response.)
E: How can two cat parents have a dog baby?
C: They can't.
E: This animal's parents were cats.
C: They probably think that two dogs are cats.
E: No, their parents really are cats.

C: Oh, that's funny.
E: Could this be a special kind of cat that looks like a dog?
C: No, it's a dog!
(Note that although the child in justifying her responses was willing to say that dog parents might look like cats, she was not willing to say that this animal that looked like a cat could really be a dog.)

K(2) Horse/cow
C: They're horses.
E: How do you know that?
C: 'Cause that could never be true, a horse could never raise a cow.
E: But the parents of this animal were cows and the insides are of a cow, so what are these animals?
C: (Impatiently) Horses.
E: And what makes you say horses?
C: Because they look like horses and I've seen horses and they have exactly the same wool, and I've seen some with white stripes there and a dot on top there and brown all over their bodies.
E: How come their babies are cows and their parents and insides are cows? How could that happen to a horse?
C: I don't know.
E: Is there any way this could be a special kind of cow that looks like a horse?
C: Oh...it is a cow-horse.
E: It can't be both, it has got to be one or the other.
C: I've heard of cow-horses before.
E: It's got to be one or the other.
C: I give up.
E: What do you think?
C: A horse.
E: Is there any way this could be a cow that looks like a horse?
C: Well, I bet anyway horses have the same inside bones of cows.
E: I thought that the insides of horses and cows were different and that they had cow bones...so what do you think they are?
C: Horses.

K(5) Pine tree/oak tree
C: Pine trees.
E: And how do you know that?
C: Because you hang things on them at Christmastime and you put presents under them.
E: Can you do that with an oak tree?

C: Nope.
E: How come it grew from an oak tree and has the insides of an oak?
C: I don't know.
E: Could this be a special kind of oak that looks like a pine?
C: No.

K(7) Dog/cat
C: Dogs...because cats do not go rooofff, and it might be just that God made them that way.
E: So even though they had the inside parts of cats and their parents and babies are cats, they're still dogs?
C: Because God wanted them to have cats...
E: To have cat babies?
C: Yes.
E: So what do you think these animals are?
C: Dogs.
(Religious justifications did not seem to predict type of response and were equally often used to justify responses scored 1 and 3.)

Most kindergartners assumed that the discovery was irrelevant to the type of the natural kind. A few, however, showed more sophisticated understanding. Consider, for example, the following kindergartner who seemed to understand the central importance of the parents (scored as a 3).

K(8) Horse/cow
C: They're horse-cows.
E: Oh, they can't be both...it's either one or the other.
C: I think they're cows.
E: And how do you know?
C: Because if it was a cow, if it had a baby, then it has to be a cow! If it was a horse, then it would have to be a baby horse.
E: These animals had baby cows.
C: Maybe if they found out the animals and the horse were taking care of the cows, they were babysitters.
E: They looked just like this, but the insides (repeats description) and had their own baby cows.
C: Maybe that's just a story.
E: So which are they?
C: Oh...can't you just tell me?
E: I can't tell you until we're all done.
C: It looks like a cow.
E: That's a funny-looking cow, how do you think that happened?

C: I think they couldn't draw a cow, so they drew a horse.
E: These are real animals, so is this really a cow?
C: Yes.

Notice that this child takes pains to distinguish between parental type behavior (babysitting) and true parentage (the biological concept). This is an important distinction discussed further in chapters 11, 12, and 13. Note also that the child distinguishes appearance from reality in her attempts to make sense of the story. (These sorts of transcripts also indicated that in later studies the relations between the animals should be made somewhat closer and more plausible.)

The older children for the most part also judged the discoveries to be relevant and usually did so with strong convictions, although these seemed to be weaker (as seen through hesitations) for the plant terms. The following transcripts are again useful illustrations (all received scores of 3):

2(1) Apple/pear
C: They're still pears, 'cause just the skin is covered with apple skin.
E: How do you think that happened?
C: They just grew that way.
E: Is there any way these could be apples?
C: No.

2(1a) Pine tree/oak tree
C: Oak trees.
E: How do you know?
C: It's a pine tree.
E: It's got to be one or the other.
C: It's a pine tree.
E: How do you know?
C: Because if it still can grow pine cones on it, it's still a pine tree.
E: How come it's got all the inside parts of an oak tree? And grew from an acorn?
C: I don't know.
E: Can a pine tree grow from an acorn?
C: No.
E: So what do you think these trees are?
C: Oak trees.
E: I know it's hard to make up your mind, so what is it?
C: Oak trees.
E: And how do you know that?
C: 'Cause (long pause) it grew from an acorn.

E: How could they look like a pine tree?
C: (Pause)...(shrug)

Note that this child was tempted to say "pine tree" for a deeper reason than younger children—namely, because of the more biological principle that it could produce pine cones, not merely because it looked like a pine tree or was used as a Christmas tree. This illustrates the subtleties of how emerging knowledge influences responses.

2(3) Horse/cow
E: Cow or horse?
C: What about just under the skin?
E: They had all the insides of cows (repeats description). What are they?
C: Cows...well, it doesn't really matter what they are outside...do they act like cows?
E: I know that people ride them, and they make a sound of a horse, but when the scientists studied the insides, and their babies (repeats description), they said cows.
C: I think they're cows, but how could they look like horses if their parents were cows?
E: I don't know...If it's a cow, how could it wind up looking just like a horse?
C: Maybe someone skinned the cow and put a horse skin on it instead.
E: But if this were a real animal, ...
C: Well, I still think it's a cow.

2(4) Horse/cow
C: Cows.
E: And how did you know?
C: Their brain and their bones.
E: They look like horses on the outside...how did that happen?
C: I don't know. Probably something happened when the baby was born.
E: Then this could be a special kind of cow that just looks like a horse?
C: Yes.
E: Then if you had to say which one this is?
C: A cow.

2(5) Pine tree/oak tree
C: Oak trees.
E: How did you decide they're oak trees?

C: Their seeds...and they just have different kinds of pines and not leaves.

E: Can it still be an oak tree if they still decorate it at Christmas?

C: Yes.

E: Can it still be an oak tree if looks like a pine tree?

C: Yes.

4(1) Apple/pear

C: Pears.

E: How do you know?

C: Because the seeds, when you plant the seeds a pear tree would grow, and if it were an apple, an apple tree would grow. They've got the insides of a pear and an apple wouldn't have the insides of a pear if it wasn't a pear.

E: Then how come it looks like this?

C: It's been sitting out for a long time and it turned red.

E: And it doesn't have a pear shape?...How did that happen?

C: (Shrug)

4(2) Horse/cow

C: Cows, they have to be.

E: And how do you know that?

C: Because, they're cows, they have a cow body and after they, um, they had cows.

E: How come they look like a horse?

C: Maybe there was something wrong with them?

E: So is it a special kind of cow that just looks like a horse?

C: Yeah...they can do that...I've seen a cow with a horse tail. They just *look* like a horse...and some cows got this white thing in front too.

(Note how these children are willing to say that the characteristic features are optional, but never the theoretically central ones.)

4(3) Dog/cat

C: They're cats, they just look like dogs.

E: Even though they go woof and chase after cars?

C: Well, I'd have to say they're still cats, because they're continuously cats, through the life of the parent one and now this one and the babies that are going to be born, it's always cats, and it's not like different animals being ground up and mushed together, looking like one thing one generation and another thing in another generation, they've been cats all along and just happen to look like dogs this time.

E: So even though everyone calls these cats dogs, they are really cats?

C: *Yes.*

For reasons of space I have omitted samples of the adult transcripts. All of them look like those of the most sophisticated fourth graders.

The consistency of the subjects' responses should be stressed. In 19 of the 27 cases when a subject gave a clearly scorable response that the discovery was irrelevant for any of the four natural kind terms, responses for the other three were scored in the same way. The pattern is even stronger if scores of 2 are excluded from the analysis. This pattern strongly suggests that the shift represents a general biological insight that extends to all common biological entities (it may not extend to the exotic or unusual) and does not occur on a case-by-case basis.

There is less to report about the artifact transcripts since they reveal no developmental change in judgments about the relevance of the discovery. Nonetheless, the patterns of justification do change with age, indicating increased sophistication in the understanding of artifact categories as well, an increase that fits nicely with the study on tool terms described in chapter 5. Consider the following excerpts from transcripts of children in each of the three grades. (Again, adult transcripts are roughly like those of the most sophisticated fourth graders.)

K(1) Cup/bowling ball

C: Cups.

E: And how do you know?

C: They look like cups? *(question intonation)*

E: Even though they are made out of the same material as bowling balls?

C: (Nods yes)

E: Is there any way at all it could be a bowling ball?

C: (Shakes head no)

K(3) Boot/sail

C: Boots.

E: And how do you know?

C: They look like you can wear them on your feet.

E: Can they still be boots if they're made of sails?

C: Yes.

K(4) Key/penny

C: Keys.

E: Why?

C: Because it's not circled.

E: What else?

C: Because it's got one of these, a straight line (pointing to the length of the key).

E: Even though it's made of the same insides as pennies, it's still a key?

C: Yes.

2(1) Boot/sail

C: A mixture of both.

E: If you had to decide?

C: I'd say boots, but they used to be sails.

E: Are they boots now?

C: (Long pause)...Boots, I think.

E: And how did you decide?

C: Because they made a piece of sail into boots.

E: Can it still be a boot if it's made of a sail?

C: Yeah, it doesn't matter what something is made of. If it's leather, it's still skin.

2(2) Boot/sail

C: Boots.

E: Why did you say boots?

C: 'Cause boots can be made of lots of different things.

E: So even though these are made of sail material, they're still boots?

C: Yes.

4(1) Cup/bowling ball

C: Cups.

E: How do you know that?

C: Because bowling balls are used to bowl down in an alley, and this is used to drink, so it's still a cup no matter what it's made of...like in the old times they used wood for cups.

E: So it doesn't matter that this is made of the same stuff that bowling balls are made of?

C: No.

4(2) Boot/sail

C: They have to be boots because you wouldn't put a boot up on a sailboat and go sailing.

E: So if it's made out of the same material, which one is it?

C: Boots, who says a boot has to be made out of leather, or plastic, or materials? The company can make them out of whatever they want.

4(4) Cup/bowling ball
C: They're used for the same purpose as cups and they look like cups and you can drink from them and you can't bowl with them, they're definitely cups!
E: Can they still be cups if they're made out of the same stuff as bowling balls?
C: Yeah...and if you could melt down a glass and make it into a bowling ball without breaking it to bits, it would still be a bowling ball and not a cup.

There is an apparent developmental pattern here of an increasing awareness of the arbitrariness of the underlying substance for artifacts. The younger children tended simply to state that if the object looked like *x*, it was *x*. These children also mentioned function, but that trait was mentioned more often with increasing age. Finally, the most sophisticated children focused more on the notion that the underlying substance was irrelevant as long as the function was satisfied. The older the children were, the less often they referred to simple appearance, a pattern that was also seen in the hand tool domain in chapter 5. An important issue for further work is whether this increasing awareness of artifacts and the arbitrariness of their substances is linked with emerging knowledge of natural kinds. A much more systematic exploration of artifact concepts along these lines would be needed, however, to determine whether this linkage is real or merely coincidental.

In sum, the results of the first discoveries study were as predicted. In the understanding of natural kinds, there seems to be a shift from representations based on salient perceptual and behavioral characteristic features to representations for which central principles of biological theory are most important. How these tenets are represented is an issue to be addressed in more detail in later chapters. Based on the data collected so far and on the transcripts, it is apparent that the children cite both internal parts/substance and origins/offspring properties in their justifications. Of course, since these are the principles provided to them, this is hardly surprising.

Perhaps the only slightly surprising finding was that no significant pattern of differences emerged in responses for animals and plants, even though these might be expected to develop at their own rates as independent conceptual domains. Other work has found some difference in how children of this age think about the properties of plants and animals (see, for example, Keil 1983), so this lack of a difference should be kept in mind as we consider the other studies described below.

The procedures used in this study were not perfectly uniform, in that the probes varied between "how could" questions and "even though" questions. There was no difference in results for these question types, but more uniformity would have been preferable.

A Replication and Lead-In Study for the Transformations Paradigm

The results of the first discoveries study were robust and basically the same for all items in the same category (natural kind or artifact). We decided to conduct an additional study to ask more detailed questions about the developmental pattern and, perhaps most important, to test a new stimulus set of term pairs that could work well in transformations studies (to be described in chapter 9). We wanted to see what the data would be for the same items using the discoveries paradigm. A broader range of natural kind categories was also used to assess whether there might not be differences among the various subdomains of animals, plants, and inanimate natural kinds. The questioning procedure was made fully consistent by always using the "even though" format. Finally, the pairs were made more similar to each other so as to reduce the occasional reactions of disbelief by older children for some of the natural kind discoveries. We could only assign scores to children's judgments if they were willing to grant that the actual scenarios described were possible. Only after that possibility is granted can the child then be asked to identify the described entity. Thus, extensive piloting was used to arrive at a set of pairs for which the scenarios were judged to be possible.

Stimuli

Many more stimuli were used in this study, creating some subject fatigue problems that were not picked up in the piloting. The stimulus pairs are shown in table 8.3.

Table 8.3
Stimulus pairs used in the second discoveries study

Natural kinds	Artifacts
Sheep/goat	Kitchen pipe/flute
Tiger/lion	Playing cards/toilet paper
Chicken/turkey	Tire/boot
Raccoon/skunk	Plastic milk bottle/flipflops
Horse/zebra	Garbage can/chair
Diamond/pearl	Coffeepot/birdfeeder
Lead/gold	Bobby pin/needle
Grapefruit/orange	Tie/shoelace

Since animal stimuli usually yielded the most interesting transcripts in the first study, they dominated the natural kind stimuli in this study. We also included one plant pair and added two inanimate pairs: lead/gold and diamond/pearl. Diamond/pearl was included as an especially difficult case given the artifact-like properties of these natural kinds described in chapter 3. It was expected that the characteristic feature to principled theory shift should occur late for the two nonbiological natural kinds and perhaps especially so for the diamond/pearl item.

The descriptions shown in table 8.4 and the accompanying illustrations shown in figure 8.2 are good examples of the stimulus set.

Procedure
The procedure was essentially the same as that used in the first discovery study except that more care was taken to standardize the probe questions. Unfortunately, our piloting did not inform us as well as we had

Table 8.4
Examples of descriptions used in the second discoveries study

---

Natural kind: Raccoon/skunk
There are animals that live out on a farm near Dryden and they look just like this (shows picture of raccoon). They prowl around houses a lot and sometimes eat garbage, and they like to wash their food in streams. Well, some scientists went and studied these animals very carefully with microscopes and other sorts of stuff, and when they looked at them and their insides, they found out that they weren't like most raccoons at all. The scientists found out that they had the blood of skunks, the bones of skunks, the brains of skunks, and all the other inside parts of skunks rather than those of raccoons. And they found out that these animals' mommies and daddies were skunks and that when they had babies their babies were skunks. So their mommies and daddies look just like this (points to picture of skunk) and their babies look just like this (points to picture of skunk). What do you think they really are, raccoons or skunks?

Artifact: Coffeepot/birdfeeder
There are these things that look just like this (shows picture of coffeepot), and they are made in a big factory in Buffalo for people to make coffee in. They put the coffee grounds in here and then they add water and heat it all up on the stove and then they have coffee. A while ago some scientists looked at these things carefully and they found out they aren't like most coffeepots at all, because when they looked at them under a microscope, they found out that they were not made out of the same stuff as most coffeepots. Instead they came from birdfeeders like this (points to picture of birdfeeder) which had been melted down and then made into these (points to picture of coffeepot) and when people were all done making coffee with these, they melted them down again and made birdfeeders out of them. What are they, birdfeeders or coffeepots?

Natural kind

Raccoon/Skunk

Artifact

Coffeepot/Birdfeeder

Figure 8.2
Examples of drawings that accompanied descriptions used in the second discoveries study

hoped of the time needed to interview each child adequately, and given the time allotted us by the school districts involved and the time available to the experimenter, all children did the whole set in only one session each. There is no doubt that this reduced the length of the transcripts and fatigued the children.

The subjects were 11 kindergartners, 18 second graders, and 17 fourth graders, the kindergarten group being smaller than the others because of illness and time constraints. (Average ages were 5:11, 7:9, 9:10 years, respectively.) All were from public schools in Syracuse, New York.

Results
The mean scores for all natural kinds and all artifacts are shown in figure 8.3. The overall pattern of results was the same as that found in the first study, although it was not as strong. The results show a significant main effect for stimulus type (artifact vs. natural kind) (p < .01), as well as an age-by-kind interaction (p < .02). In separate one-way ANOVAs, only the

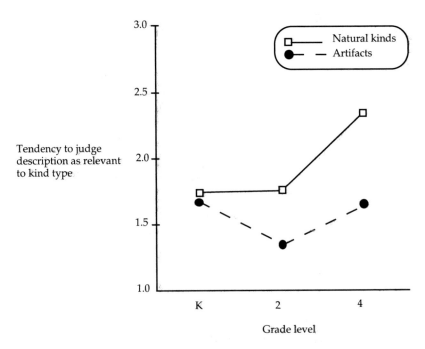

Figure 8.3
Mean scores for natural kind and artifact terms in second discoveries study. 1 = judgment that discovery did not change kind type, 2 = judgment indicating genuine indecision as to whether the discovery changed kind type, 3 = judgment that discovery did change kind type.

natural kind scores showed significant increases with age. Scheffé tests on adjacent age differences showed the second-to-fourth- grade change for natural kinds to be significant (in contrast to the kindergarten-to-second-grade change in the first discoveries study). There were no significant differences among scores on the three natural kind types although an individual t-test of plants vs. animals revealed a trend at the $p < .07$ level.

A more fine-grained item analysis again revealed strong consistency in these results. In eight out of eight cases the natural kind terms showed an increase in judgments that the discovered properties were the final arbiters of what the object was. For the artifacts, only four out of eight items showed any age increase, and all of these were smaller than those found for the natural kinds. As in the first study, a small number of children seemed to give the same answer for all items. The following examples from the transcripts should suffice to illustrate the results of this study. (In these transcripts the kindergartners' responses received scores of 1 and the fourth graders' responses received scores of 3.)

K(1) (Raccoon/skunk)
C: Raccoon.
E: Why?
C: Because a raccoon is fatter and that (points to picture of skunk)...and that has black and white and that (raccoon) is black and dark black.
E: So even though this special animal has the inside parts of a skunk and its mommy and daddy were skunks that looked just like this and its babies were skunks, you think the best name for it is what?
C: A raccoon.
E: Why?
C: Because the raccoon is fat and the skunk is skinny and it doesn't have the same skin because the skunk has black and white and the raccoon has light black and dark black.

K(2) Tiger/lion
C: Tiger.
E: Why?
C: Because it has stripes.
E: Now even though this special animal has the inside parts of a lion and its mommies and daddies were lions and when it has babies they are lions . . .(pause) . . .the best name for this special animal is what? Lion or tiger?
C: Tiger.

E: And what is your reason?
C: Because of the stripes on it.

K(3) Coffeepot/birdfeeder
C: A coffeepot.
E: Why?
C: Because it doesn't look like a birdfeeder. I wouldn't put birdseed in it . . .I would put coffee in the coffeepot.
E: So even though this special object was made from birdfeeders that look just like this and when they were done with them, they melt them down and make birdfeeders again, you think the best name for it is what? A birdfeeder or a coffeepot?
C: Coffeepot.
E: And your reason?
C: Because it doesn't look like a birdfeeder and I wouldn't put birdseed in it.

4(1) Raccoon/skunk
C: I'd say a skunk...yes, a skunk.
E: Why?
C: Because it has everything that a skunk has only it doesn't...only the outside parts of it doesn't look like that. And its babies were a skunk and its parents were a skunk.
E: Does it matter that it looks like that (points to picture of raccoon) or that it paws through your trash or that it doesn't stink?
C: Not really, not really.

4(2) Horse/zebra
C: Zebra.
E: Why?
C: Because it has the insides like a zebra, the blood like a zebra.
E: Was it important what it looked like? Did it matter that it looked like this?
C: Yes.
E: Why?
C: I don't know.
E: (Repeats story) So what is the best name?
C: Zebra.
E: Why?
C: Because it has the insides like a zebra and it has brains and cells and it's going to have babies like it.
E: Is it important what the animal looks like?
C: Yes.

E: Why?

C: Because people will think it's a horse and it's not.

In sum, the second study replicated the results of the first, although somewhat less dramatically. This seems to be a likely consequence of an older kindergarten group, a more rushed procedure, a smaller subject population, and the necessity of having the children respond to all items at one sitting.

Conclusions

The two discoveries studies show a clear difference in the development of response patterns for artifacts and natural kinds. At all ages children judge that artifacts remain the same despite the discovery that their origins and internal parts are more like those of other artifact kinds. Thus, there were no significant age trends for answers on these items. However, more subtle changes were found in the children's patterns of justifications for the artifact terms, changes that parallel those found for the tool terms in the study described in chapter 5.

The artifact results are most useful as a contrast to the developmental patterns observed for the natural kind terms. In both studies there was a definite shift in responses from those that referred almost exclusively to characteristic features and denied the importance of the discovered properties to those that focused on the discovered origins, offspring, and internal parts. This was clear both from the scores and from the transcripts. The patterns suggest an increasing appreciation of the central importance of the biological principles that organize adults' intuitive theories of biology. It seems likely that many of the younger children might have had some awareness that cows have cow blood and bones and so on, but they did not appreciate the special importance of these properties and in fact subordinated them to the behavioral and appearance-based ones, or at least they did not think of such inside parts as crucial distinguishers among species even if they are functionally very important to each animal. Other children felt that the principled features had to be in accord with the characteristic ones and, as shown by some of the sample transcripts, they tended to deny the information about the principled features, claiming that the scientists must have been wrong or that the insides of both natural kinds were the same.

This developmental pattern seems analogous to the characteristic-to-defining shift described earlier, but it does not provide a complete picture of what the children are shifting to, other than some set of principled beliefs that are not directly assessed. The studies that follow in chapters 9 through 11 seek to better understand how children come to override the characteristic features and on what sort of conceptual basis they do so.

These results should *not* be interpreted as showing that kindergartners view artifacts and natural kinds as essentially the same and then come to distinguish them. Although their responses are quite similar for the two kinds, there is good reason to expect that they fully distinguish the two broad classes. This has been shown in other work (see, for example, Keil 1983; Gelman 1987) and in studies described later in this book. The results do suggest that for both artifacts and natural kinds, the younger children have shallower theories and consequently tend to rely more on atheoretical similarity spaces of the sorts that Quine postulated. They are not completely atheoretical, as we shall see, but their theories are less useful in helping them to draw fundamental categorical distinctions.

The discoveries paradigm has certain limitations that help motivate some of the different kinds of studies that follow. Perhaps the most important limitation is that the method used here makes assumptions about the nature of the essence or underlying theoretical principles that should come to override characteristic features. For the general developmental account to be true, however, it is not at all necessary that children initially, or even eventually, come up with the same theories of essence as those of standard Western biology. The notion of a causal homeostatic cluster that comes to override mere probabilistic distributions of characteristic features does not require that the homeostatic cluster take a particular form; as noted in chapter 3, several different clusters might work quite well for the same set of terms. Consequently, children might not be as swayed by blood, bones, and lineage as by other principled properties in their own somewhat idiosyncratic theories. These might include other views on how natural kinds come into existence or on what their insides are like. It is desirable, therefore, to use a different technique that does not supply the children with a fixed set of principled features but instead allows them to rely on a variety of different features that might be more relevant to their own belief systems.

A second possible limitation of the discoveries studies is that a mature response evaluates the actions and discoveries of experts as being critically relevant to the identification of natural kinds. The differences between the natural kind and artifact responses make it clear that the older children were not blindly giving in to the priority of the features the scientists discovered regardless of the category involved, and the transcripts indicate that their justifications were based on more than simple deference to scientists. Nonetheless, it would be desirable to use a technique in which a mature response would evaluate the actions of experts as irrelevant to the true nature of natural kinds and relevant to the nature of artifacts—in other words, just the opposite of the technique used in this study. The study described in chapter 9 develops such a technique.

Chapter 9
Transformations on Natural Kinds and Artifacts

Discoveries are not the only way that our beliefs about the nature of instances can be changed. We can also encounter transformations on properties of those instances; and if the properties and method of transformation are of an appropriate sort, we may judge the instances to have become members of a different kind.

This suggests asking children whether artifacts and natural kinds remain members of the same kinds after transformations that change their most salient characteristic features into those of contrasting natural kinds. A method was therefore developed in which children were given descriptions of doctors who performed operations on natural kinds and artifacts whereby their most salient behavioral and perceptual properties were changed into those of another kind within the same general category (that is, artifact into artifact, animal into animal, and so on). The children were then asked to judge what sort of thing the object really was and to justify their responses. It was predicted that younger children, who have less well developed theories about what biological properties are central to a kind, would view the operations as changing the types of the natural kinds, whereas the older children would not; moreover, it was predicted that all children and adults should see the operation as changing the types of the artifacts.

Method
The same kind pairs were used as in the second discoveries study described in chapter 8. It was decided that if the discovered properties in that study belonged to kind x (say, a skunk) and the characteristic properties belonged to kind y (a raccoon), then in the operations paradigm the preoperation animal should have same characteristic properties as kind y, whereas the postoperation animal should have the same characteristic features as kind x. Table 9.1 shows the term pairs used in the study; in each pair the first term describes the preoperation state, and the second describes the postoperation state. The descriptions given in table 9.2 illustrate how the stimuli were constructed (the full set of descriptions is listed in appendix 6).

Table 9.1
Stimulus pairs used in the first transformations study

Natural kinds	Artifacts
Sheep/goat	Kitchen pipe/flute
Tiger/lion	Playing cards/toilet paper
Chicken/turkey	Tire/boot
Raccoon/skunk	Plastic milk bottle/flipflops
Horse/zebra	Garbage can/chair
Diamond/ pearl	Coffeepot/birdfeeder
Lead/gold	Bobby pin/needle
Grapefruit/orange	Tie/shoelace

Table 9.2
Examples of two descriptions used in the first transformations study

Natural kind: Raccoon/skunk
The doctors took a raccoon (show picture of raccoon) and shaved away some of its fur. They dyed what was left all black. Then they bleached a single stripe all white down the center of its back. Then, with surgery (explained to child in preamble), they put in its body a sac of super smelly odor, just like a skunk has (with younger children "odor" was replaced with "super smelly yucky stuff"). When they were all done, the animal looked like this (show picture of skunk). After the operation was this a skunk or a raccoon? (Both pictures were present at the time of the final question.)

Artifact: Coffeepot/birdfeeder
The doctors took a coffeepot that looked like this (show picture of coffeepot). They sawed off the handle, sealed the top, took off the top knob, sealed closed the spout, and sawed it off. They also sawed off the base and attached a flat piece of metal. They attached a little stick, cut a window in it, and filled the metal container with birdfood. When they were done, it looked like this (show picture of birdfeeder). After the operation was this a coffeepot or a birdfeeder? (Both pictures were present at the time of the final question.)

The descriptions highlighted the most salient characteristic features for the two kinds in each pair so that the operation changed virtually all the important characteristic features into those of a different kind. These features are a subset of those provided when college students were asked to generate the most typical features of the kinds shown in table 9.1, in a task very similar to that used by Rosch and Mervis (1975). Thus, it could be argued that precisely the sort of characteristic-feature-based information that has been believed to form the basis for prototype concepts (Rosch and Mervis 1975) was used in these tasks to describe animals in the pre- and postoperation states.

Procedure
The procedure was similar to that used in the discoveries studies except that many children, especially the younger ones, required more than one session over successive school days to finish all the items. Before each session a preamble was given in which the doctors were introduced and the notion of operations and surgery was described.

The follow-up questions were very similar to those used in the second discoveries study. After each judgment the experimenter asked why the child made that judgment and then posed an "even though" question stressing the features of the kind the child did *not* pick. Thus, if a child said that the raccoon/skunk animal was now a skunk, the experimenter asked, "So even though it started out as a raccoon and looked just like this, you think it's a what?" The experimenter also frequently pushed the children further to make sure they knew at the outset that the pre-operational animal was, say, a real raccoon by telling them at that point that it had real raccoon parents and real raccoon babies. The entire description was repeated if there was any reason to suspect that the child had missed parts of it. In addition, the children were often asked to repeat parts of the description. As before, children who suggested that the final animal was a blend (say, a "racunk") were told that it really was just one or the other and were asked to choose.

All responses and questions were tape-recorded and transcribed. The transcripts were scored by two independent judges on a three-point scale. A score of 1 meant that the child had relied on characteristic features throughout (and thus viewed the kind as being changed by the operation). A score of 3 meant that the child had relied on some other, deeper set of principles to overrule the characteristic features (and thus viewed type of kind as being preserved). Scores of 2 were less common and meant that the child was in a transitional state, vacillating between characteristic features and deeper principles.

The subjects in this study consisted of 21, 17, and 18 children in grades K, 2, and 4. (Average ages were 5:8, 7:6, and 9:9 years, respectively.) All were from public schools in Tompkins County, New York.

Results

Figure 9.1 summarizes the results of the study by showing the mean scores for all artifact and natural kind term pairs as a function of age. The general developmental pattern of the discoveries studies is clearly repeated. There is a strong shift in response types for the natural kind terms (p < .001) and no significant age change for the artifact terms (a two-way ANOVA shows main effect of age and kind type and an age-by-kind interaction, all significant at the p < .001 level). Separate ANOVAs showed that the scores for minerals were lower than those for both animals and plants (p < .001) (with no significant interactions); scores for plants were also significantly lower than scores for animals (p < .05). For the natural kinds, both the kindergarten/second grade and the second/fourth grade differences were significant by Scheffé tests (p < .05).

Item analysis reveals strong consistency in the results. For eight out of eight natural kind pairs, scores increased significantly with age, whereas none of the eight artifact pairs exhibited an age-related increase (as shown by one-way ANOVAs). An important new finding of this study

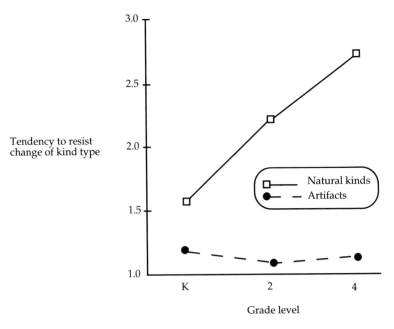

Tendency to resist change of kind type

Grade level

Figure 9.1
Mean scores for natural kind and artifact terms in the first transformations study. 1 = judgment that operation changed kind type, 2 = judgment indicating indecision as to whether operation changed kind type, 3 = judgment that operation did not change kind type.

was that not all natural kinds shifted at the same time. In particular, although all of the biological kinds (five animal pairs and one plant pair) shifted at roughly the same time, the two nonbiological kind pairs showed a highly significant lag. This lag was predicted in both the discoveries and the operations study, based on the notion that theories of the essential nature of minerals, elements, and the like should take longer to develop than such theories for biological kinds. The different curves for the two natural kind types are shown in figure 9.2.

As always, individual responses offer additional insight into the developmental process. The following excerpts from kindergartners' transcripts for the natural kind and artifact terms are typical (all received scores of 1):

Natural kinds
  K(1) Raccoon/skunk
  C: Now a skunk because they changed it into a skunk all smelly, yucky stuff.

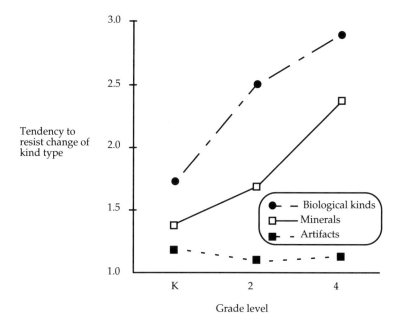

Figure 9.2
Mean scores for biological vs. mineral kinds in the first transformations study. 1 = judgment that operation changed kind type, 2 = judgment indicating genuine indecision as to whether operation changed kind type, 3 = judgment that operation did not change kind type.

E: What about the mommies and daddies? They were raccoons. Was it still a skunk?
C: Yes.
E: And when it had babies, its babies were raccoons. Was it still a skunk?
C: Yes.

K(2) Raccoon/skunk
C: They made it into a skunk.
E: Why do you think it's a skunk?
C: Because I just do.
E: Why do you think it's a skunk?
C: Because they MADE IT INTO A SKUNK!
E: What about it makes it a skunk?
C: I don't know.
E: Could it still be a raccoon or did they make it into a skunk?
C: Inside it's, I guess it's a...a...I guess it's a...raccoon.
E: Well, which do you think the animal really is? Do you think it's really a raccoon or do you think it's really a skunk?
C: A raccoon!
E: Can it be a...
C: (Interrupting) It's a skunk.
E: Which do you really mean?
C: A skunk.
E: Can it be a skunk if its mommies and daddies were raccoons?
C: Yes.
E: Can it be a skunk if its babies were raccoons?
C: Yes.
E: (Repeats entire story) Which do you think it really was?
C: A skunk. Because it looks like a skunk, it smells like a skunk, it acts like a skunk, and it sounds like a skunk. *(The child was not told this.)*
E: So it can be a skunk even though its babies are raccoons?
C: Yes!

K(3) Horse/zebra
C: Zebra, because horses don't have black and white stripes in their skin.
E: Can it be a zebra if its mommy and daddy were horses?
C: Yes.
E: And can it be a zebra if its babies were horses?
C: Yes.

K(5) Sheep/goat
C: A goat.
E: Can it be a goat even though its mommy and daddy are sheep?
C: I don't know.
E: What do you think is really right? (repeats entire story)
C: Goat.
E: Why isn't it a sheep?
C: Because they cut off all its hair.
E: Can it be a goat if its mommy and daddy were sheep?
C: Yes.
E: Can it be a goat if it has baby sheep?
C: Yes.

Several kindergartners, though ultimately deciding that kind membership was changed, were nonetheless troubled that the transformed animals had babies of the original kind of animal. The information about parents had less influence on them. They therefore may have had some inkling that the type of baby matters, but not enough to override the salient characteristic features.

As these beliefs become more sophisticated, the children start to rely on them more in their judgments. The following excerpts from the second and fourth graders' transcripts show how they used this knowledge to decide that kind membership was not changed (all were given scores of 3). When possible, at the end of sessions in which children had given different patterns of responses for artifacts and natural kinds, they were asked what it was about the two classes that made them answer differently. A few excerpts from these exchanges are given as well.

2(1) Sheep/goat
C: Sheep, because that's how they started out.
E: Even though it looked like a goat and it climbed mountains?
C: It *looked* like one.

2(3) Raccoon/skunk
C: Raccoon...just because they made it look like a skunk, it's not really one.
E: Why is it still a raccoon? It looks just likes a skunk...
C: It looks just like a skunk and it has its smell.
E: But it's still a raccoon?
C: Yes.
E: Why could you change a pipe into a flute, but you couldn't change a raccoon into a skunk?
C: One's alive and one's not.

2(4) Tiger/lion
C: It looks like a lion, but it's a tiger.
E: Why do you think it's a tiger and not a lion?
C: Because it was made out of a tiger.
E: And why isn't it a lion?
C: It's a lion a little bit, but not very much.
E: It's not both...one or the other...
C: A tiger.
E: Why did you choose tiger instead of lion?
C: Because, even though it looks more like a lion, it's a tiger.
E: What about it makes you think it's a tiger and not a lion if it looks like a lion?
C: (Pause)
E: Maybe something about the story will help you put it in words. (repeats entire story)
C: I'd say it's still a tiger.
E: What made it a tiger and not a lion?
C: The way it was before?

(Same child)
E: What is the difference between the problems where you said the thing was changed and where you said the thing wasn't changed, such as the chicken/turkey problem vs. the shoelace/tie one?
C: The animals were alive so they could have babies...so you tell what it is.
E: Why isn't that true for things like the coffeepot and the tire?
C: Because what they're made of isn't alive.

2(5) Diamond/pearl
C: Diamond.
E: Why do you think that?
C: Because...well, if you just dip it into liquid, it would just still be a diamond...because they cut off edges and everything.
E: Why?
C: I don't know.
E: It looks and feels like a pearl, why isn't it a pearl?
C: Because it came from a diamond.

4(1) Grapefruit/orange
C: It's still a grapefruit with orange flavoring.
E: Why do you say that?
C: First it was a grapefruit and then they dipped it in orange and put the flavor in it...and some people might think it was a real

orange.
E: But why do you think it's not a real orange?
C: Because when it grew, it grew like a real grapefruit, it was grown to be grapefruit.
E: So even though everyone thinks it's an orange, it's really a grapefruit?
C: Yes.

4(2) Chicken/turkey
C: Chicken, because all they did was rearrange the feathers and give it a shot and make it taste like a turkey, but if it still hatches chickens and its mother and father were chickens, it has to be a chicken.
E: So even though it looks, sounds, and tastes like a turkey, it's still a chicken?
C: Yes.

(Same child)
E: What's the difference between the lead, the grapefruit, and the tiger that couldn't be made into new things and the garbage can which was made into a chair?
C: Those things are living and have babies.
E: But lead doesn't have babies.
C: But lead's a natural resource, you can't really change it into another resource unless it's in the age that they have some special formula.
E: So natural things can't be changed?
C: Right.
E: So what would you call things that could be changed?
C: Man-made resources like if man made the pipe and so he could probably change it into something else.

As with the discoveries studies, although children at all ages received similar scores for the artifact terms, the transcripts revealed more subtle changes in their response justifications with increasing age.

Artifacts
K(1) Bobby pin/needle
C: Needle.
E: Why?
C: Because it has a sharp end and it's thin and it has a string through it.
E: And it wasn't a bobby pin anymore?
C: No.

E: Why not?
C: They changed it.
E: Why wasn't it a bobby pin? What was special about it that made it a needle?
C: Just changing everything.

K(2) Tie/shoelaces
C: They made it into a shoelace, because it looks like a shoelace.
E: Why isn't it a tie?
C: Because they cut it into small pieces.
E: Could it be a shoelace even though it came from a tie?
C: (Nods yes)

K(4) Coffeepot/birdfeeder
C: I think they made it into a birdfeeder because it doesn't have a spout, and coffeepots need spouts and it doesn't have a handle...and how are you supposed to hold onto it if it doesn't have a handle?
E: Can it be a birdfeeder even though it came from a coffeepot?
C: Yes.

K(5) Kitchen pipe/flute
C: I think they turned it into a flute.
E: Can it be a flute even though it came from a kitchen pipe?
C: Yes.
E: And how do you know it's a flute?
C: Because you can blow on it...

These younger children's responses appear to be quite similar to their answers for the natural kinds in that they refer heavily to salient characteristic features. Contrast their responses with those of older children:

2(1) Plastic milk bottle/flipflops
C: Flipflops.
E: Even though it came from a jug?
C: Yeah, but it would break.
E: Which would break?
C: The flipflops 'cause they're made out of glass. (*Note that this child thus insisted they were flipflops because of intended function even though he thought that they wouldn't qualify in real function.*)
E: No, the jug was made out of plastic. (repeats story)
C: Flipflops because they cut it up and made it into flipflops.
E: Even though it came from a jug, it couldn't be still a jug and it was flipflops instead?
C: (Nods yes)

E: Why couldn't it be a jug anymore?
C: Because they ruined it.

2(2) Tire/boot
C: Boot, because anything that isn't living you can turn into something else...but something living you can't. *(This was the second pair for this child; the first was raccoon/skunk.)*
E: Can it be a boot even though it came from a tire?
C: Yes.
(Note that although this child used the "living" explanation, he also said that neither the lead nor the diamond was changed.)

4(1) Garbage can/chair
C: Chair, because they made it sturdy enough.
E: And why wasn't it a garbage can anymore?
C: Because it was changed into a chair from a garbage can and they cut it all out and now the leftover pieces of garbage can are just pieces of junk.
E: So even though it came from a garbage can, it can be a chair?
C: Yes.

4(2) Garbage can/chair
C: Chair, because they cut off all those bits and they made it into a chair, and a person can sit on it.
E: So even though it came from a garbage can, it's a chair now?
C: Yes.

The shifts in explanations are not dramatic, but there is certainly a tendency for older children to refer more to function and less to appearance.

A Cross-Cultural Replication and Extension

Jeyifous (1986) reports on a cross-cultural replication of the operations study that explored judgments concerning the effects of operations among rural, urban poor, and urban elite members of the Yoruba people. The operations were performed on both natural kinds and artifacts, although, of course, the kinds transformed were often quite different from those used in Ithaca in an attempt to make them more culturally appropriate: for example, pig/goat, pawpaw/pineapple, chewing stick/ladle, table/chair. As with the characteristic-to-defining shift study, the most traditional, nonliterate, non-Western group exhibited shifts as dramatic as those found in Ithaca, whereas the urban poor exhibited a more complicated developmental pattern (again, see Jeyifous 1986 for much more on this topic). The following response of an 85-year-old unschooled rural farmer to one of the natural kind stimuli clearly illustrates how the more mature biological beliefs completely overrule characteristic features:

Pawpaw/pineapple
Some students took a pawpaw and stuck some green, pointed leaves on the top. Then they put small, prickly patches all over it. Now it looks like this—is it a pawpaw or a pineapple? (p. 169)

   "It's a pawpaw, because a pawpaw has its own structure from heaven and a pineapple its own origin. One cannot turn into the other." (pp. 134–135)

Conclusions

The operations paradigm clearly yielded the predicted pattern of results, which converged nicely with the results of the discoveries studies. It should be stressed that, in this paradigm, the child is only informed of characteristic features—no "essential" properties, or causal mechanisms, or paths to origins are mentioned. Nonetheless, the older children seem to rely on such "underlying" information to make a final judgment.

   In the next two chapters I describe follow-up studies using the same paradigm, which not only explore new issues arising from the results reported here but also fully replicate those results.

Chapter 10
Property Transformations and Intercategory
Distance

The transformations and discoveries studies described in chapters 8 and 9 provide evidence for a developmental shift in the sorts of features and relations that children consider important for judging an entity to belong to a given natural kind. Studies with many different stimulus pairs and widely divergent subject populations disclosed the same developmental phenomena. These phenomona raise several new questions that require further investigation.

Examining the basis for the shift uncovers concerns similar to those raised for the nominal kind studies. Given the stimulus items used, almost all the characteristic features were easily visible properties (the only exceptions being some of the behavioral statements that described habitual behaviors observed over long time spans). This correlation suggests a simpler explanation of the shift than the one I have been assuming. Perhaps it is instead a shift from perceptual to conceptual features or, more crudely, from what one can see to what one cannot. In other words, perhaps children are not incorporating underlying biological theories that undermine the characteristic features but are merely realizing that one must look beyond the immediately visible. Such an account is made less likely by children's justifications of their responses, in which they often refer to a variety of unobservable biological principles. Moreover, research by other investigators from a variety of perspectives would argue against such an explanation (see chapter 12). Nonetheless, it would be informative to demonstrate not only that there are ways in which the youngest of children can go beyond the immediately perceivable but also how these ways relate to emerging theories of biology.

A second issue raised by the discoveries and transformations studies is the extent to which young children are pure phenomenalists. Regardless of whether or not they are perceptually bound, the data presented so far do suggest that they are slavishly tied to representations in the Quinean sense—in other words, that they merely compute atheoretical similarity and feature correlations over a set of familiar instances. This conclusion may be unwarranted, and in fact seems unlikely, when one considers its developmental implications. If young children were complete, unrepenting phenomenalists, how could they ever make the transition to more principled biological knowledge? It seems more reasonable to suggest that even at the youngest ages the children might have started to build intuitive theories concerning the true nature of biological kinds and that, if these theories could be accessed, the children might well be willing to overrule characteristic features. Some conceptual distinctions may be so fundamental and theoretically central that even young children are unwilling to judge that an item's membership in one fundamental category can be changed into that of another by mere alterations in characteristic features, no matter how perceptually salient and typical they might be.

Ontological Categories and the Operations Paradigm

The possibility that the developmental shifts uncovered in the operations and discoveries studies at least partly reflect a shift from the perceptual to the conceptual must be more directly addressed, even though the transcripts from those studies would seem to argue against such a simple dichotomy. What conceptual categories would be fundamentally important to very young children? Based on prior work (Keil 1979, 1983), I decided to use so-called ontological categories that refer to some of the most fundamental conceptual cuts one can make in the world, such as those between animals and plants, artifacts and animals, and the like. Earlier work suggested that even preschoolers are sensitive to certain ontological contrasts and that they might therefore resist kind membership changes in transformations over such fundamentally different categories. Moreover, Putnam (1975) suggests that such distinctions might have a psychologically different status in thinking about natural kinds.

> Consider the stereotype of 'tiger' for a moment. This includes such features as being an animal; being big-cat-like; having black stripes on a yellow ground (yellow stripes on a black ground?); etc. Now, there is something very special about the feature *animal*. In terms of Quine's notion of *centrality* or *unrevisability*, it is qualitatively different from the others listed....Spelling this out, I repeat, is difficult, and it is curiously hard to think of the case to begin with, which is why it is easy to make the mistake of thinking that it is 'logically impossible' for a tiger not to be an animal. On the other hand, there is no difficulty in imagining a tiger that is not striped; it might look like an albino. Nor is it difficult to imagine an individual tiger that doesn't look like a big cat: it might be horribly deformed....But tigers ceasing to be animals? Great difficulties again....it is qualitatively

harder to revise 'all tigers are animals' than 'all tigers have stripes' —indeed, the latter statement is not even true....Not only do such features as 'animal', 'living thing', 'artifact', 'day of the week', 'period of time', attach with enormous centrality to the words 'tiger', 'clam', 'chair', 'Tuesday', 'hour'; but they also form part of a widely used and important *system of classification.* The centrality guarantees that items classified under these headings virtually never have to be reclassified; thus these headings are the natural ones to use in a host of contexts. (pp. 267–268)

Finally, Michael Kelly and I (Kelly and Keil 1985) demonstrated that even when authors such as Ovid and the Brothers Grimm invented metamorphoses in their stories, the transformations tended to occur more often within ontological categories than across them.

To assess the possible influence of ontological categories, a new operations study was designed that included three major types of transformations: natural kinds into other, related natural kinds (for instance, animals into animals, plants into plants), artifacts into artifacts, and natural kinds into or from ontologically different kinds. The cross-ontological category changes were as follows: animals into plants, machines into animals, animals into inanimate natural kinds. The full set of pre- and postoperation pairs is shown in table 10.1.

The stimuli were thus constructed to contrast the two types of transformations used in previous studies with new transformations that crossed ontological categories. In addition, the manner of presenting the stimuli was changed in one important respect. Because one purpose of

Table 10.1
Stimuli used in first cross-ontological category study

Natural kind into related natural kind	Artifact into artifact	Cross-ontological category shift
Horse/zebra	Nail/needle	Toy bird/real bird
Sheep/goat	Table/bookcase	Squirrel/moss
Tiger/lion	Bridge/table	Worms/silver
Maple tree/pine tree	Highchair/rocking chair	Toy dog/real dog
Rose/daisy	Belt/shoelace	Fish/stone
Pear/apple	Pants/shirt	Porcupine/cactus
Salt/sand	Lightpole/swings	Hippo/rock
Gold/lead		Lizard/stick
Oil/water		Toy mouse/real mouse

this study was to assess the extent to which children were basing their judgments on readily perceivable features, the pictorial line drawings used in prior studies were replaced with photographs so as to maximize any possible perceptual influences. If, when examining a photograph of a real mouse, children nonetheless insisted that it could not be a real one because it was transformed into that appearance from a toy, they would be giving the strongest possible evidence of overriding the perceptual features in the display. The photographs were taken with great care so as to maximize the feasibility of a transformation and minimize irrelevant differences. Thus, the two animals might be portrayed against similar backgrounds, in similar orientations and postures (for instance, both heads facing left or right), and, to the greatest extent possible, as being of equivalent sizes. Sample photographs are shown in figure 10.1. Three examples of the descriptions are shown in table 10.2.

Sixteen children in each of three grades (K, 2, 4) participated as subjects in the study. (Average ages were 5:6, 7:7, and 9:8 years, respectively.) All were from elementary schools in the Ithaca, New York, area. Four children were unable to complete the task and were replaced with new subjects.

The stimuli were presented in a partially random sequence, subject to the constraint that no more than two operations of the same type would be presented in succession. The questioning procedure was essentially the same as in prior studies. The large number of stimuli frequently required that the experimenter return on successive days to complete the interview.

All sessions were tape-recorded and transcribed. Responses were scored by a judge on a three-point scale. A score of 1 signified a judgment that type of kind was changed; a score of 2, a judgment of some uncertainty; and a score of 3, a judgment that type of kind was not changed. An independent scorer carried out extensive reliability spot-checks, and agreement was achieved 98% of the time; as a result, the original scores were used in all later analyses. In the vast majority of cases, responses were assigned scores of 1 or 3, scores of 2 being assigned only 2.8% of the time.

The means for the different kinds of transformations for each grade are shown in table 10.3. The data can be better understood, however, by considering the overall scores for each of three categories: natural-kind-to-natural-kind changes, artifact-to-artifact changes, and cross-ontological category changes. Figure 10.2 illustrates three markedly different response patterns for the three types of operations. The patterns for the artifact-to-artifact and natural-kind-to-related-natural-kind operations are the same as those described in chapter 9 and thus replicate those results. By contrast, the developmental pattern for the cross-ontological

(horse/zebra)   (maple tree/pine tree)

Natural kind into related natural kind

(bridge/table)   (table/bookcase)

Artifact into artifact

(toy bird/real bird)   (porcupine/cactus)

Cross-ontological categories

Figure 10.1
Examples of photographs accompanying descriptions used in the first cross-ontological category study.

Table 10.2
Examples of stimulus descriptions used in the first cross-ontological category study

Natural kind into related natural kind: Horse/zebra
A scientist took this horse and did an operation on it. He put black and white stripes all over its body. He cut off its mane and braided its tail like this. He taught it to run away from people. No one could ride it anymore. He taught it to eat grass instead of oats and hay. He also taught it to live out in the wild part of Africa instead of in a stable. Did he change it into a zebra, or is it still a horse?

Artifact into artifact: Table/bookcase
A scientist had this table. He cut the top up into smaller pieces with a saw. He nailed them back together a new way. This is what he ended up with. Did he change it into a bookcase, or is it still a table?

Cross-ontological category shift: Toy bird/real bird
A scientist took this toy. You wind it up with a key, and its mouth opens and a little machine inside plays music. The scientist did an operation on it. He put on real feathers to make it nice and soft and he gave it a better beak. Then he took off the wind-up key and put in a new machine so that it flapped its wings and flew, and chirped. Did he change it into a real bird, or is it still a toy bird?

Table 10.3
Mean scores for different transformation types in the first cross-ontological category study

	K	2	4
Natural kind - within category			
Animal into animal	1.79	1.92	2.87
Plant into plant	1.25	1.88	2.72
Inanimate into inanimate	1.63	1.92	2.58
Artifact into artifact	1.11	1.08	1.00
Cross-ontological category			
Animal into inanimate	2.60	2.77	3.00
Animal into plant	2.49	2.89	2.98
Machine into animal	2.50	2.88	2.96

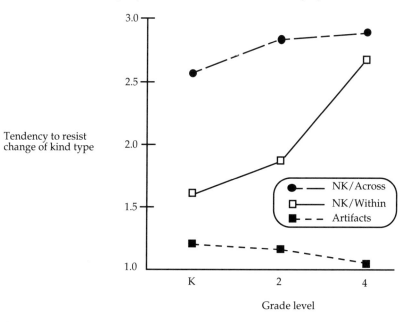

Tendency to resist change of kind type

Grade level

Figure 10.2
Mean scores for natural kind and artifact terms in the first cross ontological category study. 1 = judgment that operation changed kind type, 2 = judgment indicating genuine indecision as to whether operation changed kind type, 3 = judgment that operation did not change kind type.

category operations is totally different. At all ages the vast majority of children judge that type of kind is preserved, even while they are looking at a photograph of the transformed object that is a legitimate instance of that second kind.

Separate two-way and one-way ANOVAs reveal that there are three distinct patterns, the developmental shift for natural-kind-to-related-natural-kind operations being much more marked than the shift for cross-ontological category operations. Three two-way repeated measure ANOVAs revealed (1) for cross-category and artifact descriptions by age, no significant age differences (although a trend was observed at p < .07), but strong differences between operation types and for the operation-by-age interaction (p < .001); (2) for natural kind within-category and artifact descriptions by age, differences between ages and between operation types as well as an operation-by-age interaction, all at the p < .001 level; and (3) for natural kind within-category and cross-ontological category operations by age, differences between ages and between operation types as well as an operation-by-age interaction, all at the p < .001 level. Finally, separate one-way ANOVAs of each operation type revealed significant age changes for both cross-ontological category (p < .01) and natural kind within-category (p < .0001) types, but not for artifacts.

The differences in significance levels for the one-way ANOVAs, in conjunction with the significant interaction found in the two-way analyses, demonstrate that the age change for natural kind within-category operations is considerably stronger than that for cross-ontological category operations. Separate Scheffé tests for adjacent grade differences for within- and cross-category operations showed marginally significant differences between kindergartners and second graders for both operation types (p < .1), as well as a difference between second and fourth graders for the within-category changes (p < .05).

A second, somewhat weaker pattern was that of differences among the scores on animal, plant, and "mineral" within-category changes. Children judge the type of kind of animals to be preserved at an earlier age than that of plants (p < .005) and possibly that of animals before that of minerals (p < .16).

In this study the transcripts that best illuminate the patterns of results are those from kindergartners who simultaneously argue that type of kind is not preserved for within-category changes and that it is for cross-category changes. Consider the following examples:

K(1) Lizard/branch
C: A lizard.
E: OK. Why do you say he's a lizard still?
C: Because it is still green.
E: It's still green. OK. Even though it looks a lot like a little branch, you think it's still a lizard?
C: Yeah.
E: OK. Do you know what a branch is?
C: It's something (unintelligible) things down on trees.
E: OK. It's what comes off of trees, right?
C: Right.
E: What the leaves are on.
C: Yeah.
E: Yeah. So you don't think that's what he is now, he's not a little branch now?
C: (Shakes head)
E: No?...OK.

(Same child) Pears/apples
C: Apples.
E: Apples. OK. Why do you think they're apples now?
C: Because they have red on the outside and they have that top thing.

E: This top thing?
C: Yeah.
E: Yeah, well, that's this part. It had that before too. The stem. So even though they started out like this, used to be pears, they started out as pears, you think they're apples now?
C: Yeah.
E: OK. So you think you could do that? You think you could take a pear and change it into a real apple?
C: Yeah.
E: OK.

(Same child) Fish/rock
C: A fish, 'cause it doesn't have those white things.
E: OK. I think because he sat still for so long and didn't move that those got stuck to him. And they got hard too.
C: I think it's still a fishy because there's spots on it and it looks almost the same.
E: OK...It looks a lot like a rock too, doesn't it?
C: Yeah, but...
E: So why are you pretty sure it's a fish?
C: Because if it would be a rock, then he couldn't even move, and if it did, and I still something what he had on. (*sic*)
E: OK. If it was a rock, it couldn't move, you're right.
C: Unless someone carried it.
E: So it couldn't move by itself.

(Same child) Sheep/goat
C: A goat.
E: It's a goat now. OK. And why is it a goat?
C: 'Cause it has horns.
E: OK. 'Cause it has horns. Is that what you thought it was going to look like?
C: (Nods)
E: Yeah. Even though it used to be a lamb, you think now it's really a goat?
C: Yeah.
(Digression on details of the sheep/goat operation)
E: What I want to know is, now is it really a goat or really a sheep?
C: A goat.
E: OK. Even though it used to be a sheep, it started out...(repeats description)
C: Yeah.
E: So you think he could change a real sheep into a real goat?

C: Yeah.

E: How did he do it, do you remember what he did?

C: Cutted short hair, cutted off the hair and put some (unintelligible) and put those long nails on and then he made it skinnier, longer legs.

E: Yeah, and put that on.

C: And a beard on. Why do you need a beard on goats?

E: Some goats have beards.

C: Like not momma goats.

E: I think they do actually, some momma goats do.

This child illustrates a fairly common pattern wherein the child strongly feels that the type of kind is not changed in a cross-ontological category operation but seems unable to fully explain why and often seizes on a variety of superficial and undiagnostic features. Note that the same child, although apparently strongly swayed by the presence of new salient features for the within-category operations, discounts equally salient features in the cross-category transformations and often focuses on obscure ones to justify the preservation of type of kind.

Consider excerpts from transcripts of one more child:

K(2) Hippopotamus/rock

C: Still a hippo.

E: OK. And why do you say he's still a hippo?

C: Because he started out like a hippo.

E: Oh, OK. So even though he looks an awful lot like a big rock, you think he's a hippo?

C: (Nods)

E: OK.

(Same child) Maple tree/pine tree

C: Pine tree.

E: OK. Even though it used to be a maple tree?

C: (Nods)

E: OK. Why do you say it's a pine tree?

C: Because he just, he changed it.

E: Yeah.

C: He changed it to look different.

E: Yeah. And did that change it into a real pine?

C: (Nods)

E: OK. So do you think a scientist can do that? He can take a real maple tree and make it into a real pine?

C: (Nods)

E: OK.

(Same child) Squirrel/moss
C: A squirrel.
E: Why do you think he's a squirrel?
C: 'Cause he started out like one.
E: OK. So even though he looks like a moss plant, you think he's a squirrel?
C: (Nods)
E: OK.

(Same child) Salt/sand
C: Sand.
E: OK. Why do you say it's sand now?
C: I don't know.
E: Well, how did it start out?
C: He cooked it in the oven.
E: He cooked it in the oven...and then what?
C: And he put it in the sandbox, and it turned into sand.
E: Oh, OK. So you think a scientist really can do that? He can turn salt into real sand?
C: (Nods)
E: OK.

Although there was a very strong tendency for children to judge type of kind to be preserved for cross-ontological category operations but changed for within-category operations, rarely were children completely consistent in their judgments. For example, although the above child showed the general pattern, he also judged that a fish could be turned into a rock and denied that oil could be turned into water. Consider one final example:

K(3) Tiger/lion
C: I think he changed it into a real lion.
E: OK. Even though it started out as a tiger, you think now it's a lion?
C: Um hmm.
E: OK. Why do you say that?
C: Because a tiger doesn't have long hair on his neck.
E: OK. So you think he could change a real tiger into a lion. He could make a lion out of a tiger?
C: Um hmm.
E: Just like the other lions?
C: (Nods)
E: OK.

(Same child) Worms/silver
C: They were still really worms.
E: Why are they still really worms?
C: Because they started out as worms.
E: Oh, because they started out as worms. So even though they look like silver now, they're still worms?
C: Um hmm.
E: OK. So you don't think that you could make silver out of worms?
C: (Shakes head)
E: OK. Fine. Still worms.

(Same child) Sheep/goat
C: I think he changed it into a real goat.
E: OK. Why do you say it's a real goat now?
C: Because a sheep doesn't have horns or a beard.
E: OK. So you think even though it used to be a sheep and it came from a sheep, it's now really a goat?
C: Um hmm.
E: OK. Do you think a scientist could change a sheep into a goat? He can do that?
C: Um hmm.
E: OK.

(Same child) Porcupine/cactus
C: I think he's still really a porcupine.
E: And why do you say that?
C: Because he started out like a porcupine.
E: Oh, OK. And even though he looks like a cactus plant you think he's really a porcupine?
C: Um hmm.
E: OK. Can you think of any other reasons why he's still a porcupine? Something you know about him?
C: (Shakes head)
E: OK. Are you sure he's a porcupine?
C: Uh huh.
E: OK.

These transcripts bring out several points. First, the children were usually questioned more strongly for judgments that type of kind for natural kinds was changed than for judgments that it was not changed. Since the latter is the typical adult response, such a pattern of questioning would tend to reduce any developmental patterns by making younger children appear more adult-like. Second, children frequently were unable to justify why type of kind was preserved for the cross-ontological category operations, although one common pattern was to refer to how the entity started out or to other properties that did remain invariant. Third, the children were not perfectly consistent and occasionally made judgments contrary to the general pattern of their own responses.

The general point to keep in mind is that these results suggest that even kindergartners are not completely dominated by characteristic features and that for at least some fundamental category distinctions they do not allow type of kind to be changed. Some features demarcating ontological kinds are regarded as much closer to being necessary features than characteristic ones. For example, if an entity has a machine inside, it must not be a real animal, or if an entity eats, it cannot be a real artifact. Thus, the ontological level may give us our first clear glimpse into children's early theories and thereby illustrate one way in which they are able, with considerable confidence, to override the characteristic features.

A Conservative Replication

Although the study just described had robust results, it was possible that they might have been exaggerated by experimenter preconceptions of the results and by the details of the stimulus set. It might have been that, in subtle ways, the patterns of questioning, intonation, or accompanying nonverbal gestures served to guide the children's responses. It might also have been that the stimuli themselves contained differences that the children were exploiting, such as the occasional reference to an animal as "he" or "she" even after the operation had turned it into an artifact or plant look-alike. In addition, the stories for cross-ontological category changes carried the strong implication that some features of the initial entity were preserved. A conservative replication study was therefore conducted in which the experimenters knew neither the purposes of the experiment nor the predicted outcomes. In addition, the stimuli were slightly modified.

The two experimenters were undergraduate students at Cornell University who had taken some elementary courses in psychology but were unfamiliar with any of the research described in this book. They also had never done experimental work with children before, which made the task especially difficult for them. They were trained by being shown the stimulus stories and a rigid set of follow-up questions specified by a branching flowchart. They practiced this procedure on each other while another sophisticated observer and I watched and gave them general feedback on their technique.

In the prior study even a highly skilled experimenter had difficulty getting the younger children to attend to such a large stimulus set, so the stimuli for this experiment were limited to a subset of the original items (see table 10.4).

The subjects were selected from elementary schools in the Ithaca, New York, area. Fifteen kindergartners and twenty second graders constituted the final subject pool for which responses were scored. One kindergartner and one second grader were dropped from the study because they were uncooperative and it was not possible to get a full set of judgments from them.

The two experimenters reported difficulty in performing the task since they did not know the hypotheses. When asked at the end of the study to conjecture about the hypothesis, neither proposed anything remotely like the specific predictions of the study. Instead, they both proposed (with considerable uncertainty) that, with increasing age, children would look more like adults on all items.

The actual results of the study are summarized in figure 10.3, which shows the mean scores for children in each grade for each stimulus type. These results essentially replicated those of the previous study except that they were somewhat less dramatic. The differences between stimulus types were significant at the $p < .01$ level, however. Children of both ages judged that the cross-ontological category operations did not change type of kind whereas natural kind within-category operations did. A two-way repeated measures ANOVA revealed a trend in grade differences ($p < .1$), strong differences between operation types ($p < .001$), and a grade-by-operation interaction ($p < .05$). A separate two-way ANOVA without artifacts revealed a strong grade difference ($p < .001$) and no interaction between grade and within- and cross-category operation. These results tend to regress more toward a mean score of 2, which would be expected with less experienced experimenters who were unable to

Table 10.4
Stimuli used in conservative replication of cross-ontological category study

Natural kind into related natural kind	Artifact into artifact	Cross-ontological category shift
Salt/sand	Nail/needle	Squirrel/moss
Gold/lead	Table/bookcase	Toy bird/real bird
Horse/zebra	Bridge/table	Worms/silver
Pear/apple	Highchair/rocking chair	Toy dog/real dog
Sheep/goat	Belt/shoelace	Fish/stone
Rose/daisy	Pants/shirt	Porcupine/cactus

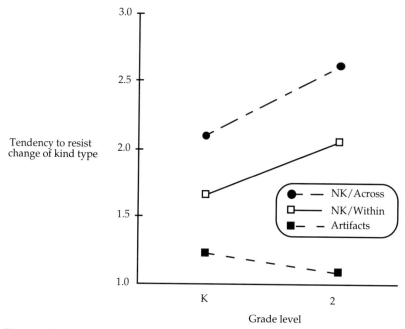

Figure 10.3
Mean scores for natural kind and artifact terms in conservative replication of cross-ontological category study. 1 = judgment that operation changed kind type, 2 = judg-ment indicating genuine indecision as to whether operation changed kind type, 3 = judgment that operation did not change kind type.

probe as effectively as possible given that they were naive regarding the procedure.

Overall, this replication should be taken as strong support for the findings of the first study reported in this chapter, especially because it employed highly conservative procedures that could have reduced the predicted effects and pushed the responses more toward a random pattern. The transcripts for this study are essentially sparser, less thorough versions of those collected in the previous study and accordingly are omitted.

Is the Ontological Level Special?

The data so far show that when one attempts to change an entity of one kind into an entity of a different ontological category by manipulating characteristic features, young children maintain that the type of kind is not changed even though they readily judge type of kind to be changed for entities within the same ontological category. These results suggest that the ontological level has a special, privileged status and that it is here that some of the first theories about natural kinds, particularly biological ones, begin to emerge. Such a conclusion is not necessarily warranted by the present data, however. It may be that any transformation between categories that are construed as being dramatically different would cause resistance to type-of-kind change, regardless of whether it crossed ontological categories. Accordingly, a study was conducted to examine four different kinds of transformations: artifact to artifact, natural kind to similar within-ontological category, natural kind to highly dissimilar within-ontological category, and cross-ontological category. The pre- and postoperation entities in each category are shown in table 10.5. Unfortunately, several months after the study was completed, some large unrecoverable gaps in the raw data were discovered, and despite very promising initial results, Susan Brudos, Karen Guskin, and I decided to repeat the entire study.

The questioning procedure was the same as that used in the blind replication study described in this chapter. The subjects were sixteen children from each of two grades (K, 2) attending public elementary schools in the Ithaca, New York, area.

Two possible accounts of how intercategory distance influences judgment of type of kind are shown in figure 10.4. The children might judge kinds to be changed in a manner that varies continuously with overall similarity ratings between kinds. Alternatively, a more principled biological understanding might well result in a discontinuous shift in judgments as the changes cross the boundaries between ontological kinds.

The results are summarized in figure 10.5. No differences were found between scores on similar within-ontological category and dissimilar within-ontological category operations, but dramatic differences emerged between scores on similar within-ontological category and cross-ontological operations (two-way ANOVA, $p < .0001$) and between dissimilar within-ontological category and cross-ontological category operations (two-way ANOVA, $p < .0001$). The differences were most pronounced with the kindergartners, as many of the second graders seemed to have already shifted to adult-like responses. Finally, at both ages the artifact scores differed significantly from all others ($p < .001$). The transcripts were similar to those collected in prior operations studies, no obvious differences being found between the responses to similar within-ontological category and dissimilar within-ontological category stimuli.

These results support the argument that mere distance between categories is not the driving force behind the child's judgment that kind is preserved. Children are just as likely to allow an insect to be turned into a mammal or an insect into a fish as they are to allow one mammal to be

Table 10.5
Stimuli used in study on the special nature of the ontological level

Natural kind into similar natural kind	Natural kind into dissimilar natural kind	Artifact into artifact	Cross-ontological category shift
Horse/zebra	Beetle/frog	Bridge/table	Toy dog/real dog
Sheep/goat	Lizard/grasshopper	Highchair/rocking chair	Fish/rock
Chicken/turkey	Butterfly/fish	Belt/shoelace	Porcupine/cactus

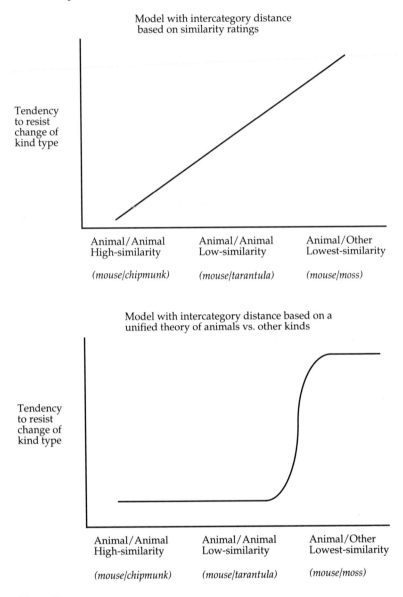

Model with intercategory distance
based on similarity ratings

Tendency
to resist
change of
kind type

Animal/Animal	Animal/Animal	Animal/Other
High-similarity	Low-similarity	Lowest-similarity
(mouse/chipmunk)	*(mouse/tarantula)*	*(mouse/moss)*

Model with intercategory distance based on a
unified theory of animals vs. other kinds

Tendency
to resist
change of
kind type

Animal/Animal	Animal/Animal	Animal/Other
High-similarity	Low-similarity	Lowest-similarity
(mouse/chipmunk)	*(mouse/tarantula)*	*(mouse/moss)*

Figure 10.4
Two models of intercategory distance effects in a transformations paradigm.

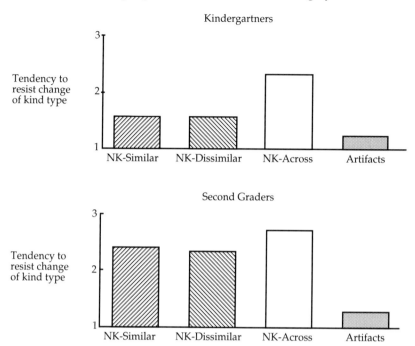

Figure 10.5
Mean scores in the study on the special nature of the ontological level.

turned into a closely related one. Since we had anticipated finding at least a small tendency for distance between categories to make a difference in children's judgments, this was a surprising result. Apparently, when biological theory develops, it does so in a way that encompasses all biological kinds, or at least all animals, at roughly the same time. Any animal can be changed into any other animal; it is only at the ontological boundaries that change is resisted.

It might be argued that young children do not consider mammals and insects to be as dissimilar as adults do and that the manipulation therefore had no real effect on them. But there is considerable evidence that children do rate mammals as being more similar to other mammals than to insects (see, for example, Carey 1985) and thus at least at some level see mice as being less like spiders than zebras are like horses. Moreover, in a separate study we collected such similarity ratings from adult subjects by requesting them to rate on a five-point scale the relative similarity of the item pairs in table 10.4. It is clear from the results summarized in figure 10.6 that these ratings are not correlated with the children's judgments and, if anything, would predict a large shift be-

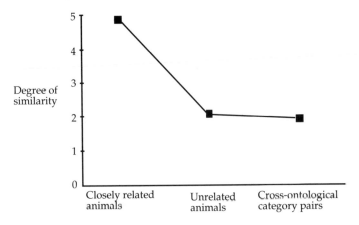

Figure 10.6
Adult similarity ratings of stimuli pairs used in the study on the special nature of the ontological level.

tween closely related animals and unrelated ones and none between unrelated animals and cross-ontological category pairs—just the opposite of the pattern found in the kindergartners' responses.

Conclusions

The studies described in this chapter argue strongly against an account portraying the young child as an unrepenting phenomenalist slavishly bound to computing correlations among salient characteristic features. They also argue against construing the mechanism underlying the observed developmental changes as any simple perceptual-to-conceptual transition. Most of the kindergartners in each of the three studies tended to override characteristic features if the pre- and postoperation entities were from different ontological categories. This was the case even though they were confronted with photographs of actual entities possessing all the characteristic features that resulted from the transformation.

Why should the ontological level be so special in guiding the emergence of biological and perhaps other natural theories? Part of the answer is suggested by the transcripts. It is very difficult to find a single feature that is unique to a particular species. Thus, tigers have stripes—but so do zebras, some fish, and other sorts of living and nonliving things. By contrast, at the ontological level there are clusters of properties that unambiguously and uniquely apply to all members of a given category at that level. All animals are alive, have offspring, and grow in ways that only animals do. Children sometimes referred to these sorts of properties in justifying why an entity had not been changed. Consider some examples from the transcripts:

2(1) Porcupine/cactus
C: It's still a porcupine.
E: What would happen when it wakes up, will it be a cactus plant or will it be a porcupine?
C: A porcupine.
E: Why would you think it would be a porcupine?
C: It will look like a cactus, but it won't be one.
E: Why not?
C: It'll be living more.
E: Are cactus living?
C: Yes, but it may be walking around.

2(2) Toy bird/real bird
C: It's still a toy.
E: Why?
C: Because you can't turn a machine into a real live thing.
E: So you think this is a toy bird?
C: Well, it looks like a real bird.
E: Yes, but you think that it is...
C: A toy bird.

2(3) Fish/rock
C: Hmm...I think...well...that it lays eggs, and it's just the outside that got crusty. So I think the inside, if they cut it open, they would see...it would still be the insides of a fish.
E: So you think that even though...(repeats transformation), it's still a fish?
C: Yeah.

These criteria are somewhat different from those voiced by older children who decide that a horse cannot be changed into a zebra. Such subjects are more likely to mention how the entity started out, that its brain remained the same, or that it had such and such origins—criteria that presumably reflect the emergence of a more systematic and coherent set of biological beliefs.

These studies make clear the need to better understand the details of the child's early beliefs. In the next chapter, I describe studies that focus specifically on biological beliefs.

Chapter 11
The Construction of an Intuitive Theory of Biological Kinds

The studies on transformations across ontological categories described in chapter 10 suggest that some of our shared assumptions about kinds (such as ontological knowledge) can be so basic and presupposed that children might appear to be completely governed by characteristic features when in fact they are not. When transformations explicitly cross ontological category boundaries, even very young children show a strong tendency to maintain that type of kind is preserved. The basic ontological distinction between "animal" and "not-animal" may not be the only biological information available to the young child. The studies described in this chapter explore other aspects of knowledge that might constrain judgments about characteristic features of biological kinds. These studies are construed as suggesting a broader developmental pattern independent of biological knowledge per se, a pattern pertaining to the theory-based structures in which emerging concepts are situated.

Manipulating the Nature of the Transformation

In chapter 10 young children's knowledge of biological kinds was demonstrated by contrasting their judgments of transformations across ontological categories with judgments of the same sorts of transformations within ontological categories. A different technique, which may ultimately yield a much more fine-grained analysis of conceptual development, is to present the subject with stories about different sorts of transformations carried out on the same class of things (say, animals). Some transformations may implicate more biologically (and therefore, theoretically) meaningful alterations than others and thereby may be more likely to elicit a judgment that type of kind has in fact changed. The transformations used in the studies reported in chapters 8 through 10 were described as permanent and, although they focused mostly on perceivable surface features, they often involved surface anatomical substitutions (horns added or removed, manes sewn on or removed, and so on). Consequently, when children judged that type of kind had been changed for a tiger/lion pair, they were not merely being swayed by the characteristic features of the lion. Perhaps only when those features are changed in a particular way that children consider biologically significant do they judge type of kind to have been changed.

If this speculation is correct, then there might be transformations that start with the same initial characteristic features and yield the same outcome features, but for which the nature of the transformation suggests that nothing biologically important has changed. As the most superficial example of this, Sheila Jeyifous and I constructed stories in which an animal was dressed in a costume that resembled another animal. Exactly the same photographs were used as in prior studies, so that the beginning and end states were exactly the same. The only difference was that the nature of the transformation might seem much less intrinsic to the animal's kind. The costume transformation descriptions are shown in table 11.1.

Superficiality of the transformation is not the only possible dimension that relates to type of kind. A second dimension may relate to the

Table 11.1
Costume changes

Yellow finch/bluebird
In the window of Mr. Davis's pet shop there was a beautiful bluebird. One day a woman bought the bluebird and took it home. Mr. Davis needed another bluebird to put in his shop window, but that was the last one. Then he had an idea—he asked his daughter to make a bluebird costume for his yellow finch. When she had finished sewing the costume, Mr. Davis carefully put the costume on the yellow finch and made sure that the snaps were covered up by the feathers. He also taught it to sing like a bluebird. Here's how it looks. Is it a bluebird or a yellow finch?

Chicken/turkey
Farmer Brown told his friend that he had a big turkey on his farm, but when he got home the turkey had died. When his friend came to visit and wanted to see the big turkey, Farmer Brown got his wife to make a beautiful turkey costume with feathers from the turkey. Then he put his largest chicken into the costume, with the zipper on the bottom so you couldn't see it. He also taught the chicken to say "gobble gobble." Here's what it looked like in the costume. Do you think it's a chicken or a turkey?

Zebra/horse
Cathy wanted to have horse rides at her birthday party, but her father couldn't find a horse in time for the party. Luckily, her father worked in the zoo and he thought of a way to keep Cathy from being sad on her birthday. He took one of the zoo's zebras, sewed it into a horse costume, and smoothed out the material so it didn't have any wrinkles. Then he took it to Cathy's party. Here's how it looks. Do you think it's a horse or a zebra?

Table 11.1 (continued)

Lion/tiger
One of the circus tigers got sick and couldn't perform in the circus act. So the animal trainer took a lion, helped him get into a tiger costume, fastened it with Velcro, then let him perform the tiger's tricks. This is how it looked. Is it a lion or a tiger?

Mouse/squirrel
A woman who made nature films wanted a squirrel for her new film. But she didn't have time to go and find one, so she made a little squirrel costume for her son's pet mouse. The costume had a nice fluffy tail and the zipper was hidden by the fur. She carefully put the mouse into the costume and made sure that the zipper underneath didn't show. She also taught the mouse to eat nuts. Here's what it looked like. Is it a mouse or a squirrel?

Goat/sheep
A young shepherd boy was watching his family's flock of sheep while they grazed on the hillside. But he fell asleep for a while and when he woke up, he discovered that one of the sheep had run away. He was afraid to tell his parents, and so he thought of an idea to keep himself from getting into trouble. He asked his aunt to make a sheep costume and to give him one of her goats. Then he carefully buttoned the goat into the sheep costume, and made sure that the buttons were hidden by all the curly hair. He also taught the goat to say "baa baa." Here's what it looked like. Is it a goat or a sheep?

perceived permanence and/or intrinsicness of the transformation. Consequently, a transformation was designed in which the beginning and end-state characteristic features were again the same as in previous studies but in which the transformation had to be repeated regularly to ensure that the animal did not revert back to its former self. For example, a lion might be transformed into a tiger by shaving its fur, adding stripes, and teaching it tiger-like behaviors exactly as in previous studies, but the child was then told that these effects wear off unless someone touches the animal up and retrains it every few nights. According to the story, because these repetitions are done so frequently and covertly, nothing ever wears off, and therefore to all observers at all times the animal looks and acts exactly like a tiger, just as in the original operations studies. It was felt that even though the appearance and even the transformation involved were identical to those used in prior studies, the added notion of impermanence might reveal yet another way in which children are willing to go beyond the merely characteristic. Examples of the descriptions for the temporary surface part changes are shown in table 11.2.

If children show a much greater resistance to kind changes when presented with these two new types of transformation, it might be

Table 11.2
Temporary surface part changes

Yellow finch/bluebird
Ms. Warren is an artist who likes to draw pictures of birds. She decided that she wanted to draw a picture of a bluebird, but she didn't have a real bluebird to copy. She did have a pet bird that was a yellow finch, and so she decided to paint her finch blue. But the blue paint started to come off when the bird jumped around in its cage, so Ms. Warren had to paint over it every morning before she started drawing. She also taught it to sing like a bluebird. Here's how it looks. Is it a bluebird or a finch?

Turkey/chicken
Susan, who lived on a farm, had the job of looking after the chickens and turkeys. One day one of the chickens ran away, and Susan was afraid to tell her mom. So Susan took one of the turkeys, pulled out some of its big feathers, spray-painted it white, and taught it to say "cluck cluck." But after a couple of days, the paint started to wear off a little bit and the feathers started growing again. So Susan used to sneak out early every morning before anyone was up, painted the turkey white, and clipped the feathers. Here's how it looked. Do you think it's really a chicken or a turkey?

Horse/zebra
The man who owns this white horse wanted the horse to be able to hide in the tall grass, so he painted black stripes all over it. But the horse spends a lot of time outside and whenever it rains the black stripes start to wash off. So every week the man has to paint the black stripes back on again. This is how it looks. Is it a horse or a zebra?

Lion/tiger
When the weather got very hot, the zookeeper shaved off the lion's mane. He also painted black stripes all over his body. But the hair soon grew back and the stripes started to wash off when the lion was bathing in his pool or when he rolled on his back. So every three or four days the zookeeper had to shave the lion hair and paint over the black stripes. Here's how he looks. Do you think it's a lion or a tiger?

Mouse/squirrel
A science teacher wanted to teach her students about squirrels, but she didn't have a live squirrel to show the students. So she took her son's pet mouse, glued some brown and black hairs to its tail, and painted its belly and around its eyes white. But the paint started to come off when the mouse played around, so every morning before the students got to class she had to paint over the white parts. She also taught it to eat nuts. Here's how it looked. Is it a squirrel or a mouse?

Sheep/goat
Farmer Brown was excited because next week he was going to take his prize goat to the county fair, and he was sure the goat would win first prize. But two days before the fair, the goat became ill and couldn't even stand up. Farmer Brown was

Table 11.2 (continued)

very disappointed, but then he had an idea. He took one of his sheep which was about the same size as the sick goat, shaved off most of its hair, attached two horns and a beard to its head, and then spray-painted it white. He also taught it to butt like a goat. The paint didn't stick to the hair very well and kept coming off a little bit, so every morning Farmer Brown had to spray-paint the animal so it would be white all over, and he reglued the beard and horns so they wouldn't come off. Here's how it looked. Is it a goat or a sheep?

because they do have more theory-based beliefs about animals than has previously been thought. If so, then it should be possible to find other transformations that will make even older children than in previous studies also judge that type of kind has been changed. In other words, if theories gradually emerge and become more differentiated with increasing age, then it should be possible to find a level of description that an older child might think is fundamental to a biological kind but an adult might consider less central.

Based on transcripts collected in prior studies, it was clear that many children seemed to place considerable emphasis on how animals grow up. This suggested that a transformation might be seen to alter more intrinsic properties if it were performed at birth and influenced later patterns of development. In addition, the transformation might be seen as more likely to change identity if it worked from the inside rather than by external manipulation of external features. Thus, stories were constructed in which animals were given either pills or injections at birth that resulted in their growing up to look and act just like animals of a different species. Again, the same photographs were used as in previous studies so that the initial characteristic features (in this case, those of the parent) and the final ones were the same (as were the behavioral features). The stories are shown in table 11.3.

The goal behind these stimulus manipulations was to explore whether, over a broad age range, children are guided by intuitive theoretical conceptions of biological kinds that go beyond mere clusters of salient characteristic features. It was predicted that, for the costume and temporary change transformations, many of the kindergartners would deny that type of kind had been changed. Although the kindergartners might not know that genetic material or other current scientific criteria are the preferred indices of belonging to a particular biological kind, they might nonetheless know that putting on a costume is simply too shallow a manipulation to change one biological kind into another. Similarly, if the transformation must be repeated regularly to prevent the old form from reappearing, even a kindergartner might conclude that something

Table 11.3
Internal/developmental changes

Bluebird/yellow finch
The person in charge of birds at the zoo always gave the baby bluebirds a shot when they were hatched, so that they would have nice healthy feathers. But one of the baby bluebirds got the wrong shot because a new person was on the job and didn't know the right shot to give. So when the baby bluebird grew up, its feathers turned yellow, it sang like a finch, and it looked like this. Is it a bluebird or a finch?

Chicken/turkey
Mr. Smith wanted to start a turkey farm, but when he went to buy some baby turkeys, they were all sold out. So the salesman gave him some baby chickens which had had a big shot. This shot made the chicks grow large black feathers and say "gobble gobble." When the chicks grew up they looked like this. Do you think they are chickens or turkeys?

Horse/zebra
An animal doctor who was taking care of some baby horses accidentally gave a baby horse the wrong injection when it was born. So when the baby horse grew up, it had black stripes all over its body. It looked like this. Do you think it's a horse or a zebra?

Tiger/lion
When this tiger was first born, it had trouble breathing, and the animal doctor gave it some pills. But there was a problem with the pills. As the tiger got better and grew bigger, it began to lose its stripes and to grow hair around its neck. Now that it's grown up, here's how it looks. Is it a lion or a tiger?

Squirrel/mouse
Mr. Lee was an old man who liked to feed the squirrels who came into his backyard. One day his favorite squirrel brought her baby, but the baby squirrel was sick. Mr. Lee gave it some pills, but the pills were too strong for the baby squirrel, and when it started to grow bigger, it didn't have a bushy tail, and its two front feet were very short and were hidden in its fur. Here's how it looked when it was grown up. Is it a squirrel or a mouse?

Goat/sheep
All Mr. Jones's goats were given vitamin shots when they were born. However, when the last little goat was born, Mr. Jones didn't realize that he had used vitamins which were very old and which didn't work the way he wanted them to. As the goat began to grow, its hair grew very long and curly, and it didn't grow a beard or horns, and it used to say "baa baa." Here's how it looked. Is it a goat or a sheep?

---

intrinsic to the original kind remains despite the animal's manifesting the surface appearance and behavior of the new kind. Surface parts must be more stable if they are to be diagnostic of a kind. Children might thus be constraining their hypotheses about how surface features are related to kinds by a theory of biologically relevant and irrelevant ways in which those features could be manifested. Using the same photographs for all three types of transformation constituted an especially strict test of the hypothesis that different mechanisms for precisely the same changes in characteristic features might have very different effects in overriding those features.

With respect to the internally triggered transformations carried out at birth, it was predicted that many of the older children might assume that type of kind was in fact changed, since this sort of transformation seemed to be linked to many biologically important concepts—what an animal's insides look like, how it grew up, and so on. Although some adults might waver on this judgment, it was felt that most adults have theories about biological kinds that do not allow essence to be altered by a shot or a pill, even one administered very early in life. Though many adults are ignorant of genetic structure, it was predicted that their theories of biological essence would assume a rich and complex internal structure, a structure that could not be easily manipulated by merely administering a chemical substance.

Procedures and design
The experimental procedure was similar to that used in prior studies. The experimenters showed children a photograph of an animal, described a transformation, and showed photographs of the end state side by side with the initial state. The children were then asked to judge what the end-state animal was and were asked to justify their judgments. As in prior studies, artifacts were also used to provide experimental controls. The full set of animal stimuli is shown in tables 11.1, 11.2, and 11.3. The artifact stimuli were the same as those used in the study reported in chapter 9.

Forty-one children (15 kindergartners, 11 second graders, and 15 fourth graders)participated as subjects, along with fifteen adults. (Average ages of the children were 5:8, 7:9, and 9:11 years respectively.) All subjects received all stimulus items. Two children were dropped from the study and replaced. All children were from public schools in the Ithaca, New York, area. All adult subjects were undergraduates at Cornell University.

Results
Many of the results can be summarized in figure 11.1, which shows the developmental curves for each of the three types of transformation as

well as for the biological transformations used in chapter 9 (dotted line). The artifact scores, which are very similar to those found in prior studies, are not shown. The predictions are clearly supported. Even the kindergartners denied roughly 80% of the time that type of kind was changed in the costume stories, and the percentage fell only slightly to 70% for the stories about temporary transformations. By contrast, almost 40% of the time fourth graders judged that type of kind was changed under the internal cause/developmental transformations. Separate one- and two-way ANOVAs reveal significant differences between each pair of transformation types and significant age changes for the transformation types. Thus, grade and item type (costume vs. temporary transformation vs. internal transformation) were both significant main effects, as was their interaction (p < .001). Separate ANOVAs on each of the item types revealed no significant age changes for costumes, although a Scheffé test did reveal a trend (p < .10) toward a difference between kindergartners and second graders. For temporary surface parts, there was a change with age (p < .01), the largest change taking place between grades K and

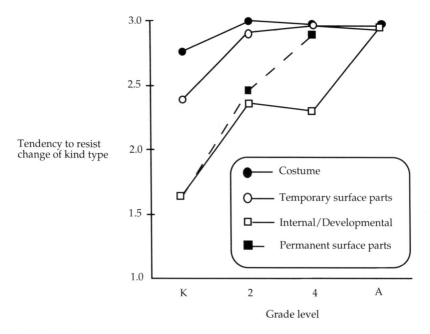

Figure 11.1
Mean scores for different transformation types in the study that manipulated the nature of the transformation. 1 = judgment that operation changed kind type, 2 = judg-ment indicating genuine indecision as to whether operation changed kind type, 3 = judgment that operation did not change kind type.

2 (p < .001). For internal/developmental transformations, there was also a general change with age (p < .001), the largest changes taking place between grades K and 2, and 4 and college (p < .05).

Finally, separate two-way ANOVAs contrasting each pair of transformation types revealed strong differences between internal/developmental changes and both temporary surface part changes and costumes (p < .001) and weaker differences between costumes and temporary surface part changes (p < .02). These analyses all fit with the visual patterns shown in figure 11.1.

Even the youngest children in this study have some beliefs about what sorts of underlying principles govern biological kind membership and therefore do not allow their beliefs to be overridden by changes in characteristic features if the mechanism behind the changes does not relate to those principles. Not just with respect to broad ontological distinctions but also with respect to distinctions between closely related species, these children seem to have beliefs about which manipulations are biologically relevant and which are not. Their beliefs are different from those of older children and adults, but they are nonetheless adequate to override characteristic features, and, as I will argue later, they seem to be specifically biological beliefs.

The transcripts provide more concrete and vivid insights into these developmental patterns. Consider the following excerpts taken from the transcripts of children of different ages.

K(1) Zebra/horse (costume)
C: Really a zebra. It is one.
E: Does it look like a zebra?
C: No.
E: What does it look like?
C: A horse.

(Same child) Goat/sheep (injection)
C: Umm...a sheep. Because he made it into one.
E: What happened?
C: The vitamins weren't working.
E: Who did he give the vitamins to?
C: The goat.
E: (Repeats entire story) So what is it really at the end...a sheep or a goat?
C: A sheep.
K(2) Zebra/horse (costume)
C: Really a zebra because he put on a costume.

(Same child) Lion/tiger (temporary surface parts)
C: Lion, because he just painted it.

(Same child) Goat/sheep (injection)
C: Sheep, because it grew long hair.

K(3) Lion/tiger (temporary surface parts)
C: A lion. Because he shaved the mane off him and put black stripes on him.

(Same child) Chicken/turkey (costume)
C: A chicken. Because he just put the costume on.
E: Who did he put the costume on?
C: The chicken.

(Same child) Squirrel/mouse (pills)
C: A mouse. Because it is very shaggy and furry and has a slippery tail. It has tiny feet in the front.
E: How did it get that way?
C: The farmer gave him the wrong kind of vitamins.
E: What did he have at first?
C: A squirrel.
E: Is this a squirrel or a mouse?
C: A mouse.

K(5) Zebra/horse (costume)
C: Did he try to trick her?
E: No—he didn't want her to be sad.
C: So how'd he make it look like a horse?
E: Remember I said he sewed it into a costume?
C: Oh yeah.
E: So do you think it's a horse or a zebra?
C: A zebra, 'cause that's just pretend.

(Same child) Goat/sheep (injection)
C: Sheep, because it doesn't have horns and it doesn't have a beard.

(Same child) Yellow finch/bluebird (temporary surface parts)
C: A finch! Because if you paint it you're just trying to trick someone; it's not really a real bluebird.
E: OK. So you think it's a yellow finch even though its color is blue?
C: Yeah, because she painted it, that's all.

Young children often justify type-of-kind change for the injection/ pills/vitamins cases by referring to the way the end-state animal looks and yet at the same time deny that appearance matters when rejecting identity changes for the costume and temporary change cases. This is a fascinating example of how they see the characteristic features as being either useful or misleading clues to biological essence depending on the transformation performed or, put differently, depending on what they see as the mechanism responsible for the transformation and consequently for the apparent features of the end-state animal.

As the children grow older, their responses change in a predictable manner. The second graders show significant increases in resistance to kind membership changes for all three types of transformation while retaining the same overall pattern as the kindergartners, being much more likely to judge that membership has changed in the injection/pills cases than in cases of the other two transformation types. Thus, their transcripts are quite similar to those of kindergartners, and some responses from one second grader should suffice as an illustration.

2(1) Lion/tiger (temporary surface parts)
C: Really a lion, because it was really a lion; but he was just shaving and put paint on him.

Yellow finch/bluebird (costume)
C: It's really a yellow finch, because he got a bluebird costume but he didn't really change.

Chicken/turkey (injection)
C: Really turkeys, because they look more like turkeys and they say "gobble gobble."
E: What happened to the baby chickens in the story?
C: They got a shot.
E: Um hmm. And what did the shot do?
C: Turned them into a turkey.

Almost half of the second graders also denied that type of kind was changed in the injection/pills case, as can be seen from the following excerpts:

2(2) Horse/zebra (injection)
C: It's still a horse because when it was a baby it was a horse, and the shot just made it look that way.

2(3) Chicken/turkey (injection)
C: That is a chicken because the insides can't change. It doesn't matter how the shot...That's on the outside, not on the inside.
E: So even though it looks like that with the big black feathers, inside it's a chicken?
C: Yes.

2(4) Bluebird/yellow finch (injection)
C: Bluebird. Because if you just give it a shot and it turns out to

look like a finch, it's still a bluebird because you can't change what it really is.

2(5) Bluebird/yellow finch (injection)
C: Really a bluebird. Well, because it was born a bluebird.

When second graders insist that type of kind cannot be changed, they do so for a variety of reasons. Some refer to the birth or origin of the animal as critical, some simply declare that no animal can be changed into any other no matter what, some mistakenly claim that nothing whatsoever happened on the inside, only on the outside, and that type therefore was not changed. Biological beliefs are beginning to emerge that question whether animal kinds can be changed by pills and injections. These beliefs continue to grow and result in the responses offered by the fourth graders, who show more of a resistance to type change than second graders. Nonetheless, almost half of the fourth graders said that type of kind was changed, revealing that the injection/pills manipulation came closer to what many of them felt to be biological essence. These differences are demonstrated by the variety of responses given by fourth graders in the following examples. The first three excerpts are from the transcripts of children who believed that type of kind changed due to the injection transformation.

4(1) Bluebird/yellow finch (injection)
C: I think it's really a finch. Well, a bluebird wouldn't go out with yellow feathers and a bluebird wouldn't sing like a finch.
E: What happened in the story?
C: Well, when it was hatched it got the wrong shot, so when they grew up they had a yellow finch.
E: So was it a finch or a bluebird at the end?
C: Really a finch.

4(2) Goat/sheep (injection)
C: (Long pause) A sheep, because it kind of turned into a sheep. It probably acted like a sheep after a while. It might have seen its reflection in a pool or something. And saw other sheep like him, and he probably started to act like it.
E: So do you think that the goat actually turned into a sheep?
C: Um hmm.
E: What do you think made it turn into a sheep?
C: The other sheep that looked like him doing things *(sic)*.
E: What did the farmer give the vitamin shot to—which animal?
C: The goat.
E: Then what happened?
C: (Repeats entire story correctly)

E: So you think it turned into a sheep?

C: Um hmm.

4(3) Goat/sheep (injection)

C: A sheep, because sheep don't have horns or beards and they have a lot of uh...wool.

E: So what happened after the baby goat got the shot?

C: It lost its horns and beard.

E: So you think this is a sheep?

C: Yeah.

Consider by contrast those children who resisted type-of-kind changes for animals:

4(4) Chicken/turkey (injection)

C: Really chickens, because there are not really shots to make a chicken turn into a turkey. And if they're already a chicken in an egg, when they're hatched they can't turn into a turkey.

4(5) Goat/sheep (injection)

C: Well, it's a goat. It just had bad vitamins so it didn't grow up to look properly.

4(6) Chicken/turkey (injection)

C: Chickens, because it still has the personality of chickens.

E: Why did they look like turkeys with big black feathers?

C: The shot—next they'll be turned into Chicken McNuggets!

4(7) Bluebird/yellow finch (injection)

C: Does this shot have to do with genetic structures of DNA to change the way it looked?

E: No, like a vitamin shot. (repeats story)

C: Well, it could either be a finch because otherwise why would it sing like a finch, it would sing like a bluebird. Or it could be...it could be bluebird. I think it would be a finch. It seems like the most logical answer, because why else would it sing like a finch? *(This is an important pattern in that only late in the development of biological knowledge do children view contraspecific behaviors as implying different underlying biological natures that must be linked to those behavioral differences. The study on contrasting feature types described below will further buttress this point.)*

E: Suppose it didn't sing like a finch.

C: Then it's a bluebird.

E: Why?

C: Well, because feathers don't really have anything to do with the bluebird. It still sings like a bluebird and all that. There's just an outside difference.

4(8) Chicken/turkey (injection)
C: Probably chickens.
E: What would make them chickens?
C: Because when they were born, they were chickens. When their mother and father had them, they were chickens. They were chickens before they got their shots. They got shots because that man wanted them to look like turkeys.

Finally, one fourth grader refused to commit herself until further information was supplied:

4(9) Goat/sheep (pills)
C: Well...the vitamins...they messed up, and so...it could be part sheep and part goat.
E: OK, how would that work? Tell me why you think it'd be part sheep and part goat.
C: Well, when it was born, it was a goat, but when he gave it the vitamin shots, it might have...uh...it just sort of changed its insides, so...maybe it turned into a sheep.
E: If you had to decide whether it was really more sheep or more goat, what would you think?
C: I'd mate it and see which way its babies came out.

The reasons these fourth graders give for resisting type-of-kind changes are similar to those given by the few second graders who also resisted them: origins, surface vs. deep features, the fundamental impossibility of such a transformation. The most obvious new type of reason involves more explicit reference to a genetic basis for kinds, ranging from the precocious reference to DNA structure to the more common remarks about who the parents were and what sorts of offspring were likely. This was the most common type of reason given by adult subjects in this study. As is clear from figure 11.1, almost all the adults felt that pills and injections at birth could not change type of kind, thus illustrating substantial further growth of biological knowledge after the fourth grade.

Overall, this study strongly indicates that kindergartners, and very possibly considerably younger children, are not the pure phenomenologists they appear to be, even when making distinctions between members of the same ontological category. They have beliefs about what sorts of mechanisms underlying characteristic feature changes are relevant to membership in a biological kind and what ones are not; and although many of these reasons may not be correct in the eyes of most adults, they are nonetheless theoretical constructs that may well be specific to biological kinds.

Unambiguously demonstrating that certain beliefs are specific to biological kinds—rather than, say, to the broader category of natural kinds—is not easy; and one must use a variety of converging measures to support such an argument. Although even the youngest children in the previous study consider that some types of bases for feature changes are relevant to an animal's essential nature and others are not, they might use the same reasoning to say that gold in a silver costume remains gold, gold painted silver that wears off remains gold, but gold painted silver that doesn't wear off is silver. I suspect that patterns of responses to such transformations for minerals would in fact be quite different than for animal kinds; and certainly notions of parentage, growth, and the effects of pills and injections are more restricted to biological kinds. This study alone, however, cannot be used as conclusive proof of biological specificity in young children; accordingly, the rest of this chapter is devoted to more exploratory studies that investigate whether young children embed their concepts of animals in theories that are specific to biological kinds.

Earlier Signs of Biological Theory

The finding that most kindergartners judge neither temporary alterations nor costumes to change type of kind leads inevitably to the question whether even younger children hold such beliefs. Karen Guskin and I developed a new set of techniques for asking these questions with younger children. A pilot study suggested that simply extending the current paradigm to younger children was not an optimal procedure for preschool-age subjects. In that study it appeared that all preschoolers were completely overwhelmed by characteristic features, even for the costume transformations. This would, in effect, replicate the findings of DeVries (1969), who found five-year-olds judging that a mask did not change a cat into a dog but three- and four-year-olds judging that it did. However, occasional remarks by these children suggested that even the preschoolers might, in a different paradigm, reveal some knowledge about the relative pertinence of costumes and biological transformations to type-of-kind changes. We conjectured that an explicit portrayal of the animal in the middle of a transformation might make the younger child think more precisely about the possible mechanisms underlying feature transformation and thereby differentially evaluate the relevance of costume and surface part transformations to type of kind. To assess this possibility, we designed transformation stories that explicitly referred to a transitional state depicted in an accompanying (doctored) photograph. Moreover, we made the transitional state especially salient by portraying it as chimeric, rather than blended, in nature. The stories in table 11.4 and the photographs in figure 11.2 illustrate the paradigm.

Thirty-seven preschool children, ranging in age from three to five years, participated as subjects. Each experimental session lasted approximately 10 minutes. Each child received only one story type (for instance, only costume stories), since piloting indicated too much confusion would otherwise occur across the story types. Two judges scored the responses on a three-point scale, assigning a score of 1 if the child judged the animal in the final picture to be what it looked like and a score of 3 if the child instead judged it to be what it started out as. The judges agreed that none of the responses should be assigned a score of 2.

The mean scores for all children were 2.62, 2.00, and 2.25 for the costume, temporary surface part, and permanent surface part changes, respectively. Only the responses to the costume items differed significantly from a random response pattern (that is, from a population mean of 2). It might be argued that the scores for the other two transformations also exhibited some tendency to override appearance, since they were greater than 1; it seems more likely, however, that these children were simply responding inconsistently.

Although this study should be pursued more systematically, it does suggest that preschoolers may differ from kindergartners in thinking

Table 11.4
Preschool transformation stories with transitional states

Horse/zebra (costume)
David was walking through a field when he saw this animal that looked just like a horse. He walked over very quietly and started to pet it. As he was patting its neck, he felt something funny. When he looked really closely he saw that there was a zipper around its neck that was all covered by hair. When David undid the zipper he saw that the animal had a costume on and there was a zebra underneath the costume! While David was standing looking at the animal with the costume head off, the person who owned the horse came into the field. She put the mask back on the animal and zipped it up so you couldn't see the zipper. When she was done, this is how it looked. What do you think it really is? A horse or a zebra?

Sheep/goat (costume)
Jane went to the county fair and while she was there, she saw an animal that looked just like a sheep. It had its neck stretched through the fence trying to get some grass. As Jane watched, the animal's head got stuck in the fence and as it tried to get loose, she heard a funny sound that sounded like Velcro. There was Velcro around its neck which held the mask onto the rest of the costume and it was coming undone! When the mask came undone, it fell onto the ground and Jane saw that there was a goat underneath the costume. Jane was very surprised but all of a sudden the farmer ran up and grabbed the mask, put it over the animal's head, and did the Velcro up. When he was finished, it looked like this. What do you think it really is? A sheep or a goat?

Table 11.4 (continued)

Horse/zebra (temporary surface parts)
Susie was walking through a field and she saw this animal that looked just like a horse. She watched it go over to a deep pond to take a drink, and when it lifted its head out of the water, this is what it looked like. It turns out that the mane had just been glued on and the stripes painted over with white paint because it was born a zebra, and when the animal put its head under the water, the paint and glue had come off. Just then, the man who owned it came out with a big can of white paint and some horse hair to glue back on his animal. He was very glad that the rest of the paint and glue hadn't come off. So he painted and glued the head again so when he was all done, this is how it looked. What do you think it really is? Is it a horse or a zebra?

Sheep/goat (temporary surface parts)
Jimmy was looking after his aunt's pet that looked just like a sheep while she went on vacation. Before she left, she told Jimmy that every morning he was supposed to rub her pet's head with a special kind of sandpaper because when it was born, it was a goat. But Jimmy kept forgetting to do that while she was gone and when his aunt came back this is how the animal looked. So she rubbed its horns with the sandpaper really hard until you couldn't see them anymore, and she shaved off the long beard that had grown, and then she painted it back to look just like a sheep. So after she painted the head again and was all done, this is how it looked. What do you think it really is? A sheep or a goat?

Horse/zebra (permanent surface parts)
Joe has this pet that looks just like a horse and one day he decided he wanted to put a picture of his pet on the wall. When he started to look through his photos, he remembered something that he'd forgotten all about. When Joe first got his pet, it was a zebra, but he'd painted it with this special paint that never came off and glued a horse mane on it with super strong glue so it looked just like a horse. Here's the picture Joe found of when he was almost done painting it and he only had the head left to paint and glue with glue and paint that never came off. After this picture was taken, he painted the head and since then, this is how it's looked and how it will always look. What do you think it really is? A horse or a zebra?

Sheep/goat (permanent surface parts)
Cindy just bought a new pet from a farm that looked just like a sheep. After a few days, however, the sheep got really lonely and homesick for its old home. So Cindy took her pet to visit all its old friends on the farm. The farmer was glad to see them and he showed them a picture of Cindy's pet that was taken two years ago. He told Cindy that when her pet was born, it was a goat. When the picture was taken, he had already glued the fur on and painted the rest of the body with special paint that never comes off and he was just about to finish the head. The next day he finished rubbing its horns down so you couldn't see them, and he had shaved the beard off so ever since then it has looked just like a sheep. What do you think it really is? A sheep or a goat?

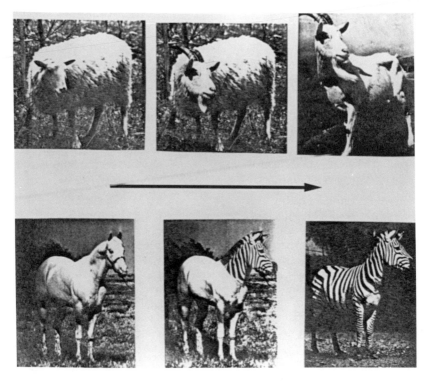

Figure 11.2
Examples of "photographs" accompanying descriptions used in the preschool study on transformations with transitional states.

that temporary changes in surface parts can change kinds; but they also believe, like older children, that costume changes are not biologically relevant. It is important to remember, however, that without explicit presentation of the chimeric displays, preschoolers do allow costumes to change type as well. Again, these differences need to be explored more fully.

Contrasting Property Types

A different way to discover what is developing in the elementary school years might be to pit one feature type against another. Michael Kelly conducted an informal study along these lines in an attempt to determine which features children consider to be most important to an animal's essence and whether they emphasize different feature types at different ages. Based on the responses given by children of different ages in the studies described above, four feature types were developed: external, internal, hereditary, and behavioral. Stimulus descriptions were constructed in which features of two types were contrasted with each other. Thus, an animal might be described as having the behavioral features of one species but the internal features of another. Because of the various feature pair contrasts in such a paradigm, it was not feasible to use the operations method of describing transformations on animals; instead, a variant of the discovery paradigm described in chapter 8 was used. Examples of the stories developed for this study are shown in table 11.5; the full set appears in appendix 7.

Illustrations were not used in this paradigm since in many conditions the relevant features could not be portrayed. If children asked about features that were not present or inferred that certain ones were, they were told the experimenters simply didn't know about those features and they shouldn't think about them in making their judgments. Six kindergartners, 8 second graders, and 10 fourth graders participated as subjects in this study.

There was a fair amount of noise in the data, probably caused by the difficulty of the task itself and the children's difficulty in focusing just on the features at hand. Moreover, only a small number of subjects were available, thus making analyses difficult. Nonetheless, two patterns do seem to emerge. First, for the youngest children, outside appearance frequently seems to override all other features. Then the insides and origins come to predominate, with no clear difference between the two. Perhaps somewhat surprisingly, the younger children never gave precedence to the behavioral features, although occasional evidence for this was found among the fourth graders. Apparently, not until that age do some children begin to think that a rich repertory of behavioral abilities must have a biological basis and must therefore be taken as evidence for that basis. This may raise some questions about accounts that presume that children's early concepts of biological kinds are based largely on behavioral criteria.

Second, the children had a strong tendency to infer appearance-based properties given other property types. This was particularly evident when behavior and insides were pitted against each other, in that children would often infer appearance-based properties that were not explicitly provided.

Overall, despite the small number of subjects, the increased difficulty of the task, and somewhat less clear intuitions about the stimuli, the results suggest an increasing reliance on internal features and matters of lineage. This, of course, is in accord with all the other studies summarized so far. Equally interesting is the suggestion (discussed at greater length in chapter 12) that younger children rarely felt that behavioral information was more important than the other three types, a point that may help argue for the biological specificity of their beliefs. These sug-

Table 11.5
Examples of descriptions used in the contrasting property types study

Porcupine/mouse (porcupine outsides and mouse insides)
The doctor went into the woods and he stumbled across this animal that he had never seen before. When he first saw it, he thought it was a porcupine because it looked just like a porcupine. Just like this guy here. It had needles and quills, just like a porcupine, and a short, stubby nose like a porcupine, and little, stubby feet, just like a porcupine. But when he took it back to the zoo and the doctor checked it out and looked inside it, he found out that it had all the inside parts of a mouse. So, it had a mouse heart instead of a porcupine heart, and a mouse stomach. Where you have a person stomach, this had a mouse stomach, and it had a mouse liver. So, on the outside, this thing looked just like a porcupine, with quills and a big nose and short, stubby feet, and it didn't have a tail, like a mouse has a tail. But on the insides it was just like a mouse, with a mouse heart and a mouse stomach and mouse insides. So, if you had to guess if it was either a mouse or a porcupine, and nothing in between, and you had to guess which one it was, what do you think it would be?

Zebra/horse (horse insides but zebra relatives)
The scientist went to Africa and he found this animal and first he thought it might be a zebra because the animal had a zebra for a mommy and a daddy, and zebra aunts and uncles, and made zebra babies. But then when he had the doctor check it out and the doctor looked inside it, they found that it had all the insides of a horse. So, it had a horse heart instead of a zebra heart and horse hearts are bigger and stuff. And it had a horse stomach. And it had horse muscles in its legs and everything. So the thing had a zebra for a mommy and a daddy and zebra aunts and uncles and made little zebra babies, but on the inside it had a horse heart and a horse stomach and horse muscles. So, if you had to guess and it was either a zebra or a horse and nothing in between, what do you think it would be?

Deer/cat (deer relatives but cat behavior)
And we came across an animal and it acted just like a cat. You know, the scientist heard it first, he didn't see it, and we don't know what the thing looks like. But he heard it and it acts like a cat, because it meows and purrs and it chases mice and stuff, because he heard mice running away from the thing. And it tried to scratch things when it was mad. But the thing was, it had a deer for a mommy and a daddy and deer aunts and uncles and made little deer babies. So, it acts just like a cat, it meows and purrs and chases mice and tries to scratch when it's mad, but it has a deer mommy and daddy, a deer aunt and uncle, and makes little deer babies. So what kind of animal do you think it was? Do you think it was a cat, or do you think it was a deer?

gestive results certainly need to be explored in a more thorough and larger scale study.

More Gradual Transformations

When young children judge that shaving a lion's mane and painting it with stripes creates a tiger, they may do so because they are overwhelmed by a large number of feature changes occurring all at once. What if the transformation is instead broken down into a graphically depicted, step-by-step process in which only a small amount of change occurs at each step? Perhaps in such a situation children are more able to see that the transformations are not so integral to the animal's essence. (For instance, when just a few stripes at a time are changed, perhaps children begin to realize that stripes per se are not that important.) In fact, perhaps just through spontaneously visualizing the transformation in this much more gradual, step-by-step fashion, children on their own come to undergo the shift that we have observed in the studies described so far. If so, then perhaps the shift reflects less an emerging biological theory than a general recognition of the somewhat arbitrary nature of transformations.

A related and equally important question is what status children decide to ascribe to the animals in the intermediate stages of transformation. If the younger children are slavishly bound to characteristic features, then perhaps they will regard the intermediate animals as, say, half tiger and half lion, whereas older children, with their better understanding of biological essence, will see the animals as switching completely at some intermediate stage and never being in a transitional stage, and the oldest children will deny not only that there were transitional cases but also that any changes have taken place at all. Thus, it might be possible to predict which children are just about to shift to overriding characteristic features by finding those who agree to a change but see it as an all-or-none process.

Sheila Jeyifous, Norma Bacillious, Karen Mulvaney, and I addressed these issues by conducting a study in which the stimuli were drawings of a pretransformation animal, a posttransformation animal, and three intermediate stages. One set of these drawings is shown in figure 11.3. As the examples in table 11.6 indicate, the descriptions were similar to those used in other operations studies, except that they were more gradual in nature. When children judged that a change had occurred, they were asked why, if in a certain stage something was an x, just adding certain features (say, more stripes and fur) would make it a y when adding the same features (same amount of stripes and fur) in an earlier stage made little or no difference.

Figure 11.3
Example of tiger/lion drawings accompanying descriptions used in the information study on gradual blended changes.

Table 11.6
Sample descriptions used in informal study on gradual blended changes

Chicken/turkey
Drawing #1: Scientists came along and snipped off the orange "crown" on top of the chicken's head with scissors. And they glued a long orange piece of material under its chin with glue that never comes off. Then they dyed its feathers brown with permanent dye that never comes off. Is it still a chicken or is it something else?

Drawing #2: Next the scientists made the orange piece under its chin longer, dyed its feathers gray on its head, neck, tail, and upper legs with dye that never comes off, and gave it a drug to make its tail feathers grow longer and fuller. Is it still a chicken or is it something else?

Drawing #3: Then the scientists dyed its feathers even more grey on its head, neck, and thighs, and its body feathers more brown with permanent dye. They also fed it more so that it gained weight and gave it more of the drug to make its tail feathers grow longer and fuller. Is it still a chicken or is it something else?

Drawing #4: Now they painted its feathers with nice designs, fed it more so that it got fatter, and gave it some more of the drug that makes its tail feathers grow longer and fuller. Is it still a chicken or is it something else?

Drawing #5: All the time they were doing these things, they changed the way it acted, so now it acts like a turkey: it says "gobble gobble," eats what turkeys eat, and stays with other turkeys. When they were all done, it looked like this which is just what a turkey looks like. What do you think it is really, a chicken or a turkey?

Goat/sheep
Drawing #1: Scientists took this goat and cut off some of its beard and filed down its horns a little. Then they put hair tonic on it to make the hair grow thick and curly on its belly. Is it still a goat or is it something else?

Drawing #2: They got the scissors and cut off more of its beard and used a file to file down more of its horns. Next they added more hair tonic to its belly and sides to make the hair thicker and curlier. Is it still a goat or is it something else?

Drawing #3: The scientists then cut off what was left of the beard, filed down the horns even shorter, and added more hair tonic all over to make the hair thick and curly. Is it still a goat or is it something else?

Drawing #4: Now they filed off the horns completely and added lots more hair so its hair is all thick and curly like wool. Is it still a goat or is it something else?

Drawing #5: All the time they were doing these things, they changed the way it acted, so now it acts like a sheep: it says "baa," eats what sheep eat, and hangs around with other sheep. When they were all done, it looked just like this, which is just what a sheep looks like. What do you think it is really, a goat or a sheep?

Horse/zebra
Drawing #1: Scientists took some scissors and made the mane shorter and the tail less bushy. They put white dye that never comes off on its legs, and they used a special black dye to make the face darker. Is it still a horse or is it something else?

Drawing #2: Then they used more white permanent dye on the legs and to make

Table 11.6 (continued)

white patches on the body. They also used the big scissors to cut off some more of the mane and tail. Is it still a horse or is it something else?

Drawing #3: Here they used the white dye to make some stripes on the body. They cut off some more of the tail and then they took a comb and made it a little bushier at the end; they also made the little bit of mane that was left stand up a little. Is it still a horse or is it something else?

Drawing #4: Next they took the black and white dye and made the stripes clear. They used scissors to cut more tail off and make it thin on top and bushier at the end. They also used some hairspray to make the little mane stand up. Is it still a horse or is it something else?

Drawing #5: All the time they were doing this, they changed the way it acted, so now it acts like a zebra: it makes zebra noises, eats what zebras eat, and hangs around with other zebras. When they were all done with it, it looked just like this, which is just what a zebra looks like. What do you think it is really, a horse or a zebra?

Tiger/lion
Drawing #1: Scientists took some dye that never comes off and dyed its black stripes orange. Then they put some hair tonic on its head and neck to make some bushy hair grow there. And they dyed the fur on its face orange where it had been white. Is it still a tiger or is it something else?

Drawing #2: Next they took the permanent dye and dyed its fur a solid brown color over most of its stripes. They added more hair tonic on its head and neck to make the hair grow in bushier and thicker. And they dyed its fur brown where it had been white. Is it still a tiger or is it something else?

Drawing #3: They used some more dye to cover all its stripes and white patches and make its fur all one color. They also added more hair tonic to make the mane really bushy and a slightly bushy end on its tail. Is it still a tiger or is it something else?

Drawing #4: Last they added more hair tonic so that the bushy hair grew in on its head, neck and chest. And they made sure that the brown permanent dye made every part of its fur brown. Is it still a tiger or is it something else?

Drawing #5: All the time they were doing this, they changed the way it acted, so now it acts like a lion: it growls like a lion, it eats what lions eat, and it hangs around with other lions. When they were all done with it, it looked just like this, which is just what a lion looks like. What do you think it is really, a tiger or a lion?

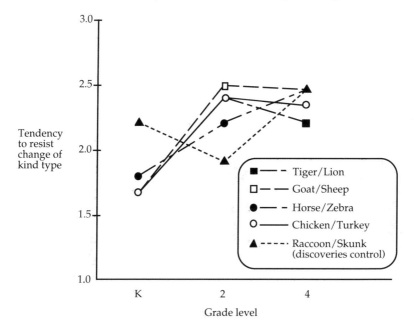

Figure 11.4
Mean scores for responses to the final picture in the sequences in the informal study on gradual blended changes. Mean scores for the skunk/raccoon control are also shown.

Fifteen kindergartners, 10 second graders, and 15 fourth graders participated as subjects in this study. Each child was seen individually for a session lasting roughly 20 minutes. In addition to posing the questions asked in prior studies, the experimenters asked specifically whether the animals in the transitional stages were animals of one species, animals of the other species, or mixtures of both. The skunk/raccoon discovery description used in chapter 8 was also included as a control item that involved neither an operation nor gradual stages.

The mean scores for responses to the final picture in the sequence as well as for the skunk/raccoon control are shown in figure 11.4. Across all picture sequences there was only a weak rise in scores with age. Thus, the kindergarten means for the final choice in the five pictures were only marginally higher than the kindergarten means in prior studies, whereas the means for grades 2 and 4 were actually somewhat lower. Moreover, the rise in scores with age could only be classified as a trend (p < .09). These patterns of responses do not mean that the children were simply regressing toward more random responding as was seen from the consistently dramatic changes in judgments as one moves from picture 1 to picture 5. For all four sequences, the change was significant at the

$p < .0001$ level; in addition, for all but one sequence (horse/zebra), there was a significant age/item interaction ($p < .05$). The kindergartners did unusually well on the control discoveries item, raising the possibility that the gradual transformations provided some insight. But given the weakness of that effect for the operations stimuli and for the second graders even on the control item, such an influence seems unlikely.

In sum, the results of this study are ambiguous with respect to whether making the transformation more gradual produced any increase in insight. Although the minimal change with age argues for such an effect, the relatively low mean scores do not. Perhaps more important was the finding that very few children seemed to judge the intermediate pictures as depicting blended animals. With only a few exceptions, children saw the animals as being completely of one kind or the other and as fully changing in kind across the critical pair of adjacent pictures. The few suggestions of blending came mostly from the oldest children. Three fourth graders, but only one second grader and one kindergartner, raised the possibility of such blends.

A Study on the Origins of Natural Kinds and Artifacts

In the operations and discoveries studies in this and prior chapters two findings are clear: (1) Although the younger children may seem to treat artifacts and natural kinds as similar by relying on characteristic features to determine the nature of both, their comments also reveal an awareness of differences between these two types. (2) When children come to regard a kind as having an essence, they frequently refer to its typical path of origin as more important to identity than conflicting characteristic features. These two findings point to a need for more direct work on origins. Although Piaget is well known for his work on origins (Piaget 1929), his investigations do not systematically manipulate the types of objects queried and instead revolve around the animacy issue. In the informal study described here Barbara Bauer and I looked at knowledge of origins about different sorts of artifacts and natural kinds.

Procedures and design

The subjects in this study participated in three tasks. Each child was first shown photographs of six familiar objects: three natural kinds (bear, hummingbird, tree) and three artifacts (shovel, boots, toy truck). The child was asked to identify each object and then watched as the experimenter put the photographs in two piles corresponding to artifacts and natural kinds. The child was then asked why the objects in each pile "go together." Given the evidence in the literature on the difficulties that young children can have with such a task, we did not expect the younger children to provide clear, consistent responses. Twelve kindergartners and fourteen second graders from elementary schools in the Ithaca, New York, area participated as subjects.

The primary reason for this initial task was to demonstrate to the children the kind of sort we were interested in. Consequently, any child who did not say that artifacts are man-made and natural kinds are not was told, "I can think of another reason why these go together...some of these things are things that people can make, and this envelope says 'People make these'...so they go in this envelope. Some of the ones might be real hard to make—you might have to know how to do special things, and you might need special materials and tools and stuff like that—but people can make some of these things. Some of these things nobody can make, no person can make them...they could never, never, never make them no matter how hard they tried, even if they tried for years and years and years. Their envelope says 'No, people couldn't make these.' Which ones of these things are the things that nobody can make...that people don't know how to make them?" The cards were shuffled, and the children were asked to sort them into the two envelopes, one bearing the picture of two smug, confident-looking people ("you can make them") and the other the picture of two puzzled-looking people, one scratching his head, the other shrugging ("you can't make them").

After children sorted these six objects, they moved on to the second task. They were told, "OK, now I've got some more things. I want you to see whether people can make them or not," reminded of what the two envelopes and the people on them meant, and instructed, "You decide where all these things go. The first one is x. X, do people make x(s)?" For all responses that an object was not made by people, children were asked where the object does in fact come from and whether there have always been objects of that type.

The stimuli, which are shown in table 11.7, were artifacts and natural kinds of three types: small familiar, large familiar, and unfamiliar. Each unfamiliar object was selected primarily because it had a highly unusual shape and bore no close resemblance to a more familiar object. Each was given a nonsense name, to eliminate any clue its real name might have given to the nature of its kind.

After the children had been queried on all the natural kinds and artifacts, they participated in the third task, in which they were asked to explain superficially analogous changes in artifacts and natural kinds. Thus, both a car and an apple tree were described as losing their typical functions, a tree and a fence changed size (got larger), and deer and bicycles of a certain type were said to have become increasingly scarce. In each case the child was asked to guess why that happened. The issue of interest here was whether they tended to give different classes of explanations for artifacts and natural kinds for at least superficially similar processes.

Table 11.7
Stimuli for origins of natural kinds vs. artifacts

	Artifacts	Natural kinds
Familiar, small	Chairs Go-cart Basket Tent	Fish Moth Grass Flower
Familiar, large	Car Farm buildings House Road Bridge	Mountain Rocks River Lake Island
Unfamiliar	Plibate (a complex, abstract wrought iron structure with many curving lines) Blope (a printed circuit board of unusual shape and dimensions) Tevye (an air ionizer machine made out of hardwood and fabric in a Danish contemporary design and with a novel shape) Snork (a brightly colored plastic plumbing valve with various protuberances)	Spritzel (an unusual cactus-type plant, white in color, somewhat similar to the century plant) Komoly (a deep-sea creature, pale white, with an oddly shaped body and head and with strange tufts growing out of parts of its skin) Clampston (a view of the front half of a manatee under water with a large amount of vegetation in the mouth area) Cantic (a 4' high, 1' wide plant consisting of a central shaft surrounded by hundreds of flowering bulbs on long stems)

Results

The results of the first part of the study merely reflect the extent to which children were able to explain why the initial two classes were sorted as they were. Not surprisingly, many children gave thematic responses (see Bruner, Olver, Greenfield, et al. 1966) such as "Birds and bears like to climb and land on trees" or "Because the man who works in the dump truck needs boots so his foots won't get dirty," in which the three items are related in a thematic, noncriterial manner. Of the twelve kindergartners, six gave unambiguously thematic responses and one gave a mixed thematic/classificatory response in which the artifacts were united thematically and the natural kinds by the common criterion of being alive. Of the remaining five, two said something like "living/nonliving" and three said something like "in nature/not in nature," sometimes referring to the artifacts as "things you work with." Of the second graders, four made judgments pertaining to living/nonliving differences with some references to the functional utility of artifacts, six gave clearly thematic responses, two gave mixed responses, and one gave unscorable responses.

These responses, however, should not be interpreted as showing that children do not understand important differences between natural kinds and artifacts. Given past research on classification (see chapter 2), it is hardly surprising that they should evince so much difficulty in escaping thematic modes of classification. The data on the other tasks in this study provide a much richer picture of their knowledge in this area. For example, consider their scores on the subsequent sorting tasks once the correct criteria were explained to them. For the original stimuli, their scores were almost perfect, with only one mistake occurring among the

Table 11.8
Percent correct sortings for the stimulus types used in the study on origins of natural kinds vs. artifacts

	K	2
Small familiar artifacts	98%	100%
Small familiar natural kinds	91%	90%
Large familiar artifacts	97%	99%
Large familiar natural kinds	90%	97%
Unfamiliar artifacts	89%	98%
Unfamiliar natural kinds	84%	93%

kindergartners and none among the second graders. Table 11.8 shows the results for the other stimulus types.

There are two notable patterns in these data. Second graders scored slightly higher than kindergartners, and children at both ages scored higher on artifacts than on natural kinds. These differences, however, should not mask the most important common finding—namely, that at both ages the children are extremely good at sorting the two groups of objects, even for totally novel objects. Moreover, these numbers are likely to be a somewhat conservative rendering of the children's competencies, since on several occasions children initially put plants with other natural kinds, then realized that humans frequently plant them, and changed their response. Unfortunately, the probe questioning was not always extensive enough to assess whether the child meant this to apply to all plants. These findings are compatible with those of Gelman (1987), who found that even preschoolers did quite well when asked whether various entities were made by people.

Conclusions

Several of the studies in this chapter are exploratory in nature, but overall they demonstrate that kindergartners and even preschoolers have systematic beliefs about what sorts of mechanisms can legitimately cause the characteristic features of animals and what sorts cannot. Put differently, they seem to understand that characteristic features on their own should not be used to diagnose membership in a kind; one also has to take into account how those features came to be manifested. Depending on the mechanisms responsible for them, exactly the same clusters of characteristic features were judged either as having no effect on the animal involved or as changing it into an entirely new kind. Thus, in contrast to the apparent Quinean pattern, these children do embed their concepts and interpret their properties in arrays of systematically connected beliefs rather than in an atheoretical similarity space.

Do these sets of beliefs constitute a naive theory of biology? An answer to this question depends on accounts of what theories are and of how the bounds of a theory are to be determined. The transcripts and the patterns of responses from these studies certainly give the impression that even the preschoolers seem to be making judgments about animals in particular and not about all natural kinds in general. But a large-scale systematic program of studies will be needed before we can fully determine the scope of these children's beliefs and the extent to which we wish to call them theories. In the next chapter I consider how such a program could be developed.

Chapter 12

Escaping the Original Sim.

From time to time we all become entranced by our "animal sense of similarity" (Quine 1977), which depends solely on theory-neutral tabulations of salient features; but at least as adults we are able to escape the immediate, atheoretical world and think in terms of the more "essential" aspects of things. Young children may be different and may have vastly more difficulty escaping the "original sim." I have suggested, especially in chapters 10 and 11, that young children do not have a general deficit along these lines but are bound to the original sim. only to the extent that theories in a particular domain fail them. This position can be evaluated more thoroughly by considering several other research programs that bear in different ways on the same issue.

The Appearance/Reality Distinction

The notion that young children move from a primitive, immediate similarity space to more theoretical spaces may well be related to their understanding of the appearance/reality distinction, a topic extensively explored by Flavell and his associates (for the most comprehensive overview of this work, see Flavell, Green, and Flavell 1986). These researchers found that most three-year-olds did not understand the appearance/reality distinction in a variety of tasks. This pattern held up even when heroic efforts were made to elicit more precocious performance by simplifying the appearance/reality task along lines that have been found to improve preschoolers' performance on other cognitive tasks. Earlier work by DeVries (1969) strongly correlates with aspects of these studies. DeVries persuaded a remarkably patient cat to serve as the stimulus and to allow a highly realistic dog mask to be put on and taken off. Most kindergartners judged the masked cat to be a cat, despite its doggish face. Preschoolers reacted in an opposite manner, however, often judging that the masked animal was in fact a dog. In a highly similar task Flavell, Green, and Flavell found a closely corresponding pattern of development.

Despite these results, preschoolers may be able to discount appearance in situations where they understand how different underlying properties might also be present. As described in chapter 11, if the nature of the transformation is made particularly salient through chimeras, it is possible to get even three-year-olds to declare that a costumed animal is no different in kind from an animal of the same species that retains its original appearance. However, it is also easy to replicate the opposite pattern by blurring over the nature of the transformation; and so the question remains why such a manipulation should have such a profound effect on preschoolers.

Three-year-olds can perform quite well on a pretend/real task for the same objects that they fail on the appearance/reality task (Flavell, Green, and Flavell 1986). Flavell and his colleagues propose that performance on these two tasks may differ because, among other reasons, in the pretend/real task "the child does not have to explicitly represent the object's appearance and differentiate it from its reality but only to indicate what sort of object it is" (p. 11). Leslie (1987), however, suggests that even in tasks involving pretense "there are two simultanous representations of the situation. One representation is for how the situation is actually perceived, while the other represents what the pretense is" (p. 417). Moreover, Leslie points out that the pretense must relate to the actual situation in highly specific, nonarbitrary ways. Thus, the reason why performance differs on the two tasks may not be simply that one requires children to think about "apparent contradictions" (Flavell, Green, and Flavell 1986, 57) between two representations whereas the other does not. Three-year-olds will override characteristic features of an animal if the ways in which those features are connected to the animal do not mesh with their intuitive notions of what causal relations underlie such features in biological kinds.

The critical difference between the appearance/reality tasks and those described in this book may be whether children are able to construct a reasonable explanation of how two sorts of representations could be simultaneously present. (This difference may also be involved in the contrasts between pretend/real and appearance/reality tasks.) Thus, Flavell, Green, and Flavell may be precisely correct in suspecting that a major part of the difficulty in the appearance/reality task lies in dealing with two simultaneous and apparently contradictory representations— not because children are intrinsically unable to do so in general, but because they cannot see a way of resolving the apparent contradiction. In the appearance/reality task relatively sophisticated beliefs about perceivers' points of view, perception, and so on, may be required to understand how the two representations are noncontradictory (which may also explain the strong correlation between level II perspective-taking tasks (Flavell, Green, and Flavell 1986) and the appearance/reality correlation). In the pretend/real task the relations between the two representations are often highly structured and hence possibly more available to children, especially since they often construct the correspondence themselves. Finally, in the natural kind transformation tasks, apparently making the intermediate stage highly salient allows the children to understand how the costumed animal and the real animal interrelate.

In sum, the results of the appearance/reality studies and those presented here are compatible if one assumes that much of what develops is an understanding of increasingly complex mechanisms that allow two apparently conflicting representations to be present simultaneously. The focus on mechanisms, or explanations, for resolving the contradictory representations offers a smoother, more continuous developmental integration of the results of the appearance/reality studies, the pretend/real studies, and the studies presented here. Even adults find some contradictions unfathomable because they lack an explanation, and even very young preschoolers can meaningfully interpret those contradictions for which they do have adequate explanatory accounts. Thus, the appearance/reality studies can be construed as supporting the notion that young children are not universally bound to the original sim. but, like adults, are locally bound in just those cases where knowledge of mechanism and explanation for surface features are not yet available to them.

Induction

Pure induction without prior constraints on the hypothesis space is doomed. (Consider, for example, the infinite set of different curves representing functions that can be drawn through any finite set of points.) For centuries it has been assumed that successful induction in humans must reflect a conceptual base, with corresponding similarity and simplicity metrics that guide those inductions (see, for example, Peirce 1931–1935; Mill 1843/1974). For this reason, studies on changing patterns of induction in childhood may provide insight into the kinds of concepts that guide those inductions and into the extent to which they are (if ever) embedded in atheoretical similarity metrics. Providing that a sufficiently comprehensive assessment is made, patterns of induction in a conceptual domain should imply features about conceptual structure that converge on those described in this book.

The most impressive systematic developmental work to date on patterns of induction in young children has been done by Carey (1985). Carey carefully documents consistent differences between younger and older children concerning inductions on what other animals would have a specific property, given that an initially presented animal does. For example, most four-year-olds, when told that humans have omenta, attributed that property only to animals that were quite similar to humans. As similarity decreased, attribution dropped precipitously. Older children showed a much smaller drop in attributions to animals that were highly dissimilar from humans. More important, when told that a dog had an omentum, the younger children were less likely to attribute it to humans and other mammals than were older children, since they seemed to adopt a generalization gradient around similarity to the taught exemplar. Most important, if younger children were told that two widely divergent animals (for example, dogs and bees) had omenta, they were much less likely to think that most other animals must have them as well and instead induced in declining gradients from the two taught exemplars.

Carey interprets these developmental patterns as indicative of an emerging coherent theory of biology. The younger children have no systematic theory of biology and of the ways in which internal organs are functionally interrelated and essential to the growth and survival of a broad class of organisms.

> They do not have an autonomous domain of biological knowledge that flags these properties as biological properties and flags what features of people, dogs, and other objects are relevant to the comparisons. For the 10-year-old, knowledge of the interrelations among the various biological functions and internal organs renders people just one mammal among many, in the context of biological properties like having particular internal organs. For the young child, on the other hand, knowledge of these functions is instead integrated into schemata for human activity. (pp.138–139)

The emphasis on emerging biological theory makes clear the special relevance of Carey's work, which is further reinforced by her discussion of some of the discoveries and operations studies described in chapters 8 and 9. For the discoveries paradigm, Carey concludes that if younger children tend to think of properties such as having babies in a social, psychological manner, then it follows that a younger child might well believe that a skunk could have raccoons for babies. For the operations paradigm, she concludes that

> if subjects have any notion of biological essence, they will know that these kinds of transformations, being nonbiological in their mechanism, cannot affect this essence. Five-year-olds have no notion of biological essence, not having differentiated the domain of biology from the domain of psychology. Therefore, their concepts of fruits,

plants, and animals must be exhausted by their knowledge of the characteristics by which they are recognized....To change these is to fundamentally change the object. (p. 180)

Carey is, of course, correct in focusing on the parallels between these two lines of research, even though they use different methods and stimuli. Moreover, I agree with her assessment that the major driving force behind these developmental patterns comes from biological theory. It may not be the case, however, that these changes represent the emergence of a totally new theory of biology that comes to replace a behavioral/psychological theory as the means for organizing animal kinds. Although the initial operations and discoveries studies would seem to support the view that five-year-olds have no notions of biological essence and rely solely on characteristic features in forming their concepts of animals, the studies presented in later chapters have demonstrated that such an account may not be correct.

Five-year-olds, and even preschoolers, do have some notions about essence and about how theoretical principles can override characteristic features. Moreover, those principles may be embedded in an emerging biological theory that is distinct from a behavioral/psychological one. Thus, what we see in these children may be not the emergence of a new theoretical domain but the further differentiation and development of a specifically biological theory that is present from the earliest ages. More work is needed to provide a detailed description of the early stages of this theory to better understand its origins and to assess the extent to which it seems to constitute an autonomous, biologically specific set of beliefs, but the studies described in chapters 10 and 11 lend feasibility to the notion that kindergartners and possibly considerably younger children have access to a rudimentary biological theory.

Further evidence that preschoolers may be able to override characteristic features comes from S. Gelman (1984) and S. Gelman and Markman (1987), who have shown that, at least in some situations involving labeled categories, even preschoolers seem to make inductions that go beyond mere appearance. Thus, even three-year-olds will go beyond perceptual information when they are told, for example, that a flamingo feeds its young mashed-up food and that a bat feeds its young milk and are then asked what a blackbird feeds its young. The pattern was much stronger when a specific label (such as "bird") was used than when it was not, but even in the latter case the children made some inferences beyond the perceptual. Gelman and Markman conclude that, in such cases, the children seem to figure out what categories are involved even in the absence of explicit labels, often by spontaneously providing such labels.

There is apparently a strong difference between the ability to make inductions about an instance's properties, given a category label, and the ability to make guesses about what an instance (category label) is, given a set of its properties (see also S. Gelman, Collman, and Maccoby 1986). Inducing properties given labels would not seem to require much in the way of rich theories of the kinds in question. The inductions are not completely atheoretical in that the young children seem to have some hunches about what sorts of features are not transferred even when labels are shared. Moreover, S. Gelman and O'Reilly (1988) has shown that preschoolers may induce differently about natural kinds and artifacts. Thus, preschoolers in Gelman's study showed a stronger tendency to assume that natural kinds with the same label shared internal parts than to assume that similarly labeled artifacts did, a phenomenon that seems restricted to the basic level (Rosch et al. 1976). In addition, in open-ended reporting on whether things have "the same kinds of stuff inside," young children assumed this to be true at the basic level but not at superordinate levels.

S. Gelman's studies therefore suggest that preschool children do have at least some crude conception that natural kinds have internal parts and that they tend to share these with other members of the same basic level category. This accords with other signs of essentialist biases in children (see chapters 8–11), often when they know very little about the specific details of the internal parts. These children, however, are still in many ways naive about the kind of role that internal parts play in a coherent biological theory. They may know that animals do have internal parts, that such parts serve certain functions (see also R. Gelman 1986, and Massey and R. Gelman 1988), and that members of similar kinds tend to share such parts. But they do not seem to understand the crucial causal roles that internal parts play in organizing surface parts and appearance-based properties. (They may have more sophisticated notions, however, about how internal parts are causally linked to movement: ibid.) Moreover, because they fail to understand such relations, they may not see internal parts as being central to a kind's nature. It is almost as though they have the relative relations between the two kinds of information reversed. Adults will say that, although all tigers share certain surface features, if most of those distinguishing surface features are missing from an instance, it is still a tiger, whereas if certain internal properties are missing, it may no longer be a tiger. Sufficiently young children, however, may view the surface features as being central and the internal ones as being more weakly correlated and less vital to decisions about a kind's essential nature.

The research by Carey and S. Gelman illustrates several points. First, even the youngest of Carey's subjects do not seem to be basing their judgments on an atheoretical original similarity metric; Carey explicitly rejects the possibility that even her youngest subjects were basing their inductions on Quine's "neutral similarity spaces." At the least, then, preschoolers are guided by a psychological/behavioral theory—perhaps one that in its vagueness is closer to the original sim., but one that possesses some degree of theoretical coherence as well. Gelman's work suggests that preschoolers' inductions may be based on some more biologically specific beliefs, although there is clearly a great deal of differentiation of those beliefs. Finally, current research that Alonso Vera and I are conducting (Vera and Keil 1988) suggests that preschoolers can exhibit quite different patterns of induction depending on what theoretical domain they think is most relevant to the properties in question. In particular, preschoolers may be capable of more sophisticated, biologically specific inductions when stimuli are presented in such a way as to access their existing biological beliefs rather than their psychological/behavioral ones. We have been able not only to replicate the patterns of induction found by Carey for such properties as bones and hearts, but also to show much more mature patterns of induction when we introduce those same properties in a biological/functional context. Although the contexts are simply 10-second descriptions of how the properties are involved in biological functions, they are sufficient to enable preschoolers to make property attributions that are indistinguishable from those of second graders.

Children, like adults, may often have several different sets of coherent beliefs that they can potentially bring to bear to make inductions about natural kinds. If so, then changes in patterns of induction with development might not represent the emergence of new theoretical perspectives, but rather a shift in which theoretical domain is initially invoked in a certain range of tasks. In any case, it seems increasingly clear that, even in preschoolers, no pattern of induction over natural kinds seems to be based on anything like an original sim.

Levels of Similarity and Analogical Thinking

Analogical thinking provides another important method for examining changing concepts and similarity relations. Successful analogies require mapping between two conceptual structures, presumably along a well-organized, predictable similarity metric. By examining the details of analogical thinking and its development, it should be possible to make reliable inferences not only about the similarity relations being used but also about the conceptual structures involved. In particular, it should be possible to tell whether young children go beyond the original sim. in drawing such analogies.

There have been increasingly precise discussions of how original sim. modes of construal might be involved both in adults' abilities to construe analogies and in the development of such abilities. For example, developmental studies repeatedly find that, for a given set of stimuli, young children tend to respond more on the basis of perceptual similarity than older children. As discussed in chapter 2, this is seen in many other kinds of tasks as well—for example, tasks involving classification and sorting, free association and free recall, word definitions, and metaphor. Young children are claimed to be "perceptually bound" or "perceptually seduced" (Bruner, Olver, Greenfield, et al. 1966)—that is to say, unduly influenced by appearances.

Accepting that younger children have a greater tendency to perceptual or original sim. seduction does not limit us to one narrow theoretical construal of why this is so. As noted in chapter 2, this bias in itself could be handled by global stage-like theories, general learning theory views, and various strong nativist views that incorporate some mode of developmental change, such as increasing access. However, if it is also recognized that such a bias varies with age as a function of the conceptual domain involved, these sorts of accounts become less tenable and a more knowledge-specific account emerges. Throughout much of this book I have argued that increasingly rich domain-specific knowledge structures, especially those that form coherent causal belief systems, are a guiding force in moving children away from holistic, atheoretical modes of construal. Recent work on analogy is particularly relevant because both developmental studies and studies with adult subjects offer explicit accounts of what the structure of the emerging belief systems must be like to allow successful analogizing to proceed.

In discussing analogy and transfer in children, Brown (1986) suggests that children, like adults, rely on appearance as a fallback option when there is no other more revealing basis on which to make a judgment. If they lack other sorts of knowledge that reveal different types of similarities, their only choice is between a random partitioning of the stimulus space and a partitioning based on general operations over the most typical features. Brown argues that supposedly profound differences in transfer skills and analogical reasoning abilities between different age groups may largely reflect the lack of richer knowledge systems that afford other sorts of relational insights. Moreover, she empirically demonstrates that preschoolers are capable of exhibiting sophisticated transfer skills (and analogical reasoning) if they have adequate relational knowledge in the two domains being juxtaposed. They also appear to be greatly helped by other, more strategic forms of task support, but the primary need seems to be for certain types of knowledge structures.

There is a second argument here as well, that the other modes of construal are more relational in nature rather than being mere tabulations, say, of feature frequencies. The details of what these different sorts of knowledge representations are like are spelled out in Gentner's structure-mapping theory (Gentner 1983; Forbus and Gentner 1986). Gentner suggests that humans map relations from one domain (the base) to another (the target) on the basis of the following three rules: (1) the properties or attributes of the objects in the base are removed from consideration, and (2) the relations among objects in the base are preserved subject to the condition that (3) higher-order relations (relations among relations) are preserved at the expense of lower-order relations. Rule (3), the principle of "systematicity," is most important; it is at this level that causal structures are especially emphasized. It has the consequence that connected sets of relations rather than isolated predicates are likely to be transported across domains.

Gentner often uses the example of analogy or transfer between the solar system and Rutherford's model of the atom. Countless high school science teachers have attempted to convey the traditional Rutherford view of the atom by comparing its structural relations to those of the solar system, which is assumed to be a domain mastered at an earlier age by most students. When teachers say that "the atom is like the solar system," they are expecting that their students will not only transfer the appropriate structural relations of solar systems over to the new domain but also not transfer irrelevant properties. Predicting what is transferred is the critical problem of analogy and one that Gentner argues can be handled in a "syntactic," objective manner that makes little or no reference to content. In the case of the solar system analogy, the first step is simply to ignore one-place predicates in the source domain (the sun), such as "is yellow" and "is gaseous," and focus on n-place predicates. The second, more interesting step is to focus on relations that are more systematic, where systematicity is defined according to several related criteria and results in "higher-order relations that connect the lower-order relations...into a mutually constraining structure" (p. 164). These criteria include a deep hierarchical embedding of relations within other relations and strong interconnections among relations.

An analogy that focuses on systematicity maps few or no object attributes and the highest-order relational ones possible. Systematicity is crucial for knowing why some two-place relations such as "more massive than" (sun, planet) are likely to be mapped, whereas others such as "hotter than" (sun, planet) are not. Systematicity obtains when "a system can be represented by an interconnected predicate structure in which higher-order predicates enforce connections among lower-order predicates" (p. 162). Consequently, "a predicate that belongs to a mappable system of interconnecting relationships is more likely to be imported into the target than an isolated predicate" (p. 162).

Gentner discusses the systematicity cluster notion in concrete detail by focusing on the relations among the following four lower-order relations and showing how changing any one of them is likely to change one or more of the others:

1. distance (sun, planet)
2. attractive force (sun, planet)
3. revolves around (planet, sun)
4. more massive than (sun, planet)

In describing this process, Gentner argues that "to the extent that people recognize (however vaguely) that the system of predicates connected with central forces is the deepest most interconnected mappable system for an analogy, they will favor relations that belong to that system in their interpretations" (p. 164).

Gentner's model assumes several different sorts of similarity: mere appearance-based similarity, in which only object attributes are used to compare kinds; literal similarity, in which both attributes and relations are used; relational similarity, in which only relations are matched; and abstract similarity, in which more systematic structured relations are considered. In discussing these different kinds of relations, Forbus and Gentner (1986) speculate on how they are differentially involved over the course of learning and development. They argue that mere appearance and literal similarity methods of construal are highly accessible and therefore appear very early in children and in adults who are novices. They cite some of the characteristic-to-defining shift studies described earlier in this book as supporting this sort of argument. They specifically suggest that prototype-like representations of the sort that Rosch has proposed are primarily consequences of literal similarity comparisons among similar experiences (p. 17). Moreover, they point out that prototype and other mere appearance or literal similarity based representations "are of limited use in deriving causal principles" (p. 17). There is a continuum of similarity relations ranging from these easily accessible representations to the abstract ones, which are the least accessible but also the most theoretically informative. DiSessa (1983) also notes a similar transition from phenomenological primitives to richer intuitive theories.

The relations between recent work on analogy and transfer and the studies described in this book are evident. There are, however, some important ways in which the account offered here may depart from this line of work.

First, preschoolers may not be sorting natural categories solely on the basis of literal similarity or mere appearance. Even if the notion of appearance is construed more broadly to include any tabulation of characteristic features, including event-related ones such as Forbus and Gentner's "protohistories," there are strong reasons for suspecting that more principle-based relations also structure their conceptual spaces.

Second, to the extent that young children do exhibit greater reliance on phenomenological primitives, such reliance is not a global developmental deficit as Gentner speculates at some points but instead is dependent on expertise in local domains. Brown (1986) also seems to recognize this alternative, as does Gentner in other passages.

Third, structure-mapping theory views the core of conceptual structure as the higher-order relations that are extracted by principles of systematicity. Although it is sometimes pointed out that causal relations tend to be common at these most systematic levels, they have no special status in organizing conceptual relations. Any other sort of conceptual relations that are heavily intertwined, such as sets of logical or mathematical relations, could, by this account, be equally important for organizing that conceptual space and for promoting transfer to other domains. For concepts concerning most naturally occurring phenomena, though, causal relations may play a particularly important role above and beyond that of other sorts of tightly compacted relations. The studies described in this book suggest the central importance of causal beliefs; however, since they did not explicitly assess the relative importance of causal and noncausal relations, it is not yet possible to be sure that causal relations are more fundamental than, for example, logical or mathematical ones.

Fourth, although Gentner's program for specifying the structure-mapping operations attains a welcome level of precision rarely seen in such discussions, it may not be adequate for capturing the kinds of belief systems that are central to natural concepts. Problems arise both with the evaluation of attributes and relations and with the principle of systematicity. It is not always easy to decide whether a predicate is relational or a simple attribute (for instance, "hot" or "hotter than"); moreover, the set of possible relational predicates that could logically apply to a domain is immense. Thus, the crucial constraining principle for narrowing the relations to a critical set is that of systematicity. Here too, however, it is not always easy to arrive at a unique solution.

There are often other sets of formally equivalent hierarchically nested relations that could apply to the elements in a domain or to the features of a kind; but somehow they seem less plausible—I suspect, because they do not provide causal explanatory insight. In chapter 13 I will attempt to specify how that insight should be structured; but one central theme is the notion of a homeostasis that—although it links to Gentner's systematicity—does not require such a hierarchical embedding and does require more explicitly causal relations. It is also important to remember that Boyd (1986), in arguing for the homeostasis account, also explicitly stresses that relational properties, not internal attributes, are critical for characterizing "essences."

Novice/Expert Differences

Novice/expert differences relate to the problem of original sim. and more general issues in cognitive development in three important ways:

1. Are novice/expert differences the same as those between child and adult; or as the issue is sometimes put, is learning the same as development? Children might differ from adults only to the extent that they are universal novices rather than local, domain-specific ones. Being a universal novice can have other consequences with respect to cognitive development (see Brown 1986 and Keil 1986a, for further discussions on this), but it generally suggests that we might approach the study of cognitive development in fundamentally the same way as we approach the study of learning in adults.

2. Assuming that the nature of knowledge does change over the course of novice to expert shifts, is that change one from an original sim. to a theory laden similarity space? Does the literature on such shifts in adults recapitulate the patterns uncovered in children?

3. This chapter and chapters 10 and 11 have been devoted primarily to the argument that indications of an original sim. early in development may only be illusory because of a failure to uncover the appropriate sets of theoretical beliefs. To what extent does such an argument also apply to adult novices?

To address these three issues, it is useful to consider a few studies on novice/expert differences. Although it is neither possible nor necessary to describe that increasingly extensive literature in detail here, even a brief overview reveals consistent patterns that bear closely on the developmental phenomena discussed in this book.

Perhaps the most heavily studied area of expertise is that of chess. The extraordinary skill of chess masters has led many investigators to ask how knowledge of chess might be organized differently in masters and novices. Following Miller's (1956) notion of knowledge being encoded in "chunks" of information, Chase and Simon (1973) assessed the size of such chunks in chess masters and adult novices in two ways: (1) They showed subjects a chess board with pieces arranged according to some stage of a legal game, removed the pieces after a brief presentation, and then asked the subjects to recall the positions by placing the pieces back on the board. In addition to recording the patterns of placement and error rates, Chase and Simon also monitored pauses during recall as a way of inferring chunk boundaries. Thus, two-second pauses were considered to be strong indices of where to segment the knowledge into chunks. (2) Chunks were independently assessed by having masters and novices copy a game configuration to a separate board. By examining the subjects' head turns as they went between the base board and the copy board, they were able to make inferences about the existence and size of chunks.

Chase and Simon's two measures of chunking did indeed converge, and the chunks were found to incorporate highly stereotyped patterns in chess such as castled-king positions, pawn chains, and spatially clustered units. The difference between novice and expert lay in the size of the chunks, with the masters' chunks containing three to six pieces and the novices, often only one. Although the experts did have larger chunks, they did not recall more chunks from the boards. They did, however, seem to relate chunks in a higher-order structure as well, a pattern that was not observed in novices.

Similar evidence that experts represent larger chunks and higher-order chunk structures is found in other domains of expertise. In electronics, skilled technicians reconstruct symbolic drawings of circuit diagrams according to the functional nature of the elements in the circuit, such as amplifiers, rectifiers, and filters. Novice technicians, however, produce chunks based more on the spatial proximity of the elements. When architects are asked to recall building plans, their reconstructions show several levels of patterns: (1) local patterns of wall segments and doors, (2) rooms and other areas, and (3) clusters of rooms or areas. Novices' reconstructions tend to show just the first level. Recall of baseball events by experts shows hierarchical structure yielding much larger sequences than recall of the same events by novices (see Chi, Glaser, and Rees 1982 for more discussion of this literature).

What do these areas of expertise have in common? Informally, it seems that functional or relational properties are more important at higher levels, whereas more attribute-like properties such as form and color are more important at lower levels. Though the number of detailed analyses along these lines is not large, this theme does seem to emerge repeatedly in the few that have been undertaken.

Some of the most relevant studies on the nature of knowledge structure changes and cognitive development have been conducted by Chi, Glaser, and their colleagues on expertise in physics. Generally, the experts in these studies were physics professors who also had considerable experience teaching introductory physics, and the novices were physics majors who had just completed their first term of undergraduate physics.

In one study Chi, Feltovich, and Glaser (1981) hypothesized that a major novice/expert difference in the realm of physics might be related to the way novices and experts group physics problems, whereby novices sort them into superficial categories and experts sort them in a more principled way. They asked eight experts and eight novices to sort 25 problems from a well-known physics text, "based on similarities in how they would solve them."

There were no significant differences in the number of categories produced by each subject (both novices and experts averaged about 8.5) or in the amount of time needed to sort the problems; but the actual categories constructed differed dramatically. The novices grouped problems on the basis of surface structure or appearance-based similarities such as (1) objects referred to in the problem (spring or inclined plane), (2) key words that are technical terms in physics (such as "center of mass" or "friction"), or (3) physical configurations involving the interaction of several object components (for instance, block on inclined plane). Experts did not categorize problems on the basis of surface features. Neither the key words used in the problems they sorted together, nor the visual appearance of the diagrams the problems involved, nor the final equations required to solve them were similar. Instead, the experts seemed to categorize according to the major principles of physics or fundamental laws such as the law of the conservation of energy or Newton's second law. Chi, Feltovich, and Glaser thus argue that the experts are referring to the "deep structure of the problem."

Chi, Feltovich, and Glaser have looked for further structure in hierarchical sorting tasks. After making the initial sorts of the type described above, subjects were asked to further subdivide each group until only single problems were left and then to combine the initial groups until no further combinations seemed reasonable. Rationales were also collected. Novices were often unable to produce rich hierarchical structures incorporating either lower-level or higher-level groupings. When asked to subdivide their initial groups, they often immediately branched into all the individual problems. When asked to combine them, they usually had very little idea of any further reasonable combinations. By contrast, the experts often produced a multilayered hierarchy of problems with well-partitioned clusterings and subclusterings leading up to two or three superordinate nodes.

The physics studies would seem to support an original sim. account of novice/expert shifts. The novice groupings might well be based on an atheoretical similarity space. Similar arguments are possible for the studies on other sorts of expertise mentioned above. As with the developmental studies, however, it may be that the novice's similarity space is not so atheoretical as it seems, nor so radically different from that of the expert. Novice physicists may well be operating under constraints imposed by theory-based intuitions about physics. For example, although novices labeled some problems as "ramp" problems or "rope and pulley" problems, they never created groups of "block" problems or "rope" problems even though blocks and ropes were clearly salient elements in the problems they were given. Some implicit notions of the importance of dynamic systems might well be guiding their sorting of the problem types. In fact, it seems almost certain that a host of interconnected beliefs about the mechanics of objects underlies and constrains the novice's choices of problem groups.

Expert knowledge is subject to other pressures as well, pressures that may structure it in ways the above accounts do not anticipate. Experts often have to make their performance rapid, smooth, and efficient, and they may do so by automatization. Anderson (1983) suggests that as a result of automatization, knowledge shifts from a declarative representation to a more procedural one that is much less accessible to introspection and awareness. Such procedural knowledge may not particularly resemble a set of clean principles for organizing a problem space. For example, Ceci and Liker (1986) have shown that racehorse touts engage in extraordinarily complex factorial analyses of many data sources to figure out where to place their bets even though they cannot verbalize their conjectures in any way or show comparable skills in other domains.

Some of the literature on medical diagnosis describes a different sort of progression to expertise (see, for example, Johnson 1983). As in other fields, novices are viewed as paying attention to a vast array of features, perhaps either ignoring a few critical ones or noticing them but not realizing their significance. Intermediate diagnosticians may have filtered everything down to a simple set of rules or procedures to be executed, almost a set of fixed routines or laws, but then the experts seem to fade back into much vaguer notions where the fixed laws have become more fuzzy. The experts may not really have lost the theoretical clarity of the intermediates, however. Rather, they have probably shifted away from attempting to characterize the problem space in terms of definition-like rules and instead have incorporated a far more complex set of intricate causal relationships more along the lines of the homeostasis model. Murphy and Wright (1984) document that expert clinicians in the field of psychology also exhibit a more complex, less definition-like set of concepts about psychological categories than do novices.

It sometimes seems that experts do not behave as intelligently as intermediates because experts do not appear to use as explicit a problem-solving routine as those who are less experienced. One might try to account for this sort of expertise with rich exemplar-based models according to which experts have much larger exemplar sets that act as "magnets" for new instances and atheoretical associative procedures are used to solve the new problems by comparing them to the old. However, pure exemplar-based accounts fail to explain what enables the experts to know how to organize their exemplar space in such a way that novel problems are usually quickly assigned a location in that space. It might well be causal functional knowledge that is responsible for this clustering of exemplars into stable subgroups, each of which has its own set of interacting laws.

In sum, much of the novice/expert literature does seem to recapitulate the apparent development shift from original sim. to theory. However, just as in the developmental case, a closer look raises questions about the purity of the original sim. Novices also seem to have elaborate sets of coherent beliefs that may well be specific to the domain in question. To the extent that they do, the developmental shift may not be as dramatic as it seems. In some areas of expertise where the domain is largely an arbitrary, highly conventionalized construct, the original sim. account may be much closer to the truth. Chess may be one such example, where prior theories are only useful in very limited ways as analogies to better understand some fragments of the chess game.

The novice/expert literature also reveals the dangers of assuming that expert representations are simple lists of discrete principles, or rules. Although this may be roughly true for classical mechanics, for many natural kinds the expert knowledge may be much more like a complexly interconnected set of beliefs and entailments that attempts to capture some causal homeostatic cluster in the world. By realizing that expert concepts may have this highly interconnected structure, we can start to integrate the studies on medical and psychological diagnosis with the work in physics. Expert diagnosticians aren't really becoming fuzzier and vaguer; they are simply coming to better understand the true causal complexity underlying their domain, a kind of structure very different from that of physics. Going further beyond the characteristic does not always mean going to the necessary and sufficient.

This brief overview cannot fully address the question of whether novice/expert can be equated with child/adult. It does, however, illustrate how such comparisons can be facile if they fail to understand both the theoretical beliefs of the novice and the rich interconnected beliefs inherent in many forms of expertise. I suspect that many models of novice/expert shifts in adults may have little relevance for the study of normal cognitive development just because the areas of expertise studied are so often those that scrupulously avoid connecting with prior belief systems. Board games, many manual skills, and some academic pursuits are often not closely connected to prior belief systems; nor are the final states of expertise structured like beliefs about many natural phenomena.

Concepts, Categorization, and Darwin

It is easy to get so caught up in current views of concepts and conceptual change as to overlook earlier discussions of similar issues. Kelly (1987) illustrates nicely that many of the current issues concerning types of similarity and category structure were anticipated in detail by Darwin (1859) in *The Origin of Species*. For example, Kelly shows that Darwin rejected classifying biological kinds on the basis of simple theory-neutral similarity in favor of an emphasis on causal explanation for the similarities among organisms. More important, he suggested that most naturalists in everyday practice also use such causal principles and that such a mode of classification may be psychologically the most natural.

Although Darwin also rejected simple definitional accounts of natural kinds, hence rejecting Aristotelian essentialism, it is important to see that he did not embrace probabilistic models of the sort considered earlier in this book. He stressed the importance of feature correlation over simple criterial lists of features (which he argued will almost always fail); but he clearly rejected simple family resemblance structures as well when he argued that "chains of affinities" do not form a legitimate basis for defining species. Kelly illustrates that Darwin's "natural system" of classification made specific reference to the importance of causal explanation of the surface feature frequencies and correlations, not surprisingly causal explanation grounded in a theory of evolution. One can use surface similarity as a rough basis for classification because it is closely related to systematic underlying causes; but the relation is clearly not fully reliable, and Darwin stressed that the final basis for classification must rest on causal principles of descent and the like.

Kelly's paper offers many more details of Darwin's arguments along these lines, including the sorts of biological evidence he used to support his claims. The general theme, however, is clear—Darwin believed neither in simple holistic sortings nor in simple definitions as the basis for classification of natural kinds, and he doubted that most naturalists ever use such systems in their real-world classificatory activities. (He argued, for example, that naturalists often ignore some features that are equally if not more salient than others because they are less relevant to a systematic theory of descent.)

It is probably wrong, however, to assume that people always find the richest causal structures the most naturalistic. As many have pointed out (see, for example, Mayr 1982; Hull 1965), there seems to be a kind of irrational essentialism that pervades much of biological thought and looks for a small set of fixed, necessary, and sufficient features at the cost of ignoring more complex, probabilistic causal interactions. Hull, for example, argues that Aristotle's view of species as having unique natural states led him to view species as discrete, and characterizable in terms of necessary and sufficient properties. According to Hull, this view was so appealing and so wrong that it caused "2000 years of stasis" in the science of taxonomy. (Kelly also notes this problem, as do Medin and Ortony (in press).) Such an essentialist bias may be quite adaptive, however, in providing a constant impetus to shift the learner away from mere appearance, and worth the expense of occasional oversimplification of principle.

Related Topics

Wellman and Gelman (1988) review a substantial body of literature concerning "children's understanding of the nonobvious" and come to conclusions in accord with those proposed here, namely, that concepts should be construed as being embedded in theories from a very early age. Wellman and Gelman focus less on the question of whether the knowledge state should be construed as an original sim. space and more on the contrasts discussed in chapter 2, such as perceptual vs. conceptual, concrete vs. abstract, and obvious vs. inferred. Nonetheless, a strong common theme emerges of attributing to the preschool child, and even the infant, coherent systematic theoretical knowledge, knowledge that guides inductions about categories and beliefs about the nature of mind. This is especially clear in Wellman and Gelman's discussions of their own work on the concept of mind and young children's knowledge of categories, but it is also reinforced in discussions of other research projects, such as those of Flavell and Carey.

Wellman and Gelman's account and mine differ somewhat in focus, however. Whereas Wellman and Gelman devote considerable attention to elegant arguments that earlier studies suggesting qualitative shifts are methodologically flawed, I have focused more on explaining why shifts of this sort seem to be so widely and frequently reported. I have described changes not as proceeding from the obvious to the nonobvious but as proceeding from the atheoretical and probabilistic tabulation of large clusters of typical features to an understanding of a smaller number of central relations and properties supported by those relations—a situation in which a kind of qualitative change is possible. The change is emphatically not one from a pure original sim. to fully theoretically interpreted knowledge, but local domains can embody a dramatic change in the extent to which properties and relations are interpreted and explained in terms of theory.

With all the recent emphasis on the importance of theories in organizing concepts and our understanding of property clusters, investigators may have neglected the information that we encode when our theories run out of explanatory power. It is important to come to terms with both modes of representation and to better understand how they relate to one another. In sum, Wellman and Gelman's review, although adopting a somewhat different perspective, is best interpreted as strong support for the sorts of arguments made in this chapter.

Conclusions

Two themes run through other accounts of original sim. tendencies. First, younger children often appear to show such tendencies and come to override them through access to increasingly sophisticated causal theories. Second, several studies suggest that even the youngest children nonetheless do not rely purely on attribute counts and correlations. They constrain their observations of feature frequencies and correlations by causal beliefs, presumably by ones that cohere to form a systematic theory. Without question, these theories are much less differentiated than those of older children and consequently the younger children must fall back more frequently to simpler, less interpreted similarity metrics. But the two modes of representation may always be intertwined in development, never undergoing a complete shift in representational type even in local domains. Rather than being biased toward the atheoretical tabulation of featural primitives, just the opposite may be closer to the truth: the child only reluctantly adopts such a model of construal when theory no longer affords any other options. The bias may always be toward theoretical coherence when possible. In the final chapter I will return to these issues.

Chapter 13
Concepts, Theories, and Development

With each succeeding chapter of this book, one theme has increasingly emerged. Coherent belief systems, or "theories," are critical to understanding the nature of concepts and how they develop. Although philosophers and some psychologists of a more classical bent have often argued about the interdependence of theories and concepts, for the most part cognitive psychologists in the last 20 years have not. As a consequence of the work done in the 1960s on concept learning and the later "anticlassical" response to that paradigm, it became the norm to talk about concepts as consisting of combinations of features or as being the result of summarizing operations on exemplars and/or dimensions. Although the classical and newer probabilistic views clashed on the issue of whether features for natural concepts were necessary and sufficient, their debate masked a shared set of assumptions that the meanings of concepts could be fully described by lists of features and simple probabilistic or correlational operations on those features.

As researchers began to look at the phenomena associated with concepts more closely, however, it became increasingly clear from several different lines of evidence that something was missing. Social and clinical psychologists talked about the illusory correlations that people see as existing between features (Chapman and Chapman 1969), and cognitive psychologists began to point out the limitations of prototype theory as a description of concepts. This malaise with older views was nicely summarized by Murphy and Medin's (1985) illustration that prior models were unable to account for the relations among features in concepts or to explain why the features comprising concepts cohere to make a cluster. They argued that in understanding concepts, we must go beyond correlation among features to causation and hence explanation. The meanings of concepts often include not just their constituent features and the statistical relations between them but also the causal relations between those features that explain their mutual presence. Part of the meaning of a concept may be the apprehension of the theoretical relations that explain its internal structure. This implication has reawakened a long dormant interest in the relation between concepts and theories in psychology, even though such relations have always been fundamentally important in the philosophy of science.

These recent developments and much of the research described in this book lead to the following general question: In what ways are theory and explanation important to understanding conceptual structure? More specifically: Are theories operations that are laid on top of concepts, or are they more intermingled with conceptual structures themselves from the start? Do they form the core of understanding conceptual structure, or are they more of an outside influence on that structure? Is theory equally important for understanding all types of concepts, or does its influence wax and wane as a consequence of the particular concepts involved (for instance, between natural kinds and artifacts)? Perhaps most important, what is the relation between theory and concept in learning? What part does theory play in trying to understand the fundamental problem of how concept induction ever succeeds? Does it have the same influence throughout all stages of concept acquisition, or are there predictable patterns of changing influence? Is new theoretical insight the driving force behind conceptual change, or is change driven by more bottom-up inputs of data?

It is obvious that the studies and ideas presented here hardly constitute a complete answer to these questions; but they do at least provide some guidance for further work and provide a context within which to evaluate issues concerning conceptual structure and conceptual change. First let us consider the implications for Quine's view of conceptual development.

Reassessing the Quinean Account

Much of Quine's orientation can be understood by considering his paper "Two Dogmas of Empiricism," which many regard as having dealt the death blow to notions of analytic vs. synthetic truths. Quine argues that few if any truths beyond those of propositional logic, and perhaps not even those, are analytically true. Rather, they only appear to be necessarily true to the extent that they are at the center of an interconnected set of beliefs. What gives statements their "analytic" look, therefore, is the centrality of the position they occupy in an interconnected set of beliefs or a theory. This attack on the analytic can easily be extrapolated as an attack on classical views of concepts, which in essence hold that one can make analytic statements of the form "Bachelors are unmarried" and "Birds have feathers." Although those who have rejected the classical view rarely cite Quine, it is clear that his account directly argues against there being necessary and sufficient features for concepts. Instead, Quine equates the structure of concepts with the positions that their constituents occupy in what he calls "the web of belief" (Quine and Ullian 1973), or theories. His position is especially clear in several later papers such as "Natural Kinds" (Quine 1977; see chapter 3).

Quine views the child's first concepts as being relatively devoid of theoretical influence, but then gradually acquiring theoretical structure not only for concepts acquired through formal instruction but also for concepts learned through more naive or intuitive means. Quine's speculation about concept development is surprisingly up to date in terms of many current developmental and instructional perspectives. Although views going back more than 50 years argued for qualitative changes in conceptual structure, most of them saw the qualitative changes as occurring in roughly the same way in all domains of knowledge; in other words, they posited a domain-general cognitive metamorphosis that restructured the knowledge in question. Quine's account, however, allows for specific theories having different structuring influences on local systems of belief. This view seems supported by novice/expert work with both adults and children. Expertise in one domain can cause dramatic restructuring in the way information is represented and/or computed in a tightly encapsulated manner that has little influence on other domains. The studies on nominal kinds and conceptual domains described in chapter 5 document such local effects.

In general, the nominal kind studies appear to support Quine's account by suggesting a one-to-many mapping in concept acquisition. In early stages atheoretical typicality tabulations organize conceptual similarity and conceptual structure, whereas later a smaller number of principled relations and properties come to override overall typicality.

As noted earlier, Quine would not approve of the characteristic/ defining contrast, because of his opposition to the notion that any features are strictly defining. The distinction can be recast, however, in a form more compatible with his outlook: it can be viewed as a shift from general atheoretical relations motivated by content-independent principles of similarity based on simple perceptual comparisons and typicality calculations, to theoretically organized relations that for these special (nominal kind) terms appear to yield defining features. The theoretical principles that organize nominal kinds are so simple and unidimensional that they may appear to be defining, but they are rarely actually so, as witnessed by philosophers' and linguists' elegant demonstrations of exceptions for "lie," "bachelor," and the like. Nonetheless, concept formation with respect to nominal kind terms can be construed as undergoing a qualitative shift.

This reinterpretation of the characteristic-to-defining shift for nominal kinds is compatible with the initial explorations of natural kind terms, using the discoveries and operations paradigms, explorations that also seem, at first glance, to support the Quinean account. Perhaps the earliest concepts are pure prototypes or other atheoretical sorts of representations, which only later shift to incorporate theory. If so, then concepts can be dissociated from theories and only gradually become intermingled with them over the course of development or, more accurately, with increasing expertise. This kind of conclusion would certainly please those who have traditionally studied concept formation using arbitrary conjuncts and disjuncts of salient features, such as the Vygotsky block tasks and countless other concept-learning tasks studied in the last 20 years. The concepts formed in such a task can hardly be embedded in theories, since they are usually meaningless outside of the task itself. Since they are nonetheless called concepts, perhaps we should take such studies as existence proofs of the ability of at least some "concepts" to exist without theories. However, such theory independence may rarely, if ever, hold for more naturally occurring concepts.

Despite its apparent harmony with a broad range of phenomena regarding concept acquisition, I have taken issue with Quine's account and suggested that it is a misleading treatment both of development and of adult concepts. But before reviewing the empirical support for this claim, I would like to consider some problems that Quine's account faces at the conceptual level. A good place to start is with Quine's own arguments for perceptual and conceptual quality spaces. He has pointed out, on several occasions, how impossible it would be for someone who did not know a language to learn the meanings of the terms of that language unless the learner shared with fluent speakers common "cuts" of the world (see, for example, Quine 1960). This argument is easily transferred to first language acquisition. All children, if they are to succeed at learning the terms of their native language, must share with speakers of that language a certain set of biases such that when an adult gestures at a rabbit and utters the word for rabbit, the child thinks of, as Quine puts it, "a whole, temporally enduring rabbit" and not "undetached rabbit parts," "temporal slices of rabbits," and the like. Quine and many others with associationistic leanings would like such early biases to be exclusively perceptual (perhaps even sensory) in nature and would like all else to be bootstrapped out of these primitives. The "animal sense of similarity" would provide a fully sufficient foundation for initial cuts in the world, which would then be modified only by experience and general laws of learning to yield all later conceptual and theoretical kinds.

Even though he clearly has such predilections, Quine is compelled to acknowledge that such early biases cannot be merely perceptual, and he concedes the existence of certain conceptual biases as well. For instance, when he argues that the infant doesn't think of brief temporal slices of rabbit (or "grue" instead of "green"), he is arguing for a conceptual bias. Having conceded that such biases are necessary, however, where is he to draw the line? Much of Quine's argument for perceptual quality spaces is based on the demonstration that since there are an indefinitely large number of logically different categorical construals of any given visual scene, there must be some limits on these construals if all children are to converge on common meanings. But once Quine opens the door to conceptual quality spaces as well, it is not clear that he can confine the biases that result from such spaces to only a few, weakly constraining ones. Although there is an indefinitely large number of construals at the perceptual level; there may be a far larger set at the conceptual and theoretical level; creating a need for conceptual biases that are even more powerful and more constraining than the perceptual ones.

It might be argued that, as one moves into more and more complex structured belief systems about natural phenomena, they tend to converge on unique solutions. However, the opposite seems equally likely— namely, that the number of conceptual possibilities explodes rather than converges, thereby creating the need for even richer sets of biases on inductions. An infant who has certain perceptual biases that allow her to pick out physical objects from their background may have a much more absolute set of biases that guide her to generate naive theories of the physical mechanics of such objects. The "object concept" may be meaningless to the infant if it is divorced from an intuitive theory of mechanics (see Spelke (in press) for expansions on this point of view).

If the number of possible hypotheses greatly increases as one moves from the "animal similarity space" to theory, then perhaps the child needs to be guided by some theoretical biases and preconceptions throughout development. Once one grants the need for some simple perceptual and conceptual biases, one may need to grant stronger and stronger sets of restrictions as one moves further into the realm of theory. Concepts for natural phenomena, at least, may never be able to part company completely from theoretical contexts because they need those contexts to yield meaning and give power to induction. Although one can make inductions given merely characteristic features (see, for example, Rips 1975; Carey 1985), those inductions succeed only to the extent that the features are linked with and diagnostic of a rich causal structure (see Medin and Ortony in press).

Another concrete model of how concepts develop within a dual representational system of associations and causal belief (or theory) invokes a feature network format. A Quinean account would assume that the initial state of knowledge acquisition is as shown in figure 13.1. This particular model supposes various sets of primitives, which are represented in this figure by ellipses, triangles, squares, circles, and

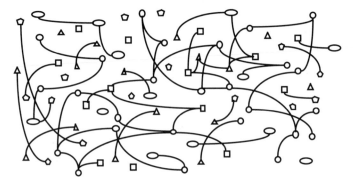

Figure 13.1
An original sim. matrix of knowledge as represented by a network of features linked by associations.

pentagons. Each shape designates a set of primitives in a particular mature theoretical domain. Early on, however, without the aid of theory, feature correlations and frequencies provide the only means of partitioning them into types. The features are presumably a set of sensory and perceptual necessities, plus perhaps one or two conceptual features that are needed to get knowledge acquisition and growth off the ground. Links between features are formed when two of them are observed to cooccur above some threshold rate. Obviously, the degree of cooccurrence is also likely to be represented, but given the difficulties of graphically representing a large range of correlation strengths, figure 13.1 and all succeeding figures represent the associative links as being simply all-or-none. Nothing crucial hinges on this simplification, and all ensuing arguments would apply equally well to continuously graded correlations.

At this point, the only constraints on the networks of links are pretheoretical and environmentally induced. Thus, they consist of the sensory primitives and general laws governing such operations as correlation detection, feature counting, and prototype abstraction. Such general laws will assuredly result in some representational distortions of the true correlations. For example, certain sequential and temporal patternings of feature cooccurrences are more likely to be misrepresented than others even though the real correlation might be the same as that of another patterning that is represented much more accurately. (Thus, a streak of perfect correlations between two features followed by a random sequence is likely to be encoded differently from a more continuous pattern of cooccurrence.) Other examples of universal tendencies that distort correlations might be biases resulting from neglect of base-rate information (Kahneman and Tversky 1973) and some of the pragmatic reasoning schemas proposed by Holland et al. (1986).

The presence of such biases means that even the patterns of links and nodes shown in figure 13.1 are not mere reflections of reality or a subset of reality where some links are omitted because of filters caused by limitations of sensory transducers. Real distortions are introduced at this level that go beyond a simple pruning of nodes and links; but the distortions are also domain general and insensitive to local content.

According to Quine, theoretical beliefs would then be overlaid on this network, thereby altering the similarity relations between elements. More accurately, such beliefs result in multiple levels of similarity, depending on which sets of relations are accessed. At this point, it is also clear that nodes in this network refer not just to sensory primitives but in fact to whole collections of such primitives. One's concept of a dog might well include links not only between dog subfeatures but also to other complexes of features such as wolves, foxes, cats, or food groups, each of which might be represented as a single node. The emergence of theory is represented in figure 13.2 by the thickened straight arrows, which stand for causal beliefs. Grey arrows stand for beliefs in causal relations that will *not* occur.

The original sim. view may be wrong, however, in assuming the initial absence of domain-specific biases acting as rudimentary precursors of specific theories. Thus, figure 13.2, and not 13.1, may represent the initial state, where some causal beliefs already bias the learner to notice circle-circle relations over other types. Ellipses might correspond to a causally homeostatic domain that humans never discover even at the correlational level or perhaps learn only with great effort through a jointly shared science (in other words, complex theory might enable one to discuss correlations that normally are not noticed). The lack of circle-

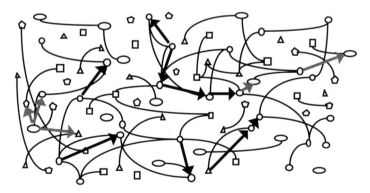

Figure 13.2
The emergence of theory in an associative net as represented by sets of causal beliefs (thickened straight arrows).

pentagon links might arise from a belief (perhaps mistaken) that the relations in two domains are causally independent of each other (such as the properties of liquids and those of prime numbers). Causal beliefs may provide an initial interpretive context for those associations, including the negative causal relations shown by gray arrows. Notice also that the causal beliefs in figure 13.2 are still quite fragmentary and are not neatly confined to one domain. Instead, although they might show a central tendency toward some domain, they are not fully coherent and overlap with other domains as well. Moreover, the causal relations do not provide much mutual support for shared sets of features.

This changes in figures 13.3 and 13.4, where the causal beliefs become more systematic and elaborated. A different progression might show a more continuously differentiating network of relations rather than the

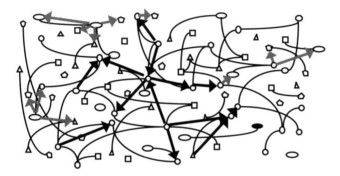

Figure 13.3
Further elaboration of causal beliefs resulting in more systematic connections that tend to demarcate domains.

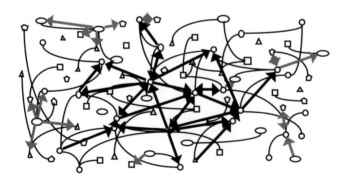

Figure 13.4
Still further elaboration of causal beliefs resulting in homeostatic clusters with several reciprocal causal relations.

fusing of formerly discrete fragments and the attrition of links to other domains. Yet another might show the complete disappearance of one set of causal relations over a set of primitives and its replacement by an entirely different set. This would presumably represent a more radical theory change. How would "defining" features emerge out of the characteristic ones in such a system? When a set of causal relations becomes extremely stable and conspires to support a very small set of primitives, which thereby become so central that without them the entire network of causal relations is radically transformed, then they might well be construed as defining. These especially central relations and features are readily apparent in figures 13.3 and 13.4. Thus, even as networks of causal beliefs may proliferate in a causally homeostatic manner, they can converge to focus on one or two central attributes. Still further theory development might again blur the definingness of one or two features as causal relations to other features become more strongly implicated. This may be a way of modeling the observation that novices are holistic, intermediates analytic and defining, and experts sometimes more vague about criterial attributes (Johnson 1983; Murphy and Wright 1984).

These figures also illustrate how networks of causal beliefs can never be fully adequate to explain all patterns of correlation. At some point they inevitably fail to provide insight into some correlations, but those correlations must be represented nonetheless. Thus, although the causal beliefs in this example come to distinguish circle features and circle-circle relations as a coherent domain, there are still relations between elements in this domain that can only be represented more associatively. Prototype abstraction might then still work to capture some circle-circle relation clusters that are outside the purview of current theory.

Even the most casual introspection suggests that we have at least two modes of construing similarity. One is a phenomenal, atheoretical tabulation of information, whereas the other is more infiltrated with causal belief and explanation. An astonishing array of thinkers who disagree on almost everything else—Quine, Putnam, Vygotsky, and Piaget, to name a few—seem to agree on this intuition. Granted, then, that the more associative and the more theoretical can coexist in our representations of things in a domain (for example, plants), we need to better understand how these two modes interact. Since we usually seem to be able to have full access to an original sim., it cannot simply be that causal beliefs obliterate conflicting associative links. They can dominate them in a more explanation-driven context and thereby yield very different similarity relations, but they can also be relaxed so as to allow the more phenomenal similarity space to reappear. One illustration of this contrast is provided by different sorts of linguistic hedges (Lakoff 1972). "Loosely speaking, which ones are fish?" produces a very different sorting of aquatic animals from "Technically speaking, which ones are fish?" "Loosely speaking" doesn't promote an alternative theory as much as it downplays rich causal relations in general.

It also seems unlikely that networks of causal beliefs develop completely independently of the more associative ones. Rather, they seem to develop within a context of correlations and frequencies as a way of providing coherence and explanation. Except for the more basic theoretical biases, causal beliefs are not rigidly attached to the associative relations. Many theories can be revised, exchanged for others, or even simply withdrawn with no detailed successor and only the loosest framework of intuitions. The representational system must be able to account for this flexibility. This flexibility, however, does not mean that the relation between theories and associative networks is arbitrary. The nonarbitrariness was stressed in chapter 3 in the arguments against a promiscuous realism and for a polygamous one.

Much too little is known at present about how expanding theoretical beliefs should interact with the more associative aspects of knowledge. I have questioned whether there could ever be a pure original sim., but the argument for ever-present fragments of theory does easily allow for a vast residual network governed heavily by atheoretical relations, especially in domains of relative ignorance. Are there certain patterns of belief that have much more dramatic effects on associative links than others? Are we really able to completely strip away all theoretical biases and see a pure original sim., or would perceptual and conceptual primitives allow so many relations that at least some skeletal theoretical biases are needed to make things computationally feasible? I suspect that some filtering by intuitive theories may always be necessary, but just how much must be determined by future studies. Can the emergence of one new theoretical belief have a sweeping effect over a whole class of beliefs? It would seem so, since one could come to believe that, in general, liquids have no important causal relations to properties of prime numbers and yet not represent this belief for each property pairing across the two domains. Some sort of hierarchical encoding of such relations may be needed.

This particular model of concepts, change, and theory growth should be viewed as only a rough approximation. Among other things, it fails to capture needed hierarchical relations, variations in correlation and belief strength, and relations among theories. Moreover, the intuition that sets of beliefs are linked to concrete mental models (see Johnson-Laird 1983) is not captured at all. Finally, the model does not distinguish between explicit causal beliefs and biases to notice certain associative patterns that are correlated with specific types and causal relations. Perhaps some psychophysical properties of trajectories compel us to directly see intentionality and a range of emotions and mental states without any mediation by a network of explicit causal beliefs. The best-known demonstration along these lines is by Heider and Simmel (1944), who created moving patterns of simple rigid geometric forms (such as triangles and squares). Subjects attributed a variety of emotional and mental states to the forms, such as aggressiveness, timidity, playfulness, and curiosity. Although the attributed states themselves each carry a great many causal entailments, it is less clear that explicit causal beliefs are involved in making the initial attributions.

The Limits of Theories

As noted in chapter 2, no theory can ever hope to continuously make principled distinctions among all the possible entities it applies to; at some point the theory "runs dry," and to further organize entities we have to fall back on our domain-general learning procedures, such as prototype abstraction, feature frequency counts, and correlation tabulations. Consider again my intuitive taxonomy of cars. There are coherent, causal, functional reasons, having to do with adaptations for specific uses and their consequent engineering solutions, that help explain to me the clusters of features that distinguish four-wheel drive vehicles from passenger sedans, sports cars, station wagons, and limousines. Among passenger cars, however, the causal relations responsible for the clusters that demarcate Chevys from Fords, for example, do not form a tight, coherent structure for me; and so to distinguish them I must by necessity fall back on more general similarity metrics based on an atheoretical abstraction over exemplars, or what I have called a characteristically based representation. There are, of course, causal laws responsible for the design differences between Fords and Chevys, but for me at least they represent a hodgepodge of historical, social, cultural, and economic factors; hence, my coherent theory has effectively run dry as an organizational aid. For another person, perhaps an expert in the history of auto design, a more coherent set of theoretical principles might guide the Chevy/Ford contrast and be used to distinguish new cases in a more inductively powerful fashion. Thus, one can (and almost invariably does) have domain-general, atheoretical principles of concept organization at work within specific theoretical contexts. (This does not mean that different truth conditions might not still hold for the two types of cars—for instance, that Fords are made at Ford plants and Chevys at GM plants.)

Depending on the chosen relations, we might in effect be able to repeatedly document qualitative shifts by successively narrowing our focus on that shrinking set of relations among which a still-growing theory cannot make principled distinctions. Only when full expertise is achieved, if it ever is, will such shifts no longer be demonstrable. Concepts may always be embedded in theories, but part of their structure may always be organized according to theory-independent principles. This is especially true for concepts of natural phenomena; for totally artificial ones, the theoretical biases may truly be absent, or composed of such a disconnected mosaic of different biases as to be uninterpretable. (Perhaps this is the case in early stages of learning chess, where biases from spatial knowledge, social interaction, math, and so on, may interact in a highly complex fashion.)

Issues of Acquisition

Each succeeding chapter of this book has also witnessed an increasingly intimate relation between views on the nature of representation and views on the nature concept acquisition and cognitive development in general. No evidence was found for global developmental shifts in the nature of representation, but local qualitative shifts did seem to occur. Later studies suggested that the shift away from characteristic features is only qualitative when examined from a perspective that presupposes common theoretical constructs as a framework within which to explore the shifts from characteristic features to either further differentiations of that theoretical framework or new theoretical perspectives. I argued that theory differentiation may be much more common than genuine theoretical revolution, especially since differentiations may appear to be revolutions if one presupposes the same initial theoretical constructs and only observes the shift from one form of organization (characteristic features) to a radically different one (theory). Both domain-specific and domain-general constraints can coexist, with the domain general principles playing a somewhat more important role early in the development of concepts.

We have also begun to see some limitations on thinking of the child as merely a universal novice. Such an account rings most true if children's early representations are totally probabilistic in nature; but to the extent that these representations already incorporate causal theories and beliefs, children cannot really be considered pure novices. Comparisons are made especially difficult because most novice/expert studies with adults investigate domains that either are highly artificial or do not seem to tap a unique natural domain of cognition. Thus, although it is almost certainly true that novice/expert studies in adults will be closely related to novice/expert studies in children, it is not at all clear how closely either of these will be related to the rest of cognitive development.

Finally, the account proposed here may offer a way out of Fodor's dilemmas concerning the reasonableness of any model of qualitative change. By arguing for the continuous presence of causal beliefs and by hypothesizing that they interact in predictable ways with associative relations, it may be possible to address the problems of incompatibility, learning, and hypothesis testing.

Developmental perspectives are useful not only for their own sake, but also because sometimes they may be the only reasonable way of answering nondevelopmental questions. I have tried to demonstrate this by suggesting that, with many adult concepts, it may be nearly impossible to understand how concepts might differ from each other and how they are internally structured without an account of how they are acquired. However, the best way to make the point may be by analogy to development in a different realm.

Consider Gould's (1983) discussion of whether a zebra is a white animal with black stripes or a black one with white stripes. As Gould points out, there are few more perennial questions; and certainly a great many who have asked that question have not been the least bit interested in how zebras develop. They simply want to know what sort of thing the adult is. Yet the clearest way to tell is to consider how stripes develop from early embryological stages. When this developmental perspective is adopted, in conjunction with some data about anomalous adult zebras, it becomes clear what they really are. (Gould's essay is too interesting to let the reader off by giving the answer here.) Gould also discusses how developmental considerations allow us to see "the difference between superficial appearance and knowledge of underlying causes" (p. 372) when applied to the puzzle of why a cross between a horse and a zebra usually has more stripes than the zebra. Superficial comparisons would predict a smaller number; but an understanding of how stripes are related to embryological development suggests strong reasons for the increase.

Many questions about concepts in particular and knowledge representation in general are like questions about zebras and their stripes. Even if one professes no interest in children, one may have to consider patterns of development to answer questions about the structure of adult knowledge. Otherwise, the nature of some structures may always remain intrinsically ambiguous.

The Structure of Theories

Perhaps the single most important problem for future research is to develop a way of describing the structure of theories and the concepts that inhabit them. If we cannot, it is difficult to see how we could ever make precise predictions about the paths of conceptual change that children will follow. So far we have not made much progress on specifying what naive theories must look like or even what the best theoretical vocabulary is for describing them, although we do have a clear idea of their importance and at least some hints about what sorts of properties theories are likely to have.

The tremendous cognitive efficiency gained by using causal connections as a kind of "glue" has been repeatedly demonstrated in other areas such as text comprehension and story understanding; but it is equally if not more evident with respect to single concepts. Causal relations make it vastly easier to remember the features that make up a concept as well as to make inductions about new instances. Just as a spatial layout provides a kind of framework to which to attach isolated concepts in Cicero's method of loci, so theory provides a framework within which to embed both the features that make up concepts and the concepts themselves.

What other principles govern the structure of intuitive theories? I would suggest the following tentative list:

1. Causal relations are essential and more useful than other sorts of relations.

2. Particular patterns of causal homeostasis may be especially useful. These may involve those that maximize symbiotic relations among all the elements that make up a concept. Thus, various combinations of the same number of causal relations among elements might differ in the extent to which each feature supports the presence of another. For example, nine causal relations might result either in each of five nodes being connected to every other one (maximally homeostatic) or in each node only being connected to one other (with some node pairs being linked by two or more relations).

3. Some hierarchical structuring of causal relations may also be especially useful for concept learning, for all the usual reasons of economy of representation and stability of substructures (Simon 1969).

4. A driving force behind the construction and differentiation of theories for apparent features may be a quasi-irrational essentialism. The belief that something stable and unique underlies the diverse members of a kind and is responsible for most of their phenomenological properties would lead even the youngest child to look beyond the level of mere feature tabulations. Such a belief can be irrational in its assumptions about both the stability and uniqueness of that "essence," as the extraordinary resistance to evolutionary thought has amply demonstrated. Mayr (1985) quite explicitly links this essentialist tendency to a kind of mechanistic bias coupled with reductionism. This bias is also seen when laypeople assume that a disease such as pneumonia, which is solely defined by its symptoms has a unique underlying biological cause. This bias seems to only apply to natural kinds; however, it is possible that a comparable bias operates with respect to beliefs about the intended

functions of artifacts with possible distortions where the intentions are a complex set of interacting goals arising out of a group.

5. Theories are intimately and inextricably linked to a matrix of associative relations. They provide explanation and interpretation of some of those relations, and the relations in turn provide data for further theory development. Moreover, theory can distort one's assessment of those relations.

6. Most concepts are partial theories themselves in that they embody explanations of the relations between their constituents, of their origins, and of their relations to other clusters of features. This is readily apparent for concepts of events but is even more important with regard to objects, since one's full concept of an object (say, a dog or a typewriter) crucially depends on understanding not only the causal relations between its properties and why they cluster as they do, but also the potential causal roles such an object stably and regularly engages in when interacting with other objects.

Questions concerning the nature of intuitive theories and how they are represented must eventually confront an issue that has only been weakly touched on in this book: just how implicit can a theory be and still be a theory? There are many phenomena that young children appear to have never considered but for which they might still be said to possess theories. For example, many kindergartners will respond that they have no idea how the common cold is caught or how food makes one grow or how children often resemble their parents; yet when asked later to choose between contrasting pairs of possible mechanisms for these phenomena, they can show strong preferences, sometimes for mechanisms that are clearly incorrect. Thus, most kindergartners (as well as many adults) strongly prefer an account of common cold infection in which the "germ" invades the entire body rather than the correct account in which the germ is primarily confined to the respiratory system. Such patterns of preferences, or constraints on hypotheses about mechanisms, might well be thought of as constituting a theory, especially where they are connected with other biases to form a coherent system. (The responses just described are part of a new research program now underway in my lab.)

How, then, is such a theory to be represented? It is hardly a set of explicit beliefs; and it seems odd to call it a set of beliefs at all if the owner of those beliefs has never entertained any thoughts about their content. One can retreat in two ways here: either by saying that the beliefs are simply innate and do not require active use, or by saying that the constraints on such mechanism choices are all consequences of domain general biases such as that causes should resemble consequences. My own guess, however, is that neither retreat is fully correct. Instead, children may be referring to a more abstract set of beliefs about biological kinds in general, beliefs that constrain guesses about the mechanisms underlying more specific biological phenomena. This may not be enough, however. A child's preferences about mechanisms of digestion may not be simply reduced to beliefs about biological kinds; other sorts of specific beliefs also seem to constrain their choices. Some may be beliefs from other general domains such as the mechanics of objects and the properties of liquids; but there may also be more specific beliefs about animals as a certain kind of machine.

Attribution of a particular theory to an individual may therefore prove to be a good bit more troublesome than it appears at first. In many cases there may be highly specific sets of coherent beliefs that children have already entertained, but in other cases these beliefs can only be inferred from preferences about mechanisms underlying phenomena that they have never considered before. Moreover, identification of the domain or domains that give rise to those biases will require an extensive series of follow-up studies devoted solely to that question. The final decision about whether the children really have an implicit theory specific to some class of phenomena will rest on a detailed characterization of the domains of knowledge that give rise to their judgments, in particular on the level of abstraction of those domains and on the extent to which they are directly linked to the phenomena in question. The difficulty of these issues should hardly be surprising, however; for they are at the core of many current debates in cognitive science.

In this book I have attempted to make progress in showing that qualitative changes in concept structure have direct implications for models of concepts in general, how such changes can and cannot be modeled, and how concepts might be embedded in larger belief systems known as theories. I have discussed how the emergence of theories can shift similarity relations and judgments of category membership and suggested that fragments of those theories may need to be present from the start. I have not shown what those theories look like in detail, where they originate, and what structural properties they all share. Nor have I considered how theories of this sort differ from other sorts of highly specialized representational complexes that go beyond the associationistic from the start, such as knowledge of a natural language grammar. Such knowledge is certainly not a theory in the same sense and embodies few if any explicit causal beliefs.

One of the primary challenges of future work in cognitive development will be to define the scope and diversity of initial theories. Are there only two primal theories, a naive psychology and a naive mechanics, and is everything else built on the foundation of metaphors based on intentionality, goal-based action, and physical mechanics? Or are there many different primitive theories—for example, economics (principles of equitable exchange among individuals and groups; see, for example, Cosmides (in press)), biology, mathematics, and navigation? These questions cannot be answered in the abstract. Instead, they require systematic exploration of the growth of beliefs in each of these domains, exploration that will indicate not only what changes and how, but also where such beliefs come from in the first place.

Undoubtedly, some of the most challenging work on concepts and conceptual change lies ahead. This challenge is an arduous one, for we must move beyond descriptions of theories as simple lists of statements (Hempel 1965) or as loosely structured nets of associations, and we have only the most tentative ideas of how to do so. But it is also an exciting one, for any progress in this area will clearly have a profound impact in many areas of cognitive and developmental psychology.

Appendix 1
Stimuli for Characteristic-to-Defining Shift Study

Lie
(+c/- d) This girl hated a boy in her class because he was so mean and did really nasty things to her. She wanted to get him into trouble, so she told the teacher all the nasty things the boy had really done. Could that be a lie?

(-c/+d) This little boy always got good grades in school and prizes for being so smart. The other children were jealous of him because of it, and he didn't want to make them feel bad and wanted them to be his friends. So, one time, when he really got a good mark on a test, he told them that he got a bad mark so they'd be his friends. Could that be a lie?

Robber
(+c/-d) This smelly, mean old man with a gun in his pocket came to your house one day and took your colored television set because your parents didn't want it anymore and told him that he could have it. Could he be a robber?

(-c/+d) This very friendly and cheerful woman came up to you and gave you a hug, but then she disconnected your toilet bowl and took it away without permission and never returned it. Could she be a robber?

Menu
(+c/-d) Suppose a waitress handed you something shaped like this (experimenter handed subject a piece of paper folded in half) that had written inside the restaurant's history—when it was built, the names of the waitresses and cooks, etc., but it didn't say anything about food inside. Could that be a menu?

(-c/+d) If there was this seashell sitting on a table in a restaurant, and on it was listed all the meals and foods that the restaurant served, could that be a menu?

Jail
(+c/-d) There is this ugly building in the slums with bars on every window and rats who live in the corners. The men who live there are so poor they can only eat bread and water. They are allowed to leave the building whenever they want to. Could that be a jail?

(-c/+d) There is this beautiful castle with horses and a swimming pool, and really delicious food. The people who live there can use all of these great things, but they are never allowed to leave unless they get special permission. They can only stay in the castle if they've done something wrong. Could that be a jail?

Twins
(+c/-d) These two girls look alike, dress alike, do well in the same subjects in school, like the same vegetables, and live in the same house. One of them, however, is two years older than the other one. Could these be twin sisters?

(-c/+d) There are these two girls who were born at the same time on the same day in the same room from the same mommy, but one of them lives in California and the other one lives in New York. Could these be twin sisters?

Sign
(+c/-d) There is this big thing on the highway shaped like this (experimenter held up rectangular piece of paper) that was built to keep the sun out of the driver's eyes, but it has no writing on it. Could that be a sign?

(-c/+d) There is this giant cupcake sitting in the middle of your street. Every day, they put out a fresh one because people come and nibble on it. In bright orange frosting, the cupcake says, "Sally's Bakeshop—one block that-a-way." Could that be a sign?

Taxi
(+c/-d) Your next-door neighbor painted his car yellow with black and white checks around the edges. The car even has a white bump on top. He likes to put on his cap and uniform and drive all over town every day. He never gives strangers rides, though, because he thinks it's too dangerous. Could that be a taxi?

(-c/+d) This purple car with three wheels and rainbows painted on the tires is driven around by a woman in a nightgown and a football helmet. Whenever you want to go somewhere, you wave to her and she takes you wherever you want to go as long as you pay her. Could that be a taxi?

Hat
(+c/-d) There is this black thing made of felt and shaped like this with a brim around the edges (experimenter held up sketch of hat) that people put ashes from their cigarette in. Could that be a hat?

(-c/+d) This man strapped a ribbon around a garbage can lid and tied it around his head to keep out the sun and the rain and the snow. Could that be a hat?

Mailman
(+c/-d) This man drives by in a red, white, and blue truck every day. His job is to clean out mailboxes with a special vacuum cleaner. He pulls his truck right up to your mailbox and sticks his vacuum cleaner in to get out all the dirt and dust from your mailbox. Could that be a mailman?

(-c/+d) This person dressed in bright orange shorts who goes around on rollerskates comes to your door every day around 1 o'clock in the morning bringing you letters and packages. Could that be a mailman?

Factory

(+c/-d) There is this big, concrete, ugly building with lots of smokestacks and chimneys on the roof. It is a warehouse where things are stored to keep warm. Nothing is ever made there, and no one ever goes in or out of the building. Could that be a factory?

(-c/+d) There is this beautiful house in the woods. Inside, people dress in beautiful clothes, tuxedos and evening gowns, and from 9 to 5 every day sit on comfortable couches making buttons. Some pour the wax, some put the buttons in boxes so they can be sold to the stores. Could that be a factory?

Island

(+c/-d) There is this place that sticks out of the land like a finger. Coconut trees and palm trees grow there, and the girls sometimes wear flowers in their hair because it's so warm all the time. There is water on all sides except one. Could that be an island?

(-c/+d) On this piece of land, there are apartment buildings, snow, and no green things growing. This piece of land is surrounded by water on all sides. Could that be an island?

Lunch

(+c/-d) It's 6 o'clock in the morning. You got up early because you're going on a trip, and you're really hungry. You make yourself a tunafish sandwich, french fries, and an ice cream soda. Could that be lunch?

(-c/+d) It's 12 o'clock in the afternoon and the sun is shining really bright. You already ate something today, but you're still very hungry so you decide to eat pancakes with syrup, orange juice, scrambled eggs, cereal, and milk. Could that be lunch?

Vacation

(+c/-d) This family leads a very interesting life. They try out different hotels all over the United States. They stay in them, eat their fine foods, and rate them so that other people know whether they are good places to stay or not. They write a book about this, and get paid for doing it. Could that be a vacation?

(-c/+d) This man decided not to go to work one week. He stayed at home, watched television, slept, and ate, but then his television broke down and he was sad and bored. Could that be a vacation?

Church

(+c/-d) This beautiful building with a point on the top and stained glass windows and a bell was built to take care of delicate plants. Nobody ever goes inside the building, and a man takes care of the plants by sticking a hose in through the beautiful stained glass windows with scenes from the Bible on them. Could that be a church?

(-c/+d) There is this huge tent with red and white stripes that floats in the middle of the ocean. People come there by boat every Sunday to sing and pray and talk about God. Could that be a church?

Uncle

(+c/-d) This man your daddy's age loves you and your parents and loves to visit and bring presents, but he's not related to your parents at all. He's not your mommy or daddy's brother or sister or anything like that. Could that be an uncle?

(-c/+d) Suppose your mommy has all sorts of brothers, some very old and some very, very young. One of your mommy's brothers is so young he's only two years old. Could that be an uncle?

Museum

(+c/-d) There is this beautiful building with columns. Mr. Johnson lives there, but he has a big problem. There are all these cracks in his floors and his walls. So he covers them with paintings and statues, and he never lets anyone inside to see them. Could that be a museum?

(-c/+d) There is this small, wooden shack in the countryside. People come from all over and pay 50 cents to get inside and see the interesting display of dirty shirts with rings around the collar and spots and stains. Could that be a museum?

News

(+c/-d) You turn on the radio and there is this man talking very seriously about foreign countries, wars, fires, and robberies. He is reading from a book that was written last year. Could that be news?

(-c/+d) You turn on the TV and these children are singing and dancing to loud rock and roll music—and they're singing everything that happened in the world that day—the weather, the fires, the robberies. They even sometimes hold up crayon drawings to show what they were talking about. Could that be news?

Appendix 2
Stimuli for Nominal Kinds and Domain Specificity Study

Lie

(+c/-d) This girl hated a boy in her class because he was so mean and did really nasty things to her. She wanted to get him into trouble, so she told the teacher all the nasty things the boy had really done. Did she lie to the teacher?

(-c/+d) This little boy always got good grades in school and prizes for being so smart. The other children were jealous of him because of it, and he didn't want to make them feel bad and wanted them to be his friends. So, one time, when he really got a good mark on a test, he told them that he got a bad mark so they'd be his friends. Did he lie to them?

Steal

(+c/-d) This smelly, mean old man with a gun in his pocket came to your house one day and took your colored television set because your parents didn't want it anymore and told him that he could have it. Did he steal your TV?

(-c/+d) This very friendly and cheerful woman came up to you and gave you a hug, but then she disconnected your toilet bowl and took it away without permission and never returned it. Did she steal your toilet bowl?

Cheat

(+c/-d) Suzy learned how to play Go Fish when she lived in California and Jimmy learned how to play in New York; and when they learned, they were taught different rules. One day Suzy moved to New York and she met Jimmy. The first time when they were playing Go Fish together, Suzy got lots and lots of pairs right away in every game they played. Jimmy got upset and said it wasn't fair! Suzy explained how she got all the pairs instead of Jimmy—it was because of the different rules she learned in California. Did Suzy cheat?

(-c/+d) Suzy and Nancy were playing Go Fish. Every time Nancy wasn't looking, Suzy would peek at Nancy's cards so she could win. But in every game they played, Nancy would win. Did Suzy cheat?

Tease

(+c/-d) One day out in the playground everyone stood behind Billy and started pointing at him. There was a BIG spider on his back. He thought they were laughing at his new haircut and he started to cry. They tried to tell him about the spider and he just cried louder and harder and wouldn't listen. He tried to walk away from them and they followed and kept pointing. He ran inside the school and told the teacher. Were the kids teasing Billy?

(-c/+d) One day outside at lunch time, all of the boys started pointing at Billy and laughing and saying, "Look at Billy's new haircut eeeeewwwwwwww how weird!! His ears stick out!" Billy only spoke Spanish...he saw them smiling and he started smiling too. He knew they were talking about his new haircut which he loved soooo much. He was happy that everyone else seemed to love it also and he thanked them in Spanish. Were the kids teasing Billy?

KINSHIP TERMS

Aunt
(+c/-d) There's a lady who's the same age as your mommy. You see her a few times a year. She loves you very much. She likes to buy you clothes and take you shopping. And sometimes she lets you sleep over at her house. She's not your mommy's or daddy's sister (and she's not married to your mommy's or daddy's brother). Could she be your aunt?

(-c/+d) There's this little girl that you've met once before. She wears her hair in braids and goes to school in California every day like you. She's your father's sister. Could she be your aunt?

Uncle
(+c/-d) There's a man who is your daddy's age. He loves you very much. When he comes to your house, he plays with you and brings presents for you. He's not your mommy's or daddy's brother (or married to your mommy's or daddy's sister). Could he be your uncle?

(-c/+d) Suppose your mommy has all sorts of brothers, some very old and some very, very young. One of your mommy's brothers is so young he's only two years old. Could that be your uncle?

Cousin
(+c/-d) There is this boy who is the same age as you are and you see him *every* Thanksgiving and on your birthday. He likes to come to your house and play with you. Sometimes he stays overnight. His mommy and daddy aren't related to you. Could he be your cousin?

(-c/+d) There's an old man who lives by himself in the woods in a little cabin. You never get to see him. His mom and your mom are sisters. Could he be your cousin?

Grandmother
(+c/-d) There's this sweet little old lady with grey hair. She always bakes cookies and knits you sweaters. And sometimes she calls you sugar plum. She's not your mommy's or your daddy's mother, but she loves them very much. Could she be your grandmother?

(-c/+d) There's this woman with long black hair. She always wears a leather jacket and she drove a motorcycle to California so she could go to see some friends there. She is your mommy's mother. Could she be your grandmother?

Grandfather
(+c/-d) There's this little old man who wears a button-down sweater. You go to visit him on Sundays and on holidays. He likes you to sit on his lap. Sometimes he smokes a pipe and gives you a quarter. He's not your mommy's or daddy's father. Could he be your grandfather?

(-c/+d) There's a man who has long blond hair in a ponytail. He sometimes rides a skateboard and plays with a yoyo. His favorite clothes are blue jeans and his favorite music is rock and roll. He's your mommy's father. Could he be your grandfather?

MEAL TERMS

Breakfast
(+c/-d) One evening at six o'clock when the sun was going down, it was time to eat. Everyone got their PJs on and came to the table. You had scrambled eggs and bacon and toast and orange juice. Your parents had a cup of coffee and read the newspaper. Were you having breakfast?

(-c/+d) One morning when your family woke up, you all put on your best clothes...Mommy wore a fancy dress and Daddy wore a suit. You had company coming over. When they arrived at 8 o'clock in the morning, you all sat down at the table. The meal was steak and potatoes and a salad. Your parents drank wine, and you got to have chocolate milk. For dessert you had apple pie and ice cream. Were you having breakfast?

Lunch
(+c/-d) It's six o'clock in the morning. You got up early because you're going on a trip, and you're really hungry. You make yourself a tunafish sandwich, french fries, and an ice cream soda. Could that be lunch?

(-c/+d) It's twelve o'clock in the afternoon and the sun is shining really bright. You already ate something today, but you're still very hungry so you decide to eat pancakes with syrup, orange juice, cereal, and milk. Could that be lunch?

Dinner
(+c/-d) One morning when your family woke up, you all put on your best clothes to go out to a fancy restaurant. The tables all had red tablecloths and candles on them and there was quiet music playing. To eat everyone ordered chicken and corn on the cob and vegetables. You had soda to drink and your parents had wine, and you had cake for dessert. Afterwards you went to school. Did you have dinner?

(-c/+d) One evening after it was dark outside, you went to stay at a friend's house overnight. When you got there, you and your friend sat down to eat because you were really hungry. Your friend's parents made waffles and bacon and orange juice for you, and afterwards you were still hungry so you had some cereal and milk. Were you and your friend having dinner?

TOOL TERMS

Screwdriver
(+c/-d) There's this thing that has a long flat metal bar and it has a wooden handle. It's used for cleaning out the grooves in the top of screws and it looks like this (shows drawing; see figure 5.1). Could this be a screwdriver?

(-c/+d) There's this round pink plastic ball and it's shaped like this (shows drawing). And it has this little edge sticking out that will fit into screws to turn them. Could this be a screwdriver?

Hammer
(+c/-d) There's this thing that has a long wood handle and on the top is a piece of metal. One end of it is round and open and empty inside and when you make cookies you hold the handle and hit the dough and the round edge cuts the dough into circles (shows drawing). Could this be a hammer?

(-c/+d) There's this thing that is made out of cement and is used to pound in nails and flatten metal. It looks just like this (shows drawing). One end is thinner so that you can hold onto it. Could this be a hammer?

Saw
(+c/-d) There's this thing that looks like this (shows drawing). The handle is made out of wood and the rest is made out of metal. One edge has blue ink on it to mark the wood so that the lumber man will know where to cut it. When a person uses it they stand like this (picture). If you rub your hands over the edges, they are really smooth. Could this be a saw?

(c/+d) There's this thin piece of purple plastic that looks like this (shows drawing). If you drop it, it can break really easily. But if you're really careful, you can rub it against a small piece of wood and cut it. Could this be a saw?

Scissors
(+c/-d) There's a thing that looks just like this (shows drawing). It's made out of metal and has black handles. You put your fingers in the holes so you can open and close it. At the pointy end, the inside edge is flat and you use it to press two pieces of metal together. Could this be a scissor?

(-c/+d) There's this thing that looks like this (shows drawing). It's made out of REAL diamonds! And it's as big as your arm. Special workmen use it to cut metal sheets. It has a small motor in the box to make the arms go up and down. Could this be a scissor?

Drill
(+c/-d) There's a thing that looks like this and special workmen use it (shows drawing). They plug it in and pull the trigger part to turn on the motor. The motor makes the part that's shaped around and around like this (points to coiled part) suck up small bits of sawdust like a straw. Could this be a drill?

(-c/+d) There's a thing that looks like this (shows drawing). People use it in offices and at schools when they want to put holes in cardboard. To use it, you slide the cardboard into the corners to hold it still. Then you turn the handle and this long part turns in circles and puts holes into the edge. Could this be a drill?

COOKING TERMS

Boil

(+c/-d) Your mother was cooking some eggs to make egg salad for lunch. So she took a pot and put a little bit of water in the the bottom. Then she put a rack in the pot to hold the eggs above the water like this (shows drawing) so that they would not roll around and break each other. She put a flame on under the pot to heat the water. Was she boiling the eggs?

(-c/+d) Michael brought a big bathtub in a truck out to a field. He filled it with water and built a fire around it...He wanted to wash his shirts out in the fresh air. When the water started bubbling, he added the soap and bleach. Was Michael boiling his shirts?

Fry

(+c/-d) One day you asked to have onion rings for dinner...the kind with the crispy stuff on the outside. Your mom cut the onions and dipped them in batter and then she put them in a pan like this (shows drawing) in the oven. When they were done, they were all crispy. Did she fry the onion rings?

(c/+d) Once Mark wanted some melted cheese. He took a big pot and put some oil in the bottom. Then he threw in some chunks of cheese. He turned on the heat, and when the cheese was melted, he spread it on some toast. Did Mark fry the cheese?

Bake

(+c/-d) Liz and Danny wanted to make a cake after school. They followed the directions for a chocolate cake mix. They poured it into a greased pan and put the cake pan on the stove and turned on the flame really low. About half an hour later, they turned off the flame and had a *yummy* chocolate cake with frosting. Did Liz and Danny bake the cake?

(-c/+d) You went to a fancy restaurant and asked for a salad with your dinner. They cut up carrots and celery and tomatoes and all that stuff. Then they put the lettuce on a plate in the oven with the heat turned on for a little while. Then when the leaves were soft, they took it out and put it in the bowl with the rest of the stuff. They put on some dressing and gave it to you. Did they bake the lettuce?

Appendix 3

Stimuli for Idiosyncratic Defining Features Study

Birthday party

A. No presents:

Suppose tomorrow some kids come over to Mary's house, and they wear funny hats, and a big cake with candles on it comes out, and they all sing a song to Mary. Mary will be five years old in the fall. Do you think that would be Mary's birthday party, or is it just a party?

B. No song:

Suppose tomorrow some kids come over to Mary's house, and they give her lots of presents, and wear funny hats, and a big cake with candles on it comes out. Mary will be five years old in the fall. Do you think that would be Mary's birthday party, or is it just a party?

C. No cake:

Suppose tomorrow some kids come over to Mary's house, and they give her lots of presents, and wear funny hats, and they all sing a song to Mary. Mary will be five years old in the fall. Do you think that would be Mary's birthday party, or is it just a party?

D. No funny hats:

Suppose tomorrow some kids come over to Mary's house, and they give her lots of presents, and a big cake with candles on it comes out, and they all sing a song to Mary. Mary will be five years old in the fall. Do you think that would be Mary's birthday party, or is it just a party?

E. Stripped story:

Suppose tomorrow some kids come over to Mary's house. Mary will be five years old in the fall. Do you think that would be Mary's birthday party, or is it just a party?

Parade

A. No people riding horses:

Last Saturday there was a lot of excitement downtown. Right on the street there were five bands with drums and baton twirlers, fancy floats and clowns, and fire engines and antique cars. The line was three blocks long. After standing still in the street for about two hours, everybody went home. Was that a parade?

B. No bands:

Last Saturday there was a lot of excitement downtown. Right on the street there were fancy floats and clowns, fire engines and antique cars, and people riding horses. The line was three blocks long. After standing still in the street for a long time, everybody went home. Was that a parade?

C. No floats and clowns:

Last Saturday there was a lot of excitement downtown. Right on the street there were five bands with drums and baton twirlers, fire engines and antique cars, and people riding horses. The line was three blocks long. After standing still in the street for a long time, everybody went home. Was that a parade?

D. No fire engines and antique cars:

Last Saturday there was a lot of excitement downtown. Right on the street there were five bands with drums and baton twirlers, fancy floats and clowns, and people riding horses. The line was three blocks long. After standing still in the street for a long time, everybody went home. Was that a parade?

E. Stripped story:

Last Saturday there was a lot of excitement downtown. The line was three blocks long. After standing still in the street for a long time, everybody went home. Was that a parade?

Uncle

A. No reminiscences:

There's this guy, a grown-up, who always comes to Pete's house for Thanksgiving dinner and brings Pete presents on Christmas and Pete's birthday. He isn't related to Pete's mom or dad. Could he be Pete's uncle?

B. No presents:

There's this guy, a grown-up, who always comes to Pete's house for Thanksgiving dinner. He and Pete's dad talk about the old days when they were just boys. He isn't related to Pete's mom or dad. Could he be Pete's uncle?

C. No age:

There's this guy who always comes to Pete's house for Thanksgiving dinner and brings Pete presents on Christmas and Pete's birthday. He and Pete's dad talk about the old days when Pete's dad was a boy. He isn't related to Pete's mom or dad. Could he be Pete's uncle?

D. No Thanksgiving:

There's this guy, a grown-up, who brings Pete presents on Christmas and Pete's birthday. He and Pete's dad talk about the old days when they were just boys. He isn't related to Pete's mom or dad. Could he be Pete's uncle?

E. Stripped story:

There's this guy who isn't related to Pete's mom or dad. Could he be Pete's uncle?

Fireman

A. No truck:

There's this guy downtown who dresses like this when he's working and has big long water hoses. When people's grass gets really brown and needs to be watered, his job is to hurry right over, blowing a siren, and water the lawns. Could he be a fireman?

B. No siren:

There's this guy downtown who dresses like this when he's working and has a big fast red truck and big long water hoses. When people's grass gets really brown and needs to be watered, his job is to hurry right over and water the lawns. Could he be a fireman?

C. No hoses:

There's this guy downtown who dresses like this when he's working and has a big fast red truck. When people's grass gets really brown and needs to be watered, his job is to hurry right over, blowing the siren on his truck, and water the lawns. Could he be a fireman?

D. No uniform:

There's this guy downtown who has a big fast red truck and big long water hoses. When people's grass gets really brown and needs to be watered, his job is to hurry right over, blowing the siren on his truck, and water the lawns. Could he be a fireman?

E. Stripped story:

There's this guy downtown. When people's grass gets really brown and needs to be watered, his job is to hurry right over and water the lawns. Could he be a fireman?

Twins

A. No confusion:

Brenda and Linda live with their parents in a house down the street. They both have short, curly red hair. They dress exactly alike. Brenda is a year older than Linda. Could Brenda and Linda be twins?

B. No red hair:

Brenda and Linda live with their parents in a house down the street. They dress exactly alike. Most people can't tell them apart. Brenda is a year older than Linda. Could Brenda and Linda be twins?

C. No home situation:

Brenda and Linda both have short, curly red hair. They dress exactly alike. Most people can't tell them apart. Brenda is a year older than Linda. Could Brenda and Linda be twins?

D. No identical clothing:

Brenda and Linda live with their parents in a house down the street. They both have short, curly red hair. Most people can't tell them apart. Brenda is a year older than Linda. Could Brenda and Linda be twins?

E. Stripped story:
   Brenda is a year older than Linda. Could Brenda and Linda be twins?

Island
A. No trees:
   This is a special place called Alboa where there are beautiful starfish and
   seashells, and where it's warm and the sun shines all the time. Some people
   dig for buried treasure there. There is water around three sides of Alboa and
   land on the other side. Could Alboa be an island?

B. No treasure:
   This is a special place called Alboa where there are beautiful palm trees,
   starfish, and seashells, and where it's warm and the sun shines all the time.
   There is water around three sides of Alboa and land on the other side. Could
   Alboa be an island?

C. No sun:
   This is a special place called Alboa where there are beautiful palm trees, and
   starfish and seashells. Some people dig for buried treasure there. There is
   water around three sides of Alboa and land on the other side. Could Alboa
   be an island?

D. No starfish and seashells:
   This is a special place called Alboa where there are beautiful palm trees, and
   where it's warm and the sun shines all the time. Some people dig for buried
   treasure there. There is water around three sides of Alboa and land on
   the other side. Could Alboa be an island?

E. Stripped story:
   This is a special place called Alboa. There is water around three sides of Alboa
   and land on the other side. Could Alboa be an island?

Appendix 4
Stimuli for Nominal Kind Teaching Study

MORAL ACT TERMS

Swindle
To swindle is to cheat someone out of something by tricking or lying to them. For example, there are crooks who ask old people to buy land which they say is worth a lot. And when the old people give the money they have saved up, they find out the land is not worth anything. It's in the middle of the desert and there's no water there, so nobody can live there, and you can't grow anything on it. The old people have been swindled. And usually they can't find the crook. So to swindle is to take money or property by tricking or lying.

(+c/-d) Mark needed a car, so he went to a car dealer. The car dealer was very pushy and showed Mark a whole bunch of cars, but he really tried to sell Mark a little red sports car by taking Mark for a drive in it and showing him the engine. Mark bought it even though he needed a station wagon. A week later, though, Mark decided the car was really too small and went back to the car dealer to sell the sports car back for a station wagon. But the car dealer said he wouldn't take it back because he only sold new cars.
　　　　Did the car dealer swindle Mark?

(-c/+d) John saw a poster for a circus with lions and tigers and elephants and got really excited. So he went out and bought a $10 ticket to get in. Inside the circus tent, though, there really wasn't anything there but an old horse and a cow. So John asked the man who sold the tickets where the other animals were. The man told John that there really weren't any other animals, but that they couldn't get anybody to come to the circus without the poster with the lions and tigers on it and they really needed the money. John could sort of understand because the man looked so poor and sad. So John went back home and had a great day playing with his friends.
　　　　Did the circus people swindle John?

Libel
To libel is to say something which is not true about someone that makes him or her look bad to other people. Newspapers and magazines are sometimes in trouble for libel if they say something about an actress or actor that isn't true. Like in *People* magazine they said that the Dukes of Hazzard were bullies and that they beat someone up and it wasn't true, so the Dukes called a lawyer to see what they

could do about the paper libeling them. To libel is to say or write something about a person which isn't true.

(+c/-d) A doctor was caught driving when he was drunk one night. The next day when he went to court, a reporter from every paper in the town came. One paper didn't like the doctor and put the story about him driving drunk across the front page, while the other papers just put it in the middle of the paper somewhere. The doctor lost his job when his boss saw the story on the front page of the one paper.
Did the paper libel the man?

(-c/+d) Have you ever seen wrestling on TV? Well, one huge wrestler is supposed to be a bad guy and he dresses all in black. People come to watch him because they love to hiss and boo. At Christmastime last year, a radio announcer decided it would be a great story to say this man was really, really nice even though the wrestler was really, really mean. So he made up a story about how the wrestler bought presents for every kid on his block, which is something he would never do. After the story, everybody hated him even more. So even more people went to watch him and he made a lot more money.
Did the reporter libel the wrestler?

Betray
To betray is to break the trust of someone who trusts you. If you told your best friend a secret and told her not to tell anyone in the world and she told everyone in your class, she would have betrayed you. To betray is to hurt someone when you've let them think that you wouldn't.

(+c/-d) Suzy told her best friend that she really liked David. Suzy wanted to tell David, but she was afraid that he might laugh at her. Suzy said that she really hoped someone else would tell him. So Suzy's best friend told David. When the friend did, David started to laugh and said how ugly Suzy was. When Suzy heard about this, she was really mad at her friend for telling David she liked him.
Did her friend betray her?

(-c/+d) Two best friends were trying out for the same part in the school play, but, of course, the teacher could only pick one. Peter couldn't read very well, but he didn't tell the teacher because he was afraid he wouldn't get the part. He only told his best friend. His friend wanted to be in the play so badly that he told the teacher all about Peter's reading problems, but the teacher said that didn't matter and picked Peter for the part. And Peter was the best student in the whole play.
Did Peter's friend betray him?

Extort
To extort is to try to take something from a person even though they don't want you to by telling that person that you will hurt them or say something about them that they don't want anybody to know. Like if a bad guy went into a store and told the owner, "Unless you give me $50 a week, I'll come over here in the middle of the night to wreck your store," he would be extorting money from the store owner. So to extort is to try to get something from someone by saying you'll hurt him or say something about him that he doesn't want anyone to know.

(+c/-d) Joe drives a taxi. One day a big, mean man got a ride in Joe's taxi, and Joe was so scared of him that he dropped the man's suitcase in a big puddle and the man's clothes got all yucky. The man got really mad and said, "You'd better not drop my bags again or I'll bash your whole taxi in with a baseball bat." Joe was so scared that he never drove near where the man lived again.

Did the man extort Joe?

(-c/+d) Sally got a 100 on her math test. That was much, much better than anybody in her class, but she didn't tell anybody except her best friend. She was afraid that the boy she liked wouldn't like her if he knew how well she did. That afternoon Sally's best friend said to her, "I really want to get a 100 too, and you better help me study or I'm going to tell everyone how well you did."

Did Sally's friend extort help from her?

COOKING TERMS

Sauté

To sauté food is to cook it slowly over a low heat in a little bit of butter or oil. Onions and mushrooms are sautéed a lot of times. You sauté them in a frying pan on top of the stove and stir them once in a while so they don't stick to the bottom of the pan. When mushrooms or onions are sautéed, they become soft and delicious. So to sauté is to cook something in a little bit of oil or butter over a little bit of heat.

(+c/-d) Peter and Josh made some mushrooms for a party. They filled a pot all the way up with oil and put it on the stove to get hot. When the oil was very hot, they dropped a lot of mushrooms in the pot, making sure they were all covered with oil. Then after a few minutes, they picked them out with forks, and they were soft and delicious.

Did Peter and Josh sauté the mushrooms?

(-c/+d) At Christmastime the French people have a special dish of nuts. They put a big, round tray on a barbecue grill that isn't very hot and heat peanut oil in it. Then they put walnuts and peanuts without their shells in the tray. Every once in a while, they shake the tray.

Do the French people sauté nuts?

To flambé

To flambé is to pour liquor over food and light it. Often they do it in really fancy French restaurants. A waiter pours liquor over cherries or bananas and then comes to the table and lights it right next to you. Flames jump up and then they go out really quickly. So to flambé food is to pour liquor over it and light it.

(+c/-d) A chef in a fancy restaurant was cooking steak over a barbecue pit. When he put a piece of steak on the grill, he'd hold it up to let the fat drip over the coals and poof, a flame would shoot up from the coals and cook the meat for a second and then go out quickly.

Did the chef flambé the steak?

(-c/+d)   By accident a bum who was sitting on a park bench spilled liquor from his bottle because he was a little drunk. It spilled all over the hot dog he was eating. Then ashes from the cigar he was smoking fell on his hot dog and set it on fire. He was so upset, he didn't want to eat it anymore.

Did the bum flambé his hot dog?

Steep

To steep is to soak something in hot water so that the taste and smell goes into the water. Like when you're making tea, you steep it. You let the tea bag sit in hot water for a while so the water tastes and smells like it. To steep is to let something soak in hot water for awhile so the water tastes and smells like it.

(+c/-d)   When I pour myself coffee from a coffeepot in the morning, I put in milk and sugar and stir it to mix it up. Then I let the coffee sit awhile to cool so I can drink it, because it's always too hot to drink at first.

Am I steeping the coffee?

(c/+d)   Some stores sell dried rose petals to make your skin beautiful. They tell you to put the rose petals in a hot, hot tub of water and leave it for one half hour so the water gets the rose oils in it and smells really pretty. Then you're supposed to sit in the bath and let your skin get really clean.

Are you steeping rose petals?

Baste

To baste is to wet a food with something while it's cooking. For example, at Thanksgiving your mom probably basted your turkey by brushing melted butter and meat juices every half hour so the meat would stay moist. So to baste is to wet something every so often with a liquid while you're cooking it.

(+c/-d)   We were having friends for dinner, so we cooked a huge roast beef. We saved the meat juices from the pan the meat was cooking in. And after we took the roast out of the oven and put it on the table, we poured the juices over the roast beef lots and lots of times so it would be nice and wet when we served it to our friends.

Did we baste the roast beef?

(-c/+d)   One Saturday two friends were making baked apples. They cut out the insides of some apples and poured in cinnamon and sugar. Then they put sugar on top and put the apples in a big black frying pan on top of the stove with a little bit of water in it. Now and then they would go into the kitchen and pour the sugar which had melted into the pan over the apples.

Did they baste the apples?

AGRICULTURAL TERMS

Irrigate

To irrigate is to bring water to plants that don't get enough normally. For example, in the Midwest when they grow corn, they need to irrigate the fields because there isn't enough rain. So the farmers put pipes all around the field and down the middle through which to pump water and spray it all over the corn so it grows green and healthy. So you irrigate by bringing water to plants that need it.

(+c/-d) The crops in Oregon, where it rains all the time, did really badly last year because of mildew. So this year the farmers built pipes and ditches to the fields and every day they pumped a liquid which kills mildew through the pipes and sprayed it in little drops all over the fields. And the crops grew much bigger and better this year.

Did the farmers irrigate the crops?

(-c/+d) There is a forest in Maine that is a hundred miles long and people go there to camp for vacations. Last year, needles kept falling off the trees because they were so dry and they weren't as pretty anymore. So this year the forest rangers rented planes and flew up in the clouds above the forest and dropped pellets. The pellets made the clouds let out all the water they had in them. And there was a rainstorm over the forest for the next three days.

Did the rangers irrigate the forest?

Fallow
To fallow is to not plant things on a piece of land so it gets healthier and plants can grow better on it the next time it's used. Farmers who have lots of cornfields, for example, usually let one cornfield stay empty every couple of years to get a rest. The field can soak in the sun and rain to get energy for itself rather than giving it to the corn growing on it. So to fallow a field is to not plant anything on the land so plants can grow better on it next time.

(+c/-d) A farmer in Ithaca was really worried that one of his fields needed a rest. He had planted corn on it for six years and the corn had taken all the good stuff, the vitamins and nutrients, out of the soil. So this year, the farmer planted really tiny beans on the field. The beans give energy back to the soil and they are so small you can hardly tell they are there.

Did the farmer fallow his field?

(-c/+d) A flower shop owner in Cortland who grows his own flowers did not plant his whole garden this year because the flowers he grew last year didn't grow very well. But in the spring, the wind blew some seeds into the garden and beautiful wildflowers bloomed there. So the flower shop owner took them to his shop and sold them. He made a lot of money on the wildflowers because they were so pretty.

Did the flower shop owner fallow his garden?

Furrow
To furrow is to make small ditches in the land. A farmer usually furrows his fields every spring. He drives a tractor with lots of hooks behind it that makes long cuts in the land. You've seen furrowed land. It looks like there are really even lines all across it that might have been made with a huge comb. Usually fields are furrowed so the farmers can plant seeds easily by dropping them in the ditches. So to furrow is to make a long, narrow cut in the land.

(+c/-d) I was watching a farmer in Ithaca plant trees one day. He pulled this thing, two shovels hooked together, behind a tractor. Every 10 feet he would stop the tractor and lower the shovels and they would scoop out a hole in the earth. Then the farmer would get off the tractor and plant the tiny trees. And when he was finished the trees were all in straight lines all across a big field.

Was the farmer furrowing the land?

(-c/+d) John just put new grass in his front yard. It rained so much, though, that his grass was getting too wet and dying. So one day he went out in the front yard with a golf club and dragged it across the lawn lots of times to make a bunch of curvy lines. When it rained then, the water ran down and flowed out to the street, off his lawn.

Did John furrow his lawn?

Mulch
To mulch is to put something over the land so that things will grow better on it. I'm sure you've seen people mulch the land in Ithaca. People put lots and lots of wood chips around rose bushes or young plants here in the winter to keep them from freezing and to keep the water in the soil. So mulching is when you cover the ground to help things you've planted there grow better.

(+c/-d) There was a huge rainstorm in Ithaca last year just before a farmer cut his straw, and it got soaking wet. So to dry it off after it was cut, the farmer picked a day when it was hot and sunny and spread the straw out carefully all over a field of carrots and left it there for half a day to get dry. But then he carefully picked it up so the carrots wouldn't get hurt by not getting enough sun.

Did the farmer mulch the carrot field?

(c/+d) Last year a friend of mine put tinfoil all over his garden because he wanted to take extra good care of the garden. He cut little holes out of the foil for the plants so they weren't covered up and could get the sun and rain they needed. The foil looked really pretty when the sun hit it because it sparkled, and it also scared the crows away when the sun shining off the foil hit their eyes.

Did my friend mulch his garden?

Appendix 5
Stimuli for First Discoveries Study

Boot/sail

This is something that you put on your feet to keep your feet warm and dry when it's raining or snowing out. Everybody calls these things boots. Some scientists went into a factory where some of these are made to be used as boots and decided to study them really carefully. They looked way deep inside with microscopes, and they found out that these things weren't like most boots. They found out that sails from sailboats were cut up to make these. Every part on this thing was made up of sails. So what do you think this is: a boot or a sail?

Horse/cow

These are animals that live on a farm. They go "neigh" and people put saddles on their backs and ride them, and these animals like to eat oats and hay and everybody calls them horses. But some scientists went up to this farm and decided to study them really carefully. They did blood tests and X-rays and looked way deep inside with microscopes and found out these animals weren't like most horses. These animals had the inside parts of cows. They had the blood of cows, the bones of cows; and when they looked to see where they came from, they found out their parents were cows. And, when they had babies, their babies were cows. What do you think these animals really are: horses or cows?

Nail/screwdriver

These things are meant for holding wood together and for hanging pictures on the wall, and everybody calls them nails. But some scientists went into a factory where some of these are made for nailing and decided to study them really carefully. They found out that these things weren't like most nails. These things that are made at this factory have the inside parts of screwdrivers. And when they looked to see how they were made, they found out that screwdrivers were melted down in order to make them. So what do you think these really are: nails or screwdrivers?

Apple/pear

These fruits are red and shiny, and they're used to make pies and cider, and everybody call these things apples. But some scientists went into an orchard where some of these grow and they decided to study them really carefully. They looked way deep inside them with microscopes and found out these weren't like most apples. These things had the inside parts of pears. They had all the cells of pears and everything like that, and when they looked to see where they came from they found out that these came off of pear trees. And, when the seeds from this fruit were planted, pear trees grew. So what are these: apples or pears?

Cup/bowling ball
These things are used for holding hot liquids like coffee and tea and cocoa or milk to drink, and everybody calls these things cups. Some scientists went to the factory where some of these are made for bowling to study them. They looked way deep inside with microscopes and found out these weren't like most cups. The ones made at this factory had the inside parts of bowling balls. And when they looked to see how they were made, they found out that bowling balls were ground up to make them. So what do you think these things really are: cups or bowling balls?

Pine tree/oak tree
This thing is used for Christmas trees and has pinecones and long green needles, and everybody calls them pine trees. Some scientists went into a forest where some of these grew and decided to study them. They looked way deep inside and found out that these weren't like most pine trees. The ones in this special forest had the inside parts of oak trees. And when they looked to see where these came from, they found out that they grew from acorns, which are oak tree seeds. When the seeds from these trees were planted, oak trees grew. So which do you think these are: pine trees or oak trees?

Key/penny
There are these things that look just like this. People use these things to open up locked doors, and also to lock up cars and houses to keep them safe. Some scientists just studied a special group of these things that came from a factory in Pennsylvania where they are made for opening locks. They looked at them very closely with a microscope to see what they were like way down inside and to see what they were made out of. They found out that they weren't like most keys; they were made out of exactly the same stuff that pennies are made out of. In fact, when they looked to see where these things came from, they found out that pennies had been melted down in order to make these things; and when they were all done, they melted them down again and made pennies again. What do you think these are: keys or pennies?

Dog/cat
This is an animal that barks and goes "woof, woof" and chases cars, and everyone calls them dogs. Some of these animals grew in a kennel, and some scientists went out to this kennel and decided to study these animals there. They did blood tests and X-rays and looked way deep inside with a microscope, and they found out these animals weren't like most dogs. They found out that these animals had the inside parts of cats. They had the blood of cats and they had the bones of cats. And when they looked to see where they came from, they found out that their parents were cats. And when these animals had babies, their babies were cats. So what do you think these animals are: dogs or cats?

Appendix 6
Stimuli for First Transformations Study

What we're going to do today is, I'm going to tell you some stories and then ask you some questions. The stories are all about a group of very good doctors who perform special operations. Have you ever heard of operations called plastic surgery operations? You know, when a doctor can change how a person's face looks so they look like someone else, totally different . . . well, that's the kind of operations these doctors are going to do. They are going to change the way things look.

NATURAL KINDS

Horse/zebra
The doctors took a horse and did an operation that put black and white stripes all over its body. They cut off its mane and braided its tail. They trained it to stop neighing like a horse, and they trained it to eat wild grass instead of oats and hay. They also trained it to live in the wilds in Africa instead of in a stable. When they were all done, the animal looked just like this. When they were finished, was this animal a horse or a zebra?

Grapefruit/orange
The doctors took a small grapefruit that looked like this. They gave it shots of orange food coloring and sugar to make it sweet. It looked just like this when they were done. When they finished the operation, was this a grapefruit or an orange?

Tiger/lion
The doctors took a big tiger that looked like this. They used special fur bleach to take away its stripes, and they sewed on a huge mane so that it ended up looking like this. Was this animal after the operation a tiger or a lion?

Sheep/goat
The doctors took a sheep that looked like this. In the operation they shaved off all its curls. They put antler horns on its head and put some long hairs under its chin. They tied a bell around its neck and taught it how to climb mountains and how to buck. When they were done, it looked just like this. Is this animal now a sheep or a goat?

Chicken/turkey
The doctors took a chicken and added a huge plume of feathers on its back. They also cut off the flaps of skin on top of its head and under its chin and instead added

one over its beak. They gave it a ruffle of feathers down its neck. They trained it to stop crowing and instead how to gobble. When they were done, it looked like this. At the end of the operation was it a chicken or a turkey?

Lead/gold
The doctors took a bar of lead. They melted it and mixed it with a shiny gold-colored dye. They molded it back into a brick. When they were done, was it lead or was it real gold?

Raccoon/skunk
The doctors took a raccoon and shaved away some of its fur. They dyed what was left all black. Then they bleached a single stripe all white down the center of its back. Then, with surgery, they put in its body a sac of super smelly odor, just like a skunk has. When they were all done, the animal looked like this. After the operation was this a skunk or a raccoon?

Coffeepot/birdfeeder
The doctors took a coffeepot that looked like this. They sawed off the handle, sealed the top, took off the top knob, sealed closed the spout, and sawed it off. They also sawed off the base and attached a flat piece of metal. They attached a little stick, cut a window in it, and filled the metal container with birdfood. When they were done, it looked like this. After the operation was this a coffeepot or a birdfeeder?

Necktie/shoelaces
The doctors took a necktie that looked like this, cut it into thin strips, and, at the ends of the strips, they attached little plastic tabs. One of the strips looked like this. After the operation what did the doctors have, a necktie or shoelaces?

Cards/toilet paper
The doctors took a deck of cards and dyed them all white. Then they soaked them in a special liquid to make them soft. Next, they mushed them all together and rolled it out in a very thin strip like dough. When it dried, they rolled it up on a cardboard tube. It looked like this. After the operation did the doctors have playing cards or did they have toilet paper?

Bobby pin/needles
The doctors took a bobby pin and shaved off thin slivers. They sharpened the end of each piece into a sharp point, and they poked a hole into the other end. When they were done, they all looked like this. After the operation did the doctors have a bobby pin or did they have sewing needles?

Garbage can/chair
The doctors took a garbage can that looked like this. They took the top rim and cut it into four strips and straightened them out. Then they cut off the bottom and attached the four strips. Next they cut a rectangle from the side of the pail and two more strips. They put all the pieces together so that they looked like this. When they were done, did they have a garbage can or did they have a chair?

Kitchen pipe/flute
The doctors took a kitchen pipe that looked like this and cut off a section. They punched holes in the section and added a mouthpiece. When they finished, it looked like this. After the operation did they have a kitchen pipe or did they have a type of flute?

Plastic bottle/flipflops
The doctors took a plastic bottle and cut two flat rectangles off the sides. They trimmed and curved the edges of the rectangles. Then they took the handle off the bottle and cut it into four strips. They attached the strips to the pieces of plastic so that it looked like this. When they were done with the operation, did they have a plastic bottle or did they have flipflop sandals?

Tire/boot
The doctors took a rubber car tire, like this, and cut an oval section. Then they shaved off some rubber from the sides of the tire and sewed that onto the oval. Then they cut off two more strips and sewed them on so that it looked like this. When they were done with the operation, did they have a tire or did they have a boot?

Appendix 7
Stimuli for Contrasting Property Types Study

Porcupine/mouse (porcupine outsides but mouse insides)
The doctor went into the woods and he stumbled across this animal that he had never seen before. When he first saw it, he thought it was a porcupine because it looked just like a porcupine. Just like this guy here. It had needles and quills, just like a porcupine, and a short, stubby nose like a porcupine, and little, stubby feet, just like a porcupine. But the thing was, when he took it back to the zoo and the doctor checked it out and looked inside it, he found out that it had all the inside parts of a mouse. So it had a mouse heart inside instead of a porcupine heart, and a mouse stomach. Where you have a person stomach, this had a mouse stomach, and it had a mouse liver. So on the outside this thing looked just like a porcupine, with quills and a big nose and short, stubby feet, and it didn't have a tail, like a mouse has a tail. But on the inside it was just like a mouse, with a mouse heart and a mouse stomach and mouse insides. So, if you had to guess whether it was either a mouse or a porcupine, and nothing in between, and you had to guess which one it was, what do you think it would be?

Zebra/horse (horse insides but zebra relatives)
The scientist went to Africa and he found this animal and first he thought it might be a zebra because the animal had a zebra for a mommy and a daddy, and zebra aunts and uncles, and made zebra babies. But then when he had the doctor check it out and the doctor looked inside it, just like with the porcupine, they found that it had all the insides of a horse. So it had a horse heart instead of a zebra heart and horse hearts are bigger and stuff. And it had a horse stomach. And it had horse muscles in its legs and everything. So the thing had a zebra for a mommy and a daddy and zebra aunts and uncles and made little zebra babies, but on the inside it had a horse heart and a horse stomach and horse muscles. So, if you had to guess and it was either a zebra or a horse and nothing in between, what do you think it would be?

Shark/dolphin (dolphin insides but shark relatives)
We found this animal in the ocean, and it had a shark for a mommy and a daddy, and shark brothers and sisters, and hatched out of a shark egg. But after it hatched out of a shark egg, the doctor took a look at it and looked inside it and found out that it had all the insides of a dolphin. So, it had dolphin brains and dolphin blood and dolphin muscles. So the thing had a shark for a mommy and a daddy and shark brothers and sisters and hatched out of a shark egg, but all its insides, its

brains, you know, and its bones and muscles were just like a dolphin. And the scientist, you know, he thought it was one or the other, and nothing in between, and he didn't tell me what it looked like. So I don't know if it looked like this or this. But all he told me was that. So what do you think it might be? Do you think it would be a shark because its parents were sharks or do you think it would be a dolphin because its insides were dolphin insides?

Goat/sheep (goat outsides but sheep relatives)
The scientist went up to a farmer and he saw this animal and he said, "Oh, that's a nice-looking goat you have there." And, you know, it looked just like a goat. It had horns like a goat, and a furry beard like a goat, and short white fur like it was a goat. But the farmer said that he wasn't sure what the thing was because it had a sheep for a mommy and a daddy and sheep brothers and sisters and made little sheep babies. So the scientist said, "Boy, I don't know what to call it. I mean, it looks just like a goat with its horns and beard and fur and everything; but it had a sheep for a mommy and a daddy and it made sheep babies and stuff." So what do you think it was, if you had to guess? A goat or a sheep?

Dog/fish (fish outsides but dog behavior)
Now, we came across this animal. And when you first looked at the way it acted, it acted just like a dog. You know, it barked and it wagged its tail and it licked your face, like a dog. But the thing was, it looked just like a fish. So it looked just like this fish right here, and this is a picture of the thing. And it had blue scales and stuff and fins and it was colored all the same as this fish here. So it acted just like this dog, but it looked just like this fish. So if you had to guess, what do you think it was, if it had to be one or the other?

Butterfly/lizard (butterfly outsides but lizard relatives)
And the scientist came along and looked at this thing and it looked just like a butterfly. It had wings like a butterfly and antennae like a butterfly and it was colored all yellow, just like this butterfly. But the thing was, they knew that it had a lizard for a mommy and a daddy and lizard grandparents and hatched out of a lizard egg. But as soon as it hatched, it looked like this butterfly here. So the scientist didn't know what to call it. On the one hand, it looked just like a butterfly, with wings and pretty yellow colors and antennae, but it had a lizard mommy and daddy and lizard grandparents and hatched out of a lizard egg. So what do you think you would call this animal? A butterfly or a lizard?

Deer/cat (deer relatives but cat behavior)
And we came across an animal and it acted just like a cat. You know, the scientist heard it first, he didn't see it, and we don't know what the thing looks like. But he heard it and it acts like a cat, because it meows and purrs and it chases mice and stuff, because he heard mice running away from the thing. And it tried to scratch things when it was mad. But the thing was, it had a deer for a mommy and a daddy and deer aunts and uncles and made little deer babies. So it acts just like a cat, it meows and purrs and chases mice and tries to scratch when it's mad, but it has a deer mommy and daddy, a deer aunt and uncle and makes little deer babies. So what kind of animal do you think it was? Do you think it was a cat or do you think it was a deer?

Turtle/rabbit (rabbit insides but turtle behavior)
We find this animal that acts just like a turtle. You know how rabbits run real fast? Well, this animal walked real slow and all the rabbits could beat it in a race; and it liked to swim in water like a turtle and it lived underground when it was cold and hibernated just like turtles do. But when you take it back to the lab and look inside, it had all the insides of a rabbit. It had rabbit blood and rabbit bones under its skin and rabbit brains. Now we don't know what the thing looked like. I mean, they do, but they didn't tell me. All I know is that it walked like a turtle, real slow, and it liked to swim in the water like a turtle and it liked to live underground when it's cold like a turtle. But on the inside it had rabbit blood and rabbit bones and a rabbit brain. So if you had to guess, what kind of animal do you think it was?

Frog/bird (frog insides but bird behavior)
Now we don't know what this animal looks like. But the scientist looked inside it and it had frog blood and frog heart and frog lungs. But the thing was, it didn't act like a frog at all. It acted just like a bird did. It could fly in the air like a bird and went south for the winter like all the Ithaca birds do or a lot of them when it's cold, and it laid eggs, like a bird does. So it had all the insides of a frog, frog blood and frog heart and frog lungs, but it flew like a bird, went south for the winter like a bird, and even laid eggs like a bird. So what kind of animal do you think it was, a frog or a bird?

Fish/snake (fish behavior but snake relatives)
We found this animal and it acted a lot like a fish. You know, it swam in water like a fish, and breathed water instead of air like a fish and even lived with all the other fish. But the scientist knew that something was a little wrong because it had a snake for a mommy and daddy and had snake cousins and hatched out of a snake egg. So we don't know what the animal looks like; and we don't know what it has on the inside. But we do know that it swims in water like fish, and breathes water instead of air like fish, and even lives with other fish. But it has a snake mommy and daddy and snake cousins and hatched out of a snake egg. So what kind of animal do you think it was? Do you think it was a snake or a fish?

Bird/chipmunk (bird outsides but chipmunk insides)
This animal looked just like a bird, because it had bird wings and yellow feathers like a bird and even had a little bird beak. But when you look inside it, it has all the insides of a little chipmunk. It has chipmunk blood inside and chipmunk bones and even a chipmunk brain. So on the outside, it's just like a bird, but on the inside it's a lot like a chipmunk. So what do you think it would be? Do you think it would be a bird, because it looks like a bird, or do you think it would be a chipmunk, because it has all the insides of a chipmunk?

Polar bear/ape (polar bear outsides but ape behavior)
We found this animal and it looked just like a polar bear. Because it had long white polar bear fur, and big white claws, and four big polar bear legs. But it acted just like an ape. It would hit its chest when it was mad like an ape, and it made all the sounds that apes make, and it would eat the same kinds of things that apes would eat, like coconuts and pineapple and bananas. So this animal looked just

like a polar bear, but it acted just like an ape. So what do you think it was? Do you think it was a polar bear, because it looked like a polar bear, or do you think it was an ape, because it acted like an ape?

References

Anderson, J. R. (1983). *The architecture of cognition*. Cambridge, MA: Harvard University Press.

Anglin, J. M. (1970). *The growth of word meaning*. Cambridge, MA: MIT Press.

Anglin, J. M. (1984). The child's expressible knowledge of word concepts: What preschoolers can say about the meanings of some nouns and verbs. In K. E. Nelson, ed., *Children's language: Volume 5*. Hillsdale, NJ: Erlbaum.

Armstrong, S., L. Gleitman, and H. Gleitman (1983). What some concepts might not be. *Cognition* 13, 263–308.

Barsalou, L. W. (1987). The instability of graded structure: Implications for the nature of concepts. In U. Neisser, ed., *Concepts and conceptual development: Ecological and intellectual factors in categorization*. Cambridge: Cambridge University Press.

Bolinger, D. L. (1965). The atomization of meaning. *Language* 41, 555–573.

Bourne, L. E., Jr. (1982). Typicality effects in logically defined categories. *Memory and Cognition* 10, 3–9.

Boyd, R. (1979). Metaphor and theory change: What is "metaphor" a metaphor for? In A. Ortony, ed., *Metaphor and thought*. Cambridge: Cambridge University Press.

Boyd, R. (1984). Natural kinds, homeostasis, and the limits of essentialism. Paper presented at Cornell University.

Brown, A. L. (1976). Semantic integration in children's reconstruction of logical narrative sequences. *Cognitive Psychology* 8, 247–262.

Brown, A. L. (1986). Paper presented at Psychonomic Society annual meeting in New Orleans.

Bruner, J. S. (1966). An overview. In Bruner, Olver, Greenfield, et al. (1966).

Bruner, J. S., R. R. Olver, P. M. Greenfield, et al. (1966). *Studies in cognitive growth*. New York: John Wiley.

Canfield, J. V. (1983). Discovering essence. In C. Ginet, ed., *Knowledge and mind: Philosophical essays*. New York: Oxford University Press.

Carey, S. (1978). The child as a word learner. In M. Halle, J. Bresnan, and G. Miller, eds., *Linguistic theory and psychological reality*. Cambridge, MA: MIT Press.

Carey, S. (1983). Constraints on the meanings of natural kind terms. In T. B. Seiler and W. Wannenmacher, eds., *Concept development and the development of word meaning*. New York: Springer-Verlag.

Carey, S. (1985). *Conceptual change in childhood*. Cambridge, MA: MIT Press.

Ceci, S. J., and J. Liker (1986). A day at the races: A study of I. Q., expertise, and cognitive complexity. *Journal of Experimental Psychology: General* 115, 255–267.

Chambers, W. G. (1904). How words get meaning. *Pedagogical Seminary* 11, 30–50.

Chapman, L. J., and J. P. Chapman (1969). Illusory correlation as an obstacle to the use of valid psychodiagnostic signs. *Journal of Abnormal Psychology* 74, 272–280.

Chase, W. G., and H. A. Simon (1973). The mind's eye in chess. In W. G. Chase, ed., *Visual information processing*. New York: Academic Press.

Chi, M. T. H. (1978). Knowledge structures and memory development. In R. S. Siegler, ed., *Children's thinking: What develops?* Hillsdale, NJ: Erlbaum.

Chi, M. T. H., P. J. Feltovich, and R. Glaser (1981). Categorization and representations of physics problems by experts and novices. *Cognitive Science* 5, 121–152.

Chi, M. T. H., R. Glaser, and E. Rees (1982). Expertise in problem solving. In R. J. Sternberg, ed., *Advances in the psychology of intelligence, Vol. I.* Hillsdale, NJ: Erlbaum.

Clark, E. V. (1973). What's in a word? On the child's acquisition of semantics in his first language. In T. E. Moore, ed., *Cognitive development and the acquisition of language.* New York: Academic Press.

Clark, E. V. (1983). Meanings and concepts. In Flavell and Markman (1983).

Coleman, L. and D. Kay (1981). Prototype semantics: The English word *lie. Language* 57, 26–44.

Copi, F. M. (1954). Essence and accident. *Journal of Philosophy* 51, 706–719.

Cosmides (in press). The logic of social exchange: Has natural selection shaped how people reason? *Cognition.*

Darwin, C. (1859). *On the origin of species by means of natural selection, or the preservation of favoured races in the struggle for life.* London: Murray.

DeVries, R. (1969). Constancy of genetic identity in the years three to six. *Society for Research in Child Development Monographs* 34 (Whole No. 127).

di Sessa, A. (1983). Phenomenology and the evolution of intuition. In D. Gentner and A. L. Stevens, eds., *Mental models.* Hillsdale, NJ: Erlbaum.

Dilger, W. C. (1962). The behavior of lovebirds. *Scientific American,* January.

Dixon, W. J., and M. B. Brown, eds. (1979). *BMDP-79: Biomedical computer programs, P-series.* Berkeley: University of California Press.

Donnellan, K. S. (1983). Intuitions and presuppositions. In C. Ginet, ed., *Knowledge and mind: Philosophical essays.* New York: Oxford University Press.

Dupré, J. (1981). Biological taxa as natural kinds. *Philosophical Review* 90, 66–90.

Feifel, H., and I. Lorge (1950). Qualitative differences in the vocabulary responses of children. *Journal of Educational Psychology* 41, 1–18.

Flavell, J. H. (1970). Concept development. In P. H. Mussen, ed., *Carmichael's manual of child psychology: Vol. I.* New York: Wiley.

Flavell, J. H., F. L. Green, and E. R. Flavell (1986). Development of knowledge about the appearance-reality distinction. *Society for Research in Child Development Monographs* 51, No. 1, Series No. 212.

Flavell, J. H., and E. M. Markman, eds. (1983). *Cognitive development.* Vol. III of P. H. Mussen, gen. ed., *Handbook of Child Psychology.* New York: Wiley.

Fodor, J. A. (1972). Some reflections on L. S. Vygotsky's *Thought and language. Cognition* 1, 83–95.

Fodor, J. A. (1975). *The language of thought.* New York: Thomas Y. Crowell.

Fodor, J. A. (1981). The current status of the innateness controversy. In *Representations: Philosophical essays on the foundations of cognitive science.* Cambridge, MA: MIT Press.

Fodor, J. A., M. F. Garrett, E. C. T. Walker, and C. H. Parkes (1980). Against definitions. *Cognition* 8, 263–367.

Forbus, K. D. and D. Gentner (1986). Learning physical domains: Towards a theoretical framework. Technical report, Dept. of Computer Science, University of Illinois.

Gardner, H. (1974). Metaphors and modalities: How children project polar adjectives onto diverse domains. *Child Development* 45, 84–91.

Garner, W. R. (1974). *The processing of information and structure.* Hillsdale, NJ: Erlbaum.

Gelman, R. (1986). First principles organize attention to and learning about relevant data. Paper presented at Psychonomic Society annual meeting in New Orleans.

Gelman, S. A. (1984). Children's inductive inferences from natural kind and artifact categories. Doctoral dissertation, Stanford University.

Gelman, S. A. (1987). Inductions about natural kinds and artifacts. Paper presented at Society for Research on Child Development, Baltimore.

Gelman, S. A., P. Collman, and E. E. Maccoby (1986). Inferring properties from categories versus inferring categories from properties: The case of gender. *Child Development 57*, 396–404.

Gelman, S. A., and E. Markman (1987). Young children's inductions from natural kinds: The role of categories and appearances. *Child Development 58*, 1532–1541.

Gelman, S. A., and A. W. O'Reilly (1988). Children's inductive inferences within superordinate categories: the role of language and category structure. *Child Development 59*, 876–887.

Gentner, D. (1983). Structure-mapping: A theoretical framework for analogy. *Cognitive Science 7*.

Gibson, E. J. (1969). *Principles of perceptual and cognitive development*. New York: Appleton-Century-Crofts.

Goodman, N. (1955). *Fact, fiction and forecast*. Indianapolis, IN: Bobbs-Merrill.

Gould, S. J. (1983). *Hen's teeth and horse's toes: Further reflections in natural history*. New York: Norton.

Hampton, J. A. (1976). An experimental study of concepts in language. Doctoral dissertation, University of London.

Hampton, J. A. (1987). Inheritance of attributes in natural concept conjunctions. *Memory and Cognition*.

Hampton, J. A. (1988a). Overextension of conjunctive concepts: Evidence for a unitary model of concept typicality and class inclusion. *Journal of Experimental Psychology: Learning, Memory and Cognition 14*.

Hampton, J. A. (1988b). Conceptual combination: Conjunction and negation of natural concepts. Unpublished paper.

Hampton, J. A. (1988c). Disjunction of natural concepts. Unpublished paper.

Hanfmann, E., and J. Kasanin (1942). *Conceptual thinking in schizophrenia*. New York: NMDM.

Harnad, S. (1987). *Categorical perception: The groundwork of cognition*. New York: Cambridge University Press.

Haviland, S., and E. Clark (1974). This man's father is my father's son: A study of the acquisition of kin terms. *Journal of Child Language 1*, 23–47.

Heider, F., and M. Simmel (1944). An experimental study of apparent behavior. *American Journal of Psychology 57*, 243–259.

Hempel, C. G. (1965). *Aspects of scientific explanation*. New York: The Free Press.

Holland, J. H., K. J. Holyoak, R. E. Nisbett, and P. R. Thagard (1986). *Induction: Processes of inference, learning, and discovery*. Cambridge, MA: MIT Press.

Hull, D. (1965). The effect of essentialism on taxonomy: 2000 years of stasis. *British Journal for the Philosophy of Science 15*, 314–326; 16, 1–18.

Inhelder, B., and J. Piaget (1964). *The early growth of logic in the child*. New York: Norton.

Jeyifous, S. (1986). Atimodemo: Semantic conceptual development among the Yoruba. Doctoral dissertation, Cornell University.

Johnson, C. (1983). Expertise in medical diagnosis. *Cognitive Science*.

Johnson, P. E., A. S. Duran, F. Hassebrock, J. Moller, M. Prietula, P. J. Feltovich and D. B. Swanson (1981). Expertise and error in diagnostic reasoning. *Cognitive Science 5*, 235–283.

Johnson-Laird, P. N. (1983). *Mental models*. Cambridge, MA: Harvard University Press.

Kahneman, D., and A. Tversky (1973). On the psychology of prediction. *Psychological Review 80*, 237–251.

Keil, F. C. (1979). *Semantic and conceptual development: An ontological perspective*. Cambridge, MA: Harvard University Press.

Keil, F. C. (1983). On the emergence of semantic and conceptual distinctions. *Journal of Experimental Psychology: General* 112, 357–385.

Keil, F. C. (1986a). On the structure dependent nature of stages of cognitive development. In I. Levin, ed., *Stage and structure*. Norwood, NJ: Ablex.

Keil, F. C. (1986b). Conceptual domains and the acquisition of metaphor. *Cognitive Development* 1, 73–96.

Keil, F. C. (1987). Conceptual development and category structure. In Neisser (1987).

Keil, F. C., and N. Batterman (1984). A characteristic-to-defining shift in the development of word meaning. *Journal of Verbal Learning and Verbal Behavior* 23, 221–236.

Kelly, M. (1987). Working paper under review.

Kelly, M. and F. C. Keil (1985). The more things change...: Metamorphoses and conceptual structure. *Cognitive Science* 9, 403–416.

Kelly, M., and F. C. Keil (1987). Conceptual domains and the comprehension of metaphor. *Metaphoric and Symbolic Activity* 2, 33–51.

Kemler, D. G. (1983). Holistic and analytic modes in perceptual and cognitive development. In T. Tighe and B. E. Shepp, eds., *Perception, cognition, and development: Interactional analyses*. Hillsdale, NJ: Erlbaum.

Kemler, D. G., and L. B. Smith (1978). Is there a developmental trend from integrality to separability in perception? *Journal of Experimental Child Psychology* 26, 498–507.

Kendler, H. H., and T. S. Kendler (1962). Vertical and horizontal processes in problem solving. *Psychological Review* 69, 1–16.

Kossan, N. E. (1978). Structure and strategy in concept acquisition. Doctoral dissertation, Stanford University.

Kozulin, A. (1986). Vygotsky in context. In Vygotsky (1934/1986).

Kripke, S. (1972a). Naming and necessity. In D. Davidson and G. Harman, eds., *Semantics of natural language*. Dordrecht, Holland: Reidel.

Kripke, S. (1972b). Identity and necessity. In M. K. Munitz, ed., *Identity and individuation*. New York: New York University Press.

Kuhn, T. S. (1970). *The structure of scientific revolutions*. Chicago: University of Chicago Press.

Kuhn, T. S. (1977). A function for thought experiments. In *The essential tension: Selected studies in scientific tradition and change*. Chicago: University of Chicago Press.

Kun, A., J. Parsons, and D. Ruble (1974). Development of integration processes using ability and effort information to predict outcome. *Developmental Psychology* 10, 721–732.

Lakoff, G. (1972). Hedges: A study in meaning criteria and the logic of fuzzy concepts. In *Papers from the eighth regional meeting, Chicago Linguistic Society*. Chicago: Chicago Linguistic Society. Reprinted in *Journal of Philosophical Logic* 2, 458–508.

Lakoff, G. (1987). *Women, fire, and dangerous things: What categories reveal about the mind*. Chicago: University of Chicago Press.

Landau, B. (1982). Will the real grandmother please stand up? The psychological reality of dual meaning representations. *Journal of Psycholinguistic Research* 11, 47–62.

Lehrer, A. (1969). Semantic cuisine. *Journal of Linguistics* 5, 39–55.

Lehrer, A. (1974). *Semantic fields and lexical structure*. Amsterdam: North-Holland.

Lehrer, A. (1978). Structures of the lexicon and transfer of meaning. *Lingua* 45, 95–123.

Leslie, A. M. (1987). Pretense and representation: The origins of "theory of mind." *Psychological Review* 94, 412–426.

Litowitz, B. (1977). Learning to make definitions. *Journal of Child Language* 4, 289–304.

Locke, J. (1690/1964). *An essay concerning human understanding*. A. D. Woozley, ed. New York: Meridian.

Luria, A. R. (1976). *Cognitive development: Its cultural and social foundations*. Cambridge, MA: Harvard University Press.

Massey, C., and R. Gelman (1988). Preschoolers deciding whether pictured unfamiliar objects can move themselves. *Developmental Psychology* 24, 307–317.

Mayr, E. (1982). *The growth of biological thought.* Cambridge, MA: Harvard University Press.

Mayr, E. (1985). Lectures at Cornell University, Spring Term.

McNamara, T. P., and R. J. Sternberg (1983). Mental models of word meaning. *Journal of Verbal Learning and Verbal Behavior* 22, 449–474.

Medin, D. L., and A. Ortony (in press). Psychological essentialism. In S. Vosniadoy and A. Ortony, eds., *Similarity and analogical reasoning.* New York: Cambridge University Press.

Medin, D. L., and E. J. Shoben (1988). Context and structure in conceptual combination. *Cognitive Psychology* 20, 158–190.

Medin, D. L., and W. D. Wattenmaker (1987). Category cohesiveness, theories, and cognitive archeology. In Neisser (1987).

Mellor, D. H., (1977). Natural kinds. *British Journal for the Philosophy of Science* 28, 299–312.

Mill, J. S. (1843/1974). *A system of logic ratiocinative and inductive.* Toronto: University of Toronto Press.

Miller, G. A. (1956). The magical number seven, plus or minus two: Some limits on our capacity for processing information. *Psychological Review* 63, 81–97.

Miller, G. A., E. Galanter, and K. H. Pribram (1960). *Plans and the structure of behavior.* New York: Holt, Rinehart and Winston.

Munn, N. L. (1965). *The evolution and growth of human behavior.* 2nd edition. Boston: Houghton Mifflin.

Murphy, G. L., (1987). Comprehending complex concepts. Unpublished manuscript.

Murphy, G. L., and D. Medin (1985). The role of theories in conceptual coherence. *Psychological Review* 92, 289–316.

Murphy, G. L. and J. C. Wright (1984). Changes in conceptual structure with expertise: Differences between real-world experts and novices. *Journal of Experimental Psychology: Learning, Memory, and Cognition* 10, 144–155.

Neisser, U., ed. (1962). Cultural and cognitive discontinuity. In T. E. Gladwin and W. Sturtevant, eds., *Anthropology and human behavior.* Washington, D.C.: Anthropological Society of Washington, D.C.

Neisser, U., (1982). *Memory observed: Remembering in natural contexts.* San Francisco: W. H. Freeman and Co.

Neisser, U., (1987). *Concepts and conceptual development: Ecological and intellectual factors in categorization.* Cambridge: Cambridge University Press.

Nelson, K. (1985). *Making sense: The acquisition of shared meaning.* Orlando: Academic Press.

Olson, D. (1982). Cognitive consequences of schooling. *The Quarterly Newsletter of the Laboratory of Comparative Human Cognition* 4, 75–78.

Osherson, D., and E. E. Smith (1981). On the adequacy of prototype theory as a theory of concepts. *Cognition* 9, 35–58.

Parfit, D. (1984). *Reasons and persons.* Oxford: Oxford University Press.

Parsons, J. E., D. N. Ruble, E. C. Klosson, N. S. Feldman, and W. S. Rholes (1976). Order effects on children's moral and achievement judgments. *Developmental Psychology* 12, 357–368

Peirce, C. S. (1931-1935). *Collected papers of Charles Sanders Peirce.* 6 vols. C. Hartshorne and P. Weiss, eds. Cambridge, MA: Harvard University Press.

Piaget, J. (1929). *The child's conception of the world.* New York: Harcourt, Brace.

Piaget, J. (1932). *The moral judgement of the child.* London: Kegan Paul.

Piaget, J., and B. Inhelder (1974). *The child's construction of quantities.* London: Routledge and Kegan Paul.

Posner, M. I., and S. W. Keele (1968). On the genesis of abstract ideas. *Journal of Experimental Psychology* 77, 353–363.

Putnam, H. (1975). The meaning of meaning. In H. Putnam, ed., *Mind, language and reality*. Vol. 2. London: Cambridge University Press.

Putnam, H. (1981). *Reason, truth, and history*. Cambridge: Cambridge University Press.

Putnam, H. (1983). *Realism and reason: Philosophical papers*. Vol. 3. Cambridge: Cambridge University Press.

Quine, W. V. O. (1951). Two dogmas of empiricism. *Philosophical Review* 60, 20–43.

Quine, W. V. O. (1960). *Word and object*. Cambridge, MA: MIT Press.

Quine, W. V. O. (1963). On simple theories of a complex world. *Synthese* 15, 107–111.

Quine, W. V. O. (1974). The nature of natural knowledge. In S. Guttenplon, ed., *Mind and language*. Oxford: Oxford University Press.

Quine, W. V. O. (1977). Natural kinds. In S. P. Schwartz, ed., *Naming, necessity, and natural kinds*. Ithaca, NY: Cornell University Press.

Quine, W. V. O., and J. S. Ullian (1973). *The web of belief*. New York: Random House.

Rey, G. (1983). Concepts and stereotypes. *Cognition* 15, 237–262.

Rips, L. J. (1975). Induction about natural categories. *Journal of Verbal Learning and Verbal Behavior* 14, 665–681

Rosch, E. (1975). Cognitive representations of semantic categories. *Journal of Experimental Psychology: General* 104, 192–233.

Rosch, E. (1978). Principles of categorization. In E. Rosch and B. B. Lloyd, eds., *Cognition and categorization*. Hillsdale, NJ: Erlbaum.

Rosch, E., and C. B. Mervis (1975). Family resemblances: Studies in the internal structure of categories. *Cognitive Psychology* 7, 573–605.

Rosch, E., C. B. Mervis, W. D. Gray, D. Johnson, and P. Boyes-Braem (1976). Basic objects in natural categories. *Cognitive Psychology* 8, 382–439.

Samett, J. (1986). Troubles with Fodor's nativism. In P. A. French, T. E. Uehling, and H. K. Wettstein, eds., *Midwest Studies in Philosophy*, Vol. X. Minneapolis: University of Minnesota Press.

Schachtel, E. G. (1947). On memory and childhood amnesia. *Psychiatry* 10, 1–26. Reprinted in Neisser (1982).

Schwartz, S. P., ed. (1977). *Naming, necessity, and natural kinds*. Ithaca, NY: Cornell University Press.

Schwartz, S. P. (1978). Putnam on artifacts. *Philosophical Review* 87, 566–574.

Schwartz, S. P. (1980). Natural kinds and nominal kinds. *Mind* 89, 182–195.

Scribner, S., and M. Cole (1973). Cognitive consequences of formal and informal education. *Science* 182, 553–559.

Seligman, M. E. P. (1970). On the generality of laws of learning. *Psychological Review* 77, 406–418.

Shepp, B. (1978). From perceived similarity to dimensional structure: A new hypothesis about perceptual development. In E. Rosch and B. Lloyd, eds., *On the nature and principle of formation of categories*. Hillsdale, NJ: Erlbaum.

Simon, H. (1969). *Sciences of the artificial*. Cambridge, MA: MIT Press.

Shepp, B. (1978). From perceived similarity to dimensional structure: A new hypothesis about perceptual development. In E. Rosch and B. Lloyd, eds., *On the nature and principle of formation of categories*. Hillsdale, NJ: Erlbaum.

Smith, C., S. Carey, and M. Wiser (1985). On differentiation: A case study of the development of the concepts of size, weight, and density. *Cognition* 21, 177–237.

Smith, E. E., E. J. Shoben, and L. J. Rips (1974). Structure and process in semantic memory: A featural model for semantic decisions. *Psychological Review* 81, 214–241.

Smith, E. E., and D. L. Medin (1981). *Categories and Concepts*. Cambridge, MA: Harvard University Press.

Smith, L. B. (1981). Importance of the overall similarity of objects for adults' and children's classifications. *Journal of Experimental Psychology: Human Perception and Performance* 7, 811–824.

Snow, C. E., and C. A. Ferguson (1977). *Talking to children*. Cambridge: Cambridge University Press.

Spelke, E. S. (in press). The origins of physical knowledge. In L. Weiskrantz, ed., *Thought without language*. Oxford: Oxford University Press.

Stevenson, H. W. (1970). Learning in children. In P. H. Mussen, ed., *Carmichael's manual of child psychology: Vol. I*. New York: Wiley.

Terman, L. M. (1916). *The measurement of intelligence*. Boston: Houghton Mifflin.

Tourangeau, R., and R. J. Sternberg (1982). Understanding and appreciating metaphors. *Cognition* 11, 203–244.

Vera, A. H., and F. C. Keil (1988). The development of inductions about biological kinds: The nature of the conceptual base. Paper presented at the 29th meeting of the Psychonomic Society, Chicago.

Vygotsky, L. S. (1934/1962). *Thought and language*. E. Hanfmann and G. Vakar, trans. Cambridge, MA: MIT Press.

Vygotsky, L. S. (1934/1986). *Thought and language*. Cambridge, MA: MIT Press.

Wellman, H., and S. A. Gelman (1988). Children's understanding of the nonobvious. In R. J. Sternberg, ed., *Advances in the psychology of human intelligence*, Vol. 4. Hillsdale, NJ: Erlbaum.

Werner, H. (1948). *Comparative psychology of mental development*. 2nd ed. New York: International Universities Press.

Werner, H., and B. Kaplan (1963). *Symbol formation: An organismic-developmental approach to language and the expression of thought*. New York: Wiley.

Wimmer, H., S. Gruber, and J. Perner (1984). Young children's conception of lying: Lexical realism—moral subjectivism. *Journal of Experimental Child Psychology* 37, 1–30.

Wittgenstein, L. (1953). *Philosophical investigations*. G. E. M. Anscombe, ed. Oxford: Blackwell.

Wolman, R. N., and E. N. Barker (1965). A developmental study of word definitions. *Journal of Genetic Psychology* 107, 159–166.

Woozley, A. D. (1964). Preface to Locke (1690/1964).

Author Index

Subject Index